with best

M. S/L

24 Ja 2009

Gulf Logistics

Blackadder's War

Tank transporters on the Tapline Road

Gulf Logistics

Blackadder's War

Edited by
Major General MS White CBE

Also from Brassey's:

CENTRE FOR DEFENCE STUDIES
Brassey's Defence Yearbook 1995

GODDEN
Shield and Storm: Personal Recollections of the Air War in the Gulf

BENSON
Rats' Tales: The Staffordshire Regiment at War in the Gulf

BELLAMY
Expert Witness: A Defence Correspondent's Gulf War 1990–1991

LAFFIN
Brassey's Battles: 3,500 Years of Conflict, Campaigns and Wars from A–Z

Brassey's Land Warfare Series:

FOXTON
Powering War: Modern Land Force Logistics

RICE & SAMMES
Command and Control Support Systems in the Gulf War

Copyright © 1995 Brassey's (UK) Ltd

All Rights Reserved. No part of this publication may be reproduced, stored in a retrieval system or transmitted in any form or by any means; electronic, electrostatic, magnetic tape, mechanical, photocopying, recording or otherwise, without permission in writing from the publishers.

First English Edition 1995

UK editorial offices: Brassey's, 33 John Street, London WC1N 2AT
UK orders: Marston Book Services, PO Box 87, Oxford OX2 0DT
North American Orders: Brassey's Inc. PO Box 960 Herndon VA22070 USA

Martin White has asserted his moral right to be identified as the author of this work.

Library of Congress Cataloging in Publication Data
available

British Library Cataloguing in Publication Data
A catalogue record for this book is available from the British Library

ISBN 1 85753 089 6 Hardcover

Typeset by Florencetype Ltd, Stoodleigh, Devon
Printed in Great Britain by BPC Wheatons Ltd., Exeter

Dedication
For Fiona and all our wives
who had the most to put up with
and to Anna who hoped I had a cunning plan.

Heidelberg May 1995   M S WHITE

Foreword

General Sir Peter de la Billière GCB CBE DSO MC

Shortly after the conclusion of the Gulf War of 1991, I wrote to my erstwhile logistic commander, the then Brigadier Martin White, and in my letter I told him 'the Gulf War was kept short, sharp, and with the minimum casualties. I am in no doubt that the efficiency of the logistic back-up was a major and critical factor in this achievement'. With the benefit of retrospect, I remain as firmly certain today that this is the case as I was when I first wrote that letter.

The scale and scope of the coalition build-up and, in particular, that of the British Services, has had no equal since the Second World War and my logistic units were the finest in the Theatre. Their achievement alone ensured that 1 (UK) Armoured Division was fit for battle and in position at the start of operations. Their subsequent support of the Division ensured that at the conclusion of the unexpectedly short operation, the British armour was poised ready to continue battle, whether that meant a pursuit towards Baghdad or further operations in the Kuwait/Iraq border area.[1]

As with any military operation, the logistic operations in the Gulf War were a critical element of my ability to fight the resources I had been given and to deploy them in the first place. They represented a remarkable feat of leadership and organisation by logistic commanders throughout the chain of command. From the United Kingdom and BAOR, across the 4,000 miles of sea lanes to the port of Jubail, 400,000 tons of freight were moved, requiring 146 cargo ships, most of which were acquired through the Baltic Exchange. Some 12,000 air lift sorties were flown, amounting to considerably more than the entire effort of the Berlin air lift. Placing these resources in theatre was only the beginning of the problem. Once they had arrived, they had to be sorted and allotted to the right portion of the front, bearing in mind that my servicemen were spread across some 2,000 miles of desert and in four different countries.

To me it was clear from the start that logistics were to present the greatest challenge and would be of the utmost importance to the success of the British operations. I therefore gave the whole logistic operation the very highest priority. I promoted Colonel White in the field to Brigadier, so that he could be on equal terms with my field commanders. I instructed him to report to me direct and particularly to keep me briefed on any shortcomings or difficulties, instructing him to by-pass the normal chain of command to do so. I personally gave the highest importance to visiting the logistic units so that not only was I familiar with their work and their problems but also that those working appreciated the importance I placed on their work.

There were, of course, particular advantages, the most important of which was the total lack of Iraqi air capability. There is no doubt that, had there been even a small Iraqi air presence, it would have delayed the logistic deployment. Furthermore, we were able to take tactical risks with forward logistic units knowing that they were safe from air attack. This should not be forgotten when assessing the logistic operations in the Gulf War.

It is of particular note that many civilian firms placed technicians into the most forward areas to give technical advice on the maintenance and repair of the armoured vehicles and other equipment.[2] This will undoubtedly be a requirement in future wars where complex technology will demand skills that it would be impractical or impossible to impart to serving soldiers. It is to the credit both of the firms concerned and particularly to the individuals who went forward with our troops, that they were prepared to share the risks and discomforts that go with modern warfare.

In the Gulf War there were three pillars which had to be constructed if the war was to be conducted effectively. They were the conduct of the theatre diplomacy; leadership at all rank levels in all three Services and, last but by no means least, effective, efficient, and speedy logistic support. This latter was forthcoming in abundance. This book is a detailed account of this massive logistic deployment and build-up, and tells how the land battle was supported and of the skill with which the necessary recovery operation was conducted. It is a worthy tribute to the outstanding servicemen and women of the various logistic units in the theatre.

Acknowledgements

It is all too easy after a military triumph to dwell only on the operational lessons of such a victory and forget some of the crucial preconditions needed for that victory. It was with that in mind that I was persuaded to undertake the editing of this book which describes the logistic effort from the point of view of those responsible commanders and staff officers actually deployed in the Gulf area of operations. I firmly believed then and still believe now that it is a story worth telling and I am very grateful to my military and civilian colleagues who were involved, in particular to the members of the Port Clearance Society, for their input and support. In addition I am grateful to Graham Ewer and Noel Muddiman for their view of the 1(UK) Armoured Division and recovery operation respectively.

All logistic activity is to support a commander's operational plan and I am most grateful to General Sir Peter de la Billière for his valuable overview of events and also for the very clear perspective given by Major General Rupert Smith, the Commander of 1(UK) Armoured Division.

I must also thank the staff of *Soldier* magazine for the use of the photographs for the frontispiece and plates 4 and 14 and those serving officers who provided the majority of photographs and charts.

My gratitude goes also to Jenny Shaw and Tony Trythall of Brassey's for their advice, but in particular to Bryan Watkins, also from Brassey's, who guided us throughout and whose knowledge and feel for logistic matters has been invaluable.

Finally, to edit a book with the individual authors living in three or four countries has been a challenge and one that I could not have met were it not for the help of Mike Moran, Les Bate and last but certainly not least Sylvia Trojand. I hope, however, that our efforts are worthwhile and that some of the lessons we learned, often the hard way, will be of use in the future.

M S WHITE
Major General
May 1995

Contents

List of Plates

Note: Except where separately acknowledged in their captions, all photographs were taken by the Author or with his camera.

Plates appear between pages 100 and 101

List of Figures

Glossary of Abbreviations and Symbols

ACC	Army Catering Corps
ACOS	Assistant Chief of Staff
ADBG	Armoured Delivery Battle Group
ADG	Armoured Delivery Group
ADP	Automatic Data Processing
ADS	Armoured Delivery Squadron
AT&T	American Telephone and Telegraph
AFN	American Forces Network
AFV	Armoured Fighting Vehicle
AG	Adjutant General
AGAA	Artillery Group Admin Area
AGC	Adjutant General's Corps
AIDT	Armoured Infantry Delivery Team
AMF (L)	Allied Command Europe Mobile Force (LAND)
AMMO	Ammunition
AMS	Army Medical Service
APU	Auxiliary Power Unit
ARAMCO	Arabian American Oil Company
ARMD	Armoured
ASMA	Air Staff Management Aid
ASOC	Air Support Operations Centre
ASP	Ammunition Supply Point
ATLO	Air Transport Liaison Officer
AVRE	Armoured Vehicle Royal Engineers
AWD	All Wheel Drive (Truck)
BAA	Brigade Administrative Area
BAOR	British Army of the Rhine
BATUS	British Army Training Unit Suffield
BCR	Battle Casualty Replacement
BERR	Battle Equipment Reliability Return

BFG	British Forces Germany
BFI	Bulk Fuel Installation
BFK	British Forces Kuwait
BFME	British Forces Middle East
BFT	Basic Fitness Test
BG	Battle Group
BMA	Brigade Maintenance Area
BMH	British Military Hospital
BN	Battalion
BR	British
C130	Hercules Transport Aircraft
C^3	Command, Control and Communications
C^3I	Command, Control, Communications and Intelligence
CA	Civil Affairs
CAM	Chemical Agent Monitor
CASEVAC	Casualty Evacuation
CAT	Catering
CGS	Chief of the General Staff
CIE	Captured Iraqi Equipment
CIS	Communication and Information System
CMA	Convoy Marshalling Area
CO	Commanding Officer
COMPO	Composite Rations
COY	Company
CP	Command Post
CPX	Command Post Exercise
CR	Challenger Main Battle Tank
CRA	Commander Royal Artillery
CRARRV	Challenger Armoured Repair & Recovery Vehicle
CSE	Combined Services Entertainment
CSS	Combat Service Support
CSUPS	Combat Supplies
DAA	Divisional Administrative Area
DACOS	Deputy Assistant Chief of Staff
DAER	Daily Ammunition Expenditure Rate
DAG	Divisional Artillery Group
DCN	Defence Communications Network
DCOS	Deputy Chief of Staff
DGEME	Director General Electrical & Mechanical Engineers
DICS	Desert Interim Computer System
DISCOM	Divisional Support Command
DMA	Divisional Maintenance Area
DMO	Director of Military Operations
DMSD	Defence Medical Services Directorate
DNBI	Disease and Non Battle Injury

DOAST	Desired Order of Arrival Staff Table
DOMS	Defence Operational Movement Staff
DP	Distribution Point
DRG	Divisional Reconstitution Group
DROPS	Dismountable Rack Off Loading and Pick-Up System
DS	Dressing Station
E&MA	Engine and Major Assembly
EFI	Expeditionary Forces Institutes
EOD	Explosive Ordnance Disposal
EPW	Enemy Prisoner of War
EW	Electronic Warfare
F46	Petrol
F54	Diesel
F58	Kerosine
FAA	Forward Assembly Area
FADG	Forward Armoured Delivery Group
FCO	Foreign and Commonwealth Office
FCU/OCU	Fuel/Oil Consumption Unit
FD AMB	Field Ambulance
FFMA	Forward Force Maintenance Area
FMA	Force Maintenance Area
FPM	Force Provost Marshal
FPO	Forces Post Office
FPT	Field Psychiatric Team
FRG	Federal Republic of Germany
FRO	Field Records Office
FRST	Field Records Support Team
FRT	Forward Repair Team
FST	Field Surgical Team
FTX	Field Training Exercise
G1	Personnel Staff Branch
G2	Intelligence and Security Staff Branch
G3	Operations and Training Staff Branch
G4	Logistic Staff Branch
G5	Civil/Military Cooperation Staff Branch
GDP	General Deployment Plan
GFA	Government Freight Agency
GOC	General Officer Commanding
GP	Group
GPS	Global Positioning System
GRT	Graves Registration Team
GT	General Transport
HET	Heavy Equipment Transporter
HF	High Frequency
HLS	Helicopter Landing Site

HN	Host Nation
HNS	Host Nation Support
HQ	Headquarters
HQ DAA	Headquarters Divisional Administrative Area
HRS (hrs)	Hours
IDR	In Depth Repairs
IO	Intelligence Officer
IRG	Immediate Replenishment Group
IRS	Individual Reinforcements
JHQ	Joint Headquarters
JHSU	Joint Helicopter Support Unit
KKMC	King Kahlid Military City
K143	Secure Communications Equipment
Km	Kilometre
KOSB	King's Own Scottish Borderers
LAD	Light Aid Detachment
LBE	Logistic Base Echo
LIM	Linear Metres
LO	Liaison Officer
LOA	Local Overseas Allowance
LOC	Line of Communications
LofC	Lines of Communications
LOGEX	Logistic Exercise
LPG	Liquid Petroleum Gas
LRS	Local Resources Section
LRU	Line Replacement Unit
LSG	Logistic Support Group
LSL	Landing Ship Logistic
LT	Lieutenant
M48	US Tank
M548	US Tracked Ammunition Carrier
M60	US Tank
M&E	Mines and Explosives
MAOT	Mobile Air Operations Team
MAPEX	Map Exercise
MCC	Movement Control Centre
MCCP	Movement Control Check Point
MCTG	Mobile Civilian Transport Group
MDBF	Mean Distance Between Failures
MEF	Marine Expeditionary Force
MHE	Mechanical Handling Equipment
MLRS	Multiple Launch Rocket System
MOD(A)	Ministry of Defence (Army)
MODA	Saudi Arabian Ministry of Defence and Aviation
MOU	Memorandum of Understanding

MOV	Movement
MP	Military Police
MRE	Meals Ready to Eat
MRG	Main Repair Group
MSR	Main Supply Route
NAAFI	Navy, Army, Air Force Institute
NAIAD	Nerve Agent Immobilized Enzyme Alarm and Detector
NATO	North Atlantic Treaty Organisation
NBC	Nuclear, Biological and Chemical Warfare
OC	Officer Commanding
ONMA	Other Nations Medical Assistance
OPCON	Operational Control
OPS	Operations
OPSEC	Operational Security
ORBAT	Order of Battle
ORD	Ordnance
ORP	Operational Ration Pack
OVI	Operationally Vital Items
PICSITREP	Pictorial Situation Report
PLOD	Pipeline Over the Desert
PLS	Palletised Load System
PLSU	Pioneer Labour Support Unit
POL	Petroleum, Oil and Lubricants
PTI	Physical Training Instructor
PUE	Prestocked Unit Equipment
PW	Prisoner of War
PWGF	Prisoner of War Guard Force
PX	Post Exchange
QDG	The Queen's Dragoon Guards
RA	Royal Artillery
RAC	Royal Armoured Corps
RAF	Royal Air Force
RAMC	Royal Army Medical Corps
RAOC	Royal Army Ordnance Corps
RAP	Regimental Aid Post
RAPC	Royal Army Pay Corps
RCT	Royal Corps of Transport
RDBG	Route Development Battle Group
RECCE	Reconnaissance/Reconnoitre
REME	Royal Electrical and Mechanical Engineers
RETT	Royal Engineers Training Team
RFA	Royal Fleet Auxiliary
RHQ	Regimental Headquarters
RLC	The Royal Logistic Corps
RMA	Rear Maintenance Area

RMO	Regimental Medical Officer
RMP	Royal Military Police
RN	Royal Navy
RO	Retired Officer
RO/RO	Roll On/Roll Off
RP	Replenishment Park
RPC	Royal Pioneer Corps
RRF	The Royal Regiment of Fusiliers
RSG	Return Stores Group
RSM	Regimental Sergeant Major
RV	Rendezvous
RVD	Residual Vapour Detector
SA80	Small Arms 80 (Rifle)
SACEUR	Supreme Allied Commander Europe
SAS	Special Air Service
SH	Support Helicopters
SIMMO	Simulated Ammunition
SIXCON	Six Container (Water Tanks)
SMO	Senior Medical Officer
SNCO	Senior Non Commissioned Officer
SO1	Staff Officer Grade 1 (Lieutenant Colonel)
SO2	Staff Officer Grade 2 (Major)
SO3	Staff Officer Grade 3 (Captain)
SOP	Standing Operating Procedure
SQMS	Staff Quartermaster Sergeant Major
SQN	Squadron
SSGT	Staff Sergeant
SSVC	Services Sound and Vision Corporation
TA	Territorial Army
TAA	Tactical Assembly Area
TAC HQ	Tactical Headquarters
TACON	Tactical Control
TAT	Tactical Advisory Team
TCN	Third Country National
TCV	Troop Carrying Vehicle
TOPO	Topographic
TP	Troop
TPT	Transport
TSU	Transport Support Unit
TTF	Truck, Tanker Fuel
UKMF	United Kingdom Mobile Force
UNIKOM	United Nations in Kuwait Observer Mission
UOR	Urgent Operational Requirement
USMC	United States Marine Corps
VC10	UK Strategic Transport Aircraft

VDU	Visual Display Unit
VEH	Vehicle
VHF	Very High Frequency
WKSP	Workshop
WMR	War Maintenance Reserve
WO1	Warrant Officer Class 1
WO2	Warrant Officer Class 2
WR	Warrior Fighting Vehicle
XP	Exchange Point

Military Symbols

Units and Formations

⬚   Basic symbol for a military unit

⬚   Troop/Platoon

⬚   Squadron/Battery/Company

⬚   Regiment/Battalion

⬚   Group (Colonel's Command)

⬚   Brigade (or equivalent)

⬚   Division

(Note: Tactical boundaries are marked to show relevant level of command. Thus: —x—x— Brigade boundary)

Command and Control

⊢   A Military Headquarters
(Like boundaries, these are marked to show the appropriate level of command.

Thus: ⊢   Divisional Headquarters)

⚲   Control Point

◯   Installation

Unit Functions and Commodities

Units

	Armour
	Armoured Recce
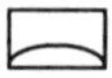	Air Defence
	Army Air Corps
	Artillery
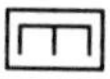	Engineer
	Helicopter
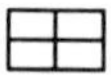	Medical
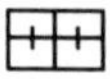	Hospital
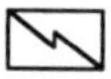	Signals
	Transport

Functions & Commodities

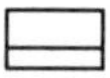	Multi Commodity Supply
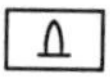	Ammunition
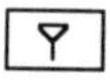	Fuel
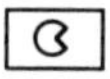	Rations
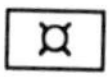	Materiel
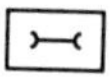	Maintenance
	Postal & Courier
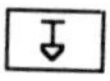	Labour
	Aviation Repair

Note: All these symbols can be used in combination with others. Thus:

	Tracked Artillery
	Transport Helicopters
	Mechanised Infantry
	Supply and Transport

Chapter One

The Support of the War in Perspective

Major General M S White CBE
(Commander Force Maintenance Area, Gulf)

The experience of the campaign again confirmed that the established principles on which administration is based were sound. The campaign confirmed time and time again that the principles of Foresight and Flexibility were of paramount importance and, within that framework, varying methods of practice could be employed with success.

I begin this account of the logistic support of the Gulf War (1990/91) with a quotation taken from the Administrative History of 21st Army Group (6 June 1944–8 May 1945) that I found just as relevant in the Gulf War as when it was written; of course the complexity, scale and speed of modern warfare has risen exponentially since 1945 but the underpinning requirements of sound logistic organisation, command, control, communications and intelligence (C^3I) and training are still valid, indeed they apply throughout the history of war.

In the middle of January 1991, I was sitting in the Headquarters of the Forward Force Maintenance Area (FFMA) wondering if the latest SCUD alert would herald a chemical strike on our logistic build up to support the forthcoming battle to liberate Kuwait or, more important, whether we had enough ammunition and fuel in the right place, when Major Peter Cross, my Chief of Staff, asked me if I had considered writing a book of my experiences; the reply is unprintable!

The political background, air battle and short land war are all well documented and our (the logisticians) problem has been how to recount the massive movement and logistic operation in support of our forces within Saudi Arabia, involving virtually half of all the servicemen and women deployed on the operation, whilst at the same time acknowledging and paying tribute to the literally thousands of soldiers and civilians who worked tirelessly in the United Kingdom, British Army of the Rhine and Cyprus to make the operation the success it was. What

follows in this opening chapter, therefore, is an overview of our participation in the Gulf War which became the largest and most complex
deployment and support operation since the Second World War and one
which pointed the way for logistics in the post-Cold War era in a world
of shrinking military budgets and multinational UN-type operations.
This then is the story of the logistic support of Operations GRANBY/
DESERT SHIELD/DESERT STORM and DESERT SABRE.[1]

UK Mobilisation and Deployment

It was not until late August 1990 that it became apparent that the UK
would make a major contribution to the liberation of Kuwait. I was a
logistic planner in Headquarters British Army of the Rhine (BAOR) at
Rheindahlen near Düsseldorf, and our lives at that time were dominated
by events in Eastern Europe[2] and the prospect of major reductions in
the Army. It seemed inconceivable that we could take a heavy armoured
formation from Europe, where it had been since the Second World War,
and deploy it to the desert.

Hence, when the political and military decisions were made to deploy
7 Armoured Brigade (Figure 1.1) as our contribution to the Allied ground
forces in Saudi Arabia, we had to follow up with some very rapid
and creative organisational activity, because we had no standing logistic
structure designed for the support of an armoured brigade operating away
from its parent division and, behind that, the Corps operational support
base in North–West Europe. However, my previous experience as
Commander of the Logistic Support Group (LSG) assigned to the United
Kingdom Mobile Force (UKMF)[3], which was just such an organisation,
was invaluable in setting up a baseline of units and specialisations for the

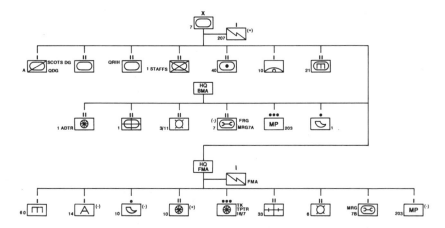

Figure 1.1 Operation GRANBY I: Order of Battle, 7 Armoured Brigade Group

Force Maintenance Area (FMA) (Figure 1.2). This was refined and confirmed after a very short reconnaissance (recce) in Saudi Arabia. The problems encountered in this preparatory phase, particularly the shortage of time to structure the FMA Headquarters (HQ), to confirm the logistic order of battle (ORBAT) and to assemble the many individuals and mass of equipment for operations, strengthened the case for the permanent establishment of some sort of HQ FMA in peace. This would give greater credence to our ability to provide support within the future NATO structure or in out of area operations in support of UN missions.

At this early stage of our preparations, life was extremely hectic and I recall being given very firm and wise guidance both from the Commander-in-Chief, General Sir Peter Inge, and from Brigadier Mike Betts (the senior logistic planner in Germany and responsible, with Brigadier Noel Muddiman, the Commander Transport and Movements, for mounting the operation) on how vital my task was. It is worth saying at this stage that the support and guidance I received from both senior colleagues and friends was superb. Brigadier Simon Firth and Colonels Jeremy Lucas and Bill Allen at the Joint Headquarters (JHQ) in High Wycombe were a tower of strength and support, and Brigadier Roland Notley, the senior operational logistic planner in the Ministry of Defence (MOD), responded swiftly and with fairly good humour to the many and perhaps unreasonable demands of our Force preparing to deploy.

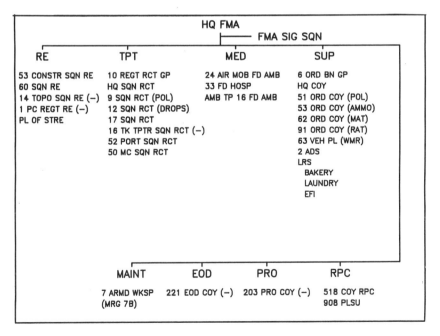

Figure 1.2 Order of Battle, The Force Maintenance Area, October 1990

However, underlying the unfailing efforts to make the Force ready for war, there was a substantial reallocation of equipment and manpower, throughout the Army (described in later chapters). For instance, to provide the ever expanding size and nature of the Force, regular units, normally brought up to strengthen on transition to war by individual reservists,[4] had to be reinforced with personnel from other regular units. For constitutional reasons, which were far from clear, we were unable to deploy Territorial Army (TA) units which provide a large part of our support in war, most critically in logistics; the resultant capability gap had therefore to be filled by regular units and equipment. In consequence, there were therefore severely detrimental effects on our standing commitment to NATO, particularly in BAOR. Just to emphasise the support requirement let me say that, in total, the Army had some 14,000 logistic personnel in Saudi Arabia, supporting over 100 types of armoured and logistic vehicles, as well as several thousand other equipments. That figure actually includes a number of TA medical personnel who were allowed to volunteer without actually being mobilized.

From the outset, a massive movements operation was necessary to ensure that the forces and equipment were transported safely and in good time to the theatre of operations. The deployment of 7 Armoured Brigade Group, followed subsequently by the remainder of 1 (UK) Armoured Division, took place during the period September 1990 to January 1991. As I have said, many equipment modifications and enhancements were required to adapt a force equipped to fight in North-West Europe to one capable of effective desert operations; not the least of these was the need to repaint the entire force from green and black to desert camouflage! Many of these modifications were still being completed in Saudi Arabia, right up to the start of the ground war.

Contracts were speedily placed for items such as desert uniforms and desert camouflage nets. Over 200 Urgent Operational Requirements (UOR) were placed for off-the-shelf or advanced delivery items to improve the operational effectiveness of the force; all of these had to be moved as and when they became available. Approximately £75m was expended on improving equipment and procuring vital items, all of which enhanced the combat preparedness of the troops on the ground. The items procured and moved covered an extraordinary diversity. Examples are water carriage equipment (the planning requirement is 45 litres per person per day, which meant over two million litres per day for the force), mine clearance vehicles from Germany, laser-guided bombs from America, stretcher posts and fittings from Norway for use in RAF aircraft and narrow bodied civil aircraft, and a complete supply of special hot-weather underwear for our female contingent! The response of industry was magnificent, as was the cooperation with our Allies.

The Force Maintenance Area

As Commander of the Force Maintenance Area (FMA) and senior logistician I was responsible for receiving the force into Saudi Arabia through the port of Jubail in the Eastern Province of Saudi Arabia and airports at Dhahran, Jubail and Riyadh, and for its support thereafter. I was initially part of the 7 Armoured Brigade Group, where I forged a close personal and professional relationship with Brigadier Patrick Cordingley, the Commander, for whom I have the greatest respect, and also Colonel John Milne, his deputy, a thoroughly professional soldier. With the deployment of 1(UK) Armoured Division, I reported directly to General Sir Peter de la Billière in Riyadh but of course supported General Rupert Smith, Commander of the Division. My mission in the FMA was perfectly simple and straightforward; it was:

'To maintain 7th Armoured Brigade Group'.

Of course, this included deployment.

Stock levels of combat supplies[5] (ammunition, fuel, rations and water) had been worked out on the basis of a defensive battle of 10 days at intense rates[6] of consumption. We therefore planned, in conjunction with JHQ, the delivery to the Gulf, mainly from Germany and by ship, of 30 days at normal rates (intense rates were approximately three times normal rates) with a reserve afloat of a further 12 days. We knew that, once deployed to the Gulf, the FMA would have to receive some 13,000 personnel, 5,000 vehicles, 14,000 tons of ammunition and 2,000 containers of materiel and unit stores. We gratefully accepted the offer of assistance from the United States Marine Corps (USMC) on the recce and, as a prerequisite, we also knew that Host Nation Support (HNS) would be essential from the Saudi Arabian authorities.

We had met the extremely professional Marine Corps logisticians commanded by Brigadier General Jim Brabham and his Chief of Staff, Colonel Tom Stopher, during our brief recce. True to their promise, they provided virtually every life support means until we could establish ourselves in the port area of Jubail. This included all our food and accommodation, and it would have been difficult to survive without their advice and guidance. Indeed, our initial links were fostered by Lieutenant Colonel Barry Aitken, one of my staff, whom I left in Saudi Arabia following the recce in September 1990. All he had was a secure phone and the most sketchy instructions from me and Brigadier Mike Walker, who led the recce. He did a magnificent job, eventually returning to Germany after we were set up in October 1990.

Barry was joined in Jubail during September by 39 Engineer Regiment commanded by Lieutenant Colonel Bob Pridham, elements of 518 Coy Royal Pioneer Corps (RPC), a local resources section, and postal and communications assets. They were our first foot on the ground and provided a head start to our operations.

Once we had established the FMA in the area of Jubail and its port, our immediate aim was to marry up personnel arriving by air and equipment arriving by sea as soon as possible and to deploy them to the desert for training. The first ship arrived on 18 October and from then on ships and aircraft arrived daily. We had to make use of the huge hangars of Jubail port as temporary accommodation for our personnel, supplemented by an Engineer-constructed 2,000 man tented camp known as Baldrick Lines. The initial build-up went well, it was well balanced and provided, coincidentally, a model for the later deployment of the remainder of 1 (UK) Armoured Division, although we did not expect this at the time. In those early days, it was planned to support defensive operations in the Eastern Province or offensive operations through Khafji into Kuwait (Figure 1.3). We were confident that we could sustain this Line of Communication (LofC) by establishing a Forward FMA (FFMA), although I was concerned that it would over extend the limited staff resources, state of training and the communications of my ad hoc Headquarters. By 14 November, when 7 Armoured Brigade Group was declared operationally ready, the FMA had sufficient combat supplies and materiel in theatre to support the Brigade Group on operations.

*   *   *

Just to illustrate what may be done with the proper expertise, our Local Resources Section (LRS) (just six men, under Lieutenant Tom Lishman, and later expanded to 15), our interface with local agencies for the provision of fuel, food, rental vehicles and so on, had, by the start of the land battle, made over 2,300 local purchase orders; in addition 40 contracts had been let for transport hire, laundry and cleaning etc at a cost of over £29 m. This illustrates not only how lucky we were to be able to tap into the rather substantial local infrastructure but how vital this civil–military interface for such operations is in modern warfare.

Arrival of 1(UK) Armoured Division

From the logistic point of view the decision to deploy 1(UK) Armoured Division, involving a huge increase in the overall size of the British force in Saudi Arabia, together with the resubordination of the UK ground forces from USMC to 7(US) Army Corps, presented some enormous challenges and I may say created a good deal of tension at the time. You only have to look at the distances involved to gain an impression of the command, control and communications problems that faced us, let alone the necessity to move stock out of Jubail, all the while conforming to a

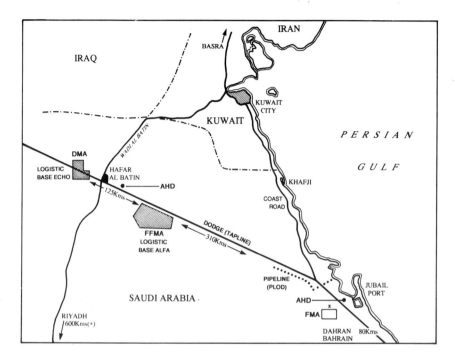

Figure 1.3 Logistic Bases

sophisticated deception plan. However, I felt very much part of the planning process and was consulted frequently by General de la Billière on the feasibility of moving our logistic effort in this way and on the detail by Major General Rupert Smith. It was at this stage that the planner from Joint Headquarters in High Wycombe briefed General Schwarzkopf on our logistic ability to support his evolving plan.

The arrival of the Division meant the reception of over 80 more ships, straining the facilities in Jubail to the limit but we worked in harmony both with our Saudi hosts and with the USMC, who were also receiving their own reinforcements, as were the US Army. Newly arrived logistic units were put to work as soon as they could marry up personnel and equipment. As the Division started training to the north of Jubail the shape of the future operation became clear and the FMA staff planned on setting up a Forward Force Maintenance Area (FFMA) 350 km northwest of Jubail at what was known by the Americans as Log Base Alpha. It was now that the Division became responsible for its own integral logistic support (first and second line) leaving HQ FMA/FFMA with a third line role.[7] The Divisional Deputy Chief of Staff for Logistics, Colonel Graham Ewer (a close personal friend) was General Rupert Smith's logistic commander and advisor on all administrative and combat service support (CSS) matters whilst I retained that role for General de la Billière at theatre level, an arrangement that worked well but one that had to be thrashed out early.

Forward Deployment

Forward deployment of logistic stocks and units was based on a 21 day time frame and started on 3 January 1991. Our major concerns were the limited capacity (number of vehicles and stock holding) of our logistic units, the fact that stocks were still arriving at Jubail, the overriding operational security situation, the Nuclear, Biology and Chemical (NBC) threat and the distances and going involved. The main supply route (MSR) along the tapline road (Route DODGE) was about 700 km for the round trip, the time for which varied between 24 and 36 hours, depending on the weather and the density, invariably immense, of Allied deployment and logistic traffic. Ammunition stock levels in the FFMA were set at 15 days for artillery, 8 days for tank and infantry, that is 18,000 tons of ammunition, together with 7 million litres of fuel, 6,000 tons of materiel and, of course, rations and water. We were constantly testing in our minds whether we had got the logistic balance right for offensive operations. We made use of the two FMA Transport Regiments (10 and 27 Regiments Royal Corps of Transport (RCT) as well as the two Divisional Regiments (1 and 4 Regiments RCT); our Tank Transporters (7 Regiment RCT) and as many local transporters as we could hire were heavily involved in deploying the Division forward. A fuel pipeline to a point some 100 km north-west of Jubail, designed and constructed by British and American Engineers, helped to shorten the resupply loop for fuel. This pipeline over the desert (PLOD) was designed and commissioned by British Royal Engineers (RE) of 516 Specialist Team RE under the command of Major Jim Kingham. PLOD was commissioned on 26 February 1991 and named the 'Kingham Line' in recognition of the effort put in by Jim Kingham who, tragically, died in a road accident during the construction. (More details can be seen in Chapter 6.)

As the inload clock ticked away (towards the 21 day limit), personnel and assets moved forward and on 17 January I moved to command from HQ FFMA, leaving my deputy, Lieutenant Colonel Chris Bradley (later Colonel Tony Welch) to run the operation in Jubail. This, of course, remained enormous, with stock continuing to arrive in theatre and elements such as Battle Casualty Replacements (BCRs) and the Prisoner of War Guard Force (PWGF) also arriving and deploying.

At this stage the Division had completed the first part of its training in Jubail and began to move along DODGE, a vast operation in itself, using every available tank transporter and as many host nation vehicles as possible. In this latter regard we found ourselves in competition with both the USMC and US Army. The lesson here, if time permits, is to establish some form of multinational control mechanism to direct priorities, it would also save a great many arguments!

The Division moved to its Forward Assembly Area (FAA) and we began the inload to a Divisional Maintenance Area (DMA) of 10 days of all ammunition natures, together with reserve fuel and materiel. Again we had concerns about the logistic balance at this point; steady nerves were much needed. In the meantime, the FFMA stock levels were being topped up from Jubail; the third line logistic support for the Division was in place and we were fairly happy that it was well balanced for the forthcoming operation.

The outline concept for the resupply of the Division is shown at Figure 1.5. In short, the intention was to resupply the Division from either the DMA or the FFMA depending on the progress of the battle and the location of Divisional CSS[8] units. A system of Exchange Points (XPs) was established where individual commodities could be transferred. We had practised this rather complex operation with the Division and Graham Ewer and I were reasonably content that it would work! The aim was to give the Division the maximum logistic mobility and flexibility possible for their advance. These XPs were simply patches of desert and our transport units had to rely heavily on the satellite navigation system (GPS) to find their way. Incidentally we employed our DROPS[9] (Dismountable Rack Off Loading and Pick-Up System) vehicles in this situation solely for the resupply of water and multi-launch rocket system (MLRS)[10] pods. We had not planned on the ground dumping of stocks during the preparatory phase or during the battle itself but, in fact, dumping of artillery ammunition was possible as a result of low expenditure rates. This provided a welcome logistic bonus when the Division was projected east towards Kuwait.

So far I have talked only about stocks and transport operations. Let me touch briefly on medical support, which will be covered in detail in Chapter 5 and was crucial to operations. At the start of the land battle there were some 5,000 medical personnel in support of the Division and the FMA. We had a well-established and reasonably well-practised evacuation system, involving our three hospitals, support helicopters[11] (SH) and C130 Hercules aircraft as well as coordination and mutual support from the US medical services and other Allies. Thankfully, our casualties were few, but the medical services were kept busy treating Iraqi prisoners, many of whom had been left untreated on the battlefield for several days.

The Land Battle

Turning now to a brief résumé of the land battle (see Figure 1.4). From 14–23 February, the Divisional Artillery Group (DAG) took part in the

7 Corps programme of preparatory fire plans known as artillery raids. These had the aims of destroying high value targets, deceiving the Iraqis as to where the main attack would occur, assessing enemy action and allowing training to continue up to the last moment as units were still deploying.

The ground war was launched at 0400 hrs on 24 February. Things went so well – except for bad weather that delayed the initial attack of 101 (US) Air Assault Division – part of 18 (US) Corps – that the main attack was brought forward by 14 hours. The Divisional Artillery Group supported 1 (US) Infantry Division in the breaching and counter reconnaissance battle whilst the rest of the Division received radio orders to cancel a planned tank transporter move and, at 1400 hrs on 24 February, the Division moved forward on tracks to be in the staging area just south of the breach by 2300 hrs on that day.

On 25 February, the Division literally crept forward behind the Americans, waiting to conduct a forward passage of the lines, which happened at 1200 hrs. At 1515 hrs, 7 Brigade crossed their line of departure. They were in the north of the Divisional area and were followed in the south by 4 Brigade some four hours later. The first major attack was launched by 7 Brigade at 2000 hrs.

Opposition on the night of 25–26 February was significant as demonstrated by enemy counter-attacks of up to tank company strength. Although it was already clear that the unexpected speed, direction and firepower of the brigades would overwhelm the opposition, it was not until first light on the 26th that the Division effectively dominated its sector. With the divisional recce troops bringing air and MLRS depth fire down, attacks continued during the 26th to clear all objectives to Phase Line SMASH.

Phase Line SMASH was reached at 0600 hrs on the 27th after 33 hours of action – 15 hours quicker than the operational analysis had predicted. The division had destroyed the best part of the 46 Mechanised Brigade and 52 Armoured Brigade, together with the manoeuvre elements of at least three infantry divisions.

A number of options were then planned to assist the Corps main effort in the north against the withdrawing Republican Guards. These included a pursuit north-east towards Basra but in fact at 0730 hrs on the 27th, 7 Brigade attacked due east across the Wadi Al Batin into Kuwait, achieving their objective on the far side of the Wadi against only light opposition at 1130 hrs. The division was then halted before receiving orders to clear a route south west down the line of the Wadi starting at 1930 hrs. Counter orders were then received and the Division resumed its advance east at 2110 hrs.

This final advance continued until the ceasefire at 0800 hrs the following morning – the 28th – the leading battle group of 7 Brigade having reached the Kuwait to Basra road at 0725 hrs. The Division had advanced

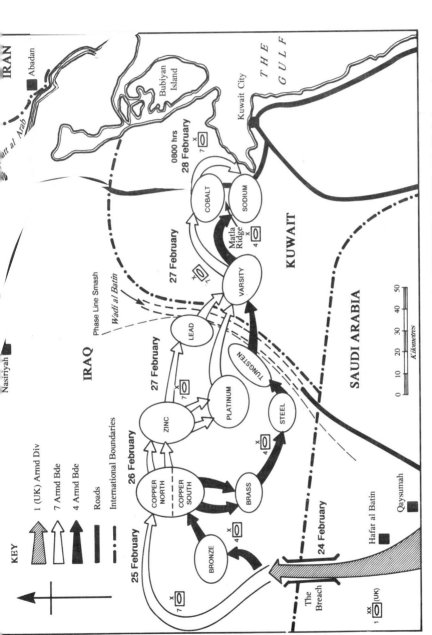

Figure 1.4 Operations of 1 (UK) Armoured Division in Operation DESERT SABRE (24–28 February)

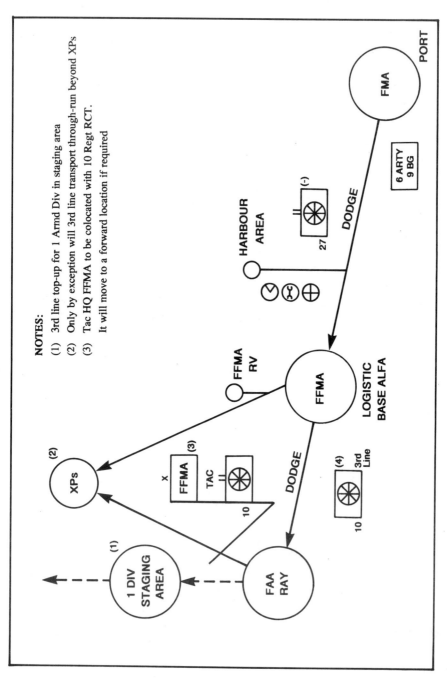

NOTES:

(1) 3rd line top-up for 1 Armd Div in staging area

(2) Only by exception will 3rd line transport through-run beyond XPs

(3) Tac HQ FFMA to be colocated with 10 Regt RCT. It will move to a forward location if required

Figure 1.5 Outline Concept of Logistic Operations

290 km in 90 hours, destroyed the best part of at least three Iraqi divisions, taken some 8,000 prisoners, including two enemy divisional commanders, and captured over 400 equipments and 2,000 small arms.

Support of the Land Battle

The divisional and brigade logistic units were heavily involved in supporting the battle (Chapter 10). Meanwhile, the first elements of FMA transport committed to resupplying the operations were the squadrons allocated to artillery ammunition resupply. The plan was to deliver to artillery exchange points (XPs). There the ammunition would be crossloaded for forward distribution by divisional transport. The initial resupply of the guns was by divisional transport but, on 22 February, FMA vehicles loaded artillery ammunition in the FFMA and moved forward to a holding area in the DMA. Shortly after this, the vehicles were called forward to an artillery XP just south of the breach, to support the artillery raids. Here some of the loads were exchanged and some were dumped on the ground.

As I have said, it had never been planned to dump stock at the XPs but, because of the lower than expected rate of fire during the breaching operation, approximately three days worth were dumped in this area. This proved a bonus when the Division raced east into Kuwait and, as further XPs were established, transport was able to resupply them from the rear.

* * *

We must now move on from artillery resupply and turn to the resupply of the land battle in general. As it crossed the breach, the Division was in good shape logistically, with substantial stocks held forward on wheels or held with units, in the divisional area and FFMA. The majority of the battle was fought with unit and divisional stock carried on wheels. Fuel resupply, however, did take place in the latter stages of the land battle. The forward movement of the large low mobility 22,500 litre tankers was restricted by muddy conditions and to alleviate this, a fuel XP was established forward in the area of the Iraq/Kuwait border. This forward XP shortened the resupply loop by nearly 120 km. The account of the Division's logistic operations is told in Chapter 10.

Once 1 (UK) Division was well established in Kuwait, FMA resupply did become necessary to top up a wide range of commodities expended throughout the land battle. Unfortunately the supply loop was 240 kms long (one way), north of the DMA, through the breach and then east into Kuwait. It was taking between 36 and 48 hours to complete the whole 480 km round trip. This loop was considerably shortened, however, when, on 2 March, a new MSR (Route 363), running north east of Hafr Al Batin, parallel to the Wadi Al Batin and joining a major tarmac road running directly east into Kuwait City, was opened by the FMA Engineer Squadron. Shortly before this, from 28 February, after the declaration of a cessation in hostilities, transport from the FMA in Jubail began running directly up the coast road into Kuwait City.

Summary

This first chapter sets the scene for the rest of the book. I am very aware that it is thin on detail and that I have excluded many crucial aspects of the logistic operations, rear area security, command, control and communications, replacement of armoured vehicles, battle casualty replacements, prisoners of war, engineer logistics, the recovery operation to name but a few. However, the purpose of succeeding chapters is to explore some of these areas in more detail, including that most vital ingredient, the commander's view by Major General Rupert Smith, Commander 1 (UK) Armoured Division. There is, inevitably, some duplication and for this I make no apology as I believe it underscores our unity of purpose.

Finally, there was much talk in the Army of why the FMA had such strong connection with the popular TV Series, Blackadder. It has definitely nothing to do with a certain Brigadier (known in the Army as Blackadder) but more to do with my daughter Anna, a fan of the TV Series, who on the outside of her letters to me invariably wrote 'I hope you have a cunning plan'. This catchword from the programme stuck throughout the force and led to the naming of our temporary camps Baldrick Lines and Blackadder Camp and to the production of the FMA insignia, the Blackadder.

Chapter 2

The Commander's Role

Lieutenant General R A Smith DSO OBE QGM
(Commander 1 (UK) Division)

Having been told I was to take my Headquarters and command the Armoured Division that was to be built up on 7 Armoured Brigade and the Force Maintenance Area (FMA) that were already in Saudi Arabia, I carried out a reconnaissance in November 1990.

I was to be the commander of the UK's land forces in a coalition offensive operation to free Kuwait from Iraq's occupation. The planning for this offensive had not been completed and whether the 1 (UK) Armoured Division was to be subordinated to the United States Marine Corps (USMC) or to a US Army Corps had not been decided. The burden of this particular decision lay with a judgement as to whether or not the UK could support its forces logistically if they were grouped with the US Army on the western flank. In principle the responsibility for logistic and medical support lay with the nation providing the contingent, although in practice the contingents helped each other out with what they had to spare at the time. If we were to be subordinated to the US Army then our logistic arrangements, predicated initially on a defensive operation on the eastern flank and subordinated to the USMC, would have to be reinforced and stretched: first, to deploy some 350 kms from the coast and then to support an attack into Iraq and up to the Euphrates. Our aim was to destroy the Republican Guard, the core of the enemy's army.

The Critical Decision

With planning at a formative stage, this operational level logistic problem was difficult to quantify let alone solve at the time of my reconnaissance. While it was evidently an important decision, my primary concern was to decide how I was going to fight the Division and here the logistics and the medical factors weighed just as heavily. I had to reach this decision by the end of my reconnaissance so as to direct my commanders' efforts, organise the force and, importantly, agree that the forces and resources I had been allocated were sufficient for the purpose or alternatively demand more. I thought this decision was the most critical because all else depended on it.

In deciding how to fight my command, I was conscious that I was about to be given very nearly all that the British Army could sustain in a campaign as far away as Saudi Arabia. There was not going to be very much in the way of reinforcements of equipment once the battle started. Wherever we went, my subordinate groupings, the brigades and the battle groups, would have to be as self-contained as possible, which argued for an increase in the stocks held forward at unit level (first line) with a consequent increase in transport. Because we were attacking and could expect to bypass enemy positions and be counter attacked, the supply routes and those travelling along them would need protecting. These considerations were complicated by the unreliability of some of our equipments, but beyond knowing this was so, I and my staff were unable to quantify the extent of this worrying factor. In deciding on my concept, I thought I had to reach a balance which I have described with Figure 2.1. The left hand stool concerns the tactical concept and is arrived at by striking a balance between the factors of firepower, mobility and acquisition of Information, in relation to the enemy and the circumstances at the time. The right hand stool, the logistic concept, must strike a balance between a further three factors: the duration of the anticipated battle, the distance over which supplies must be carried, and the anticipated demand for those supplies. The plank resting on the two stools must be level and be kept level; it being unwise to start a battle you cannot supply, or alternatively, not to be prepared to fight to your full capacity. The connection between the stools, the plank, and

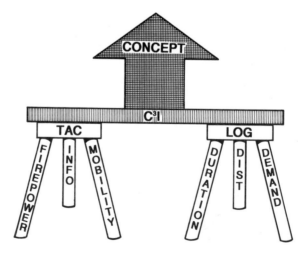

Figure 2.1 The Development of an Operational Concept

to an extent the method of keeping them level is the business of the command and control arrangements which includes how the force is organised.

By the end of my reconnaissance, I was reasonably confident that provided I had an increase in drivers, so that my transport could be run continuously, and suitable cross country transport to carry the extra stocks I wished to hold at first line and plant to construct and maintain routes, I could supply and maintain the Division. I was less confident about the reliability of our equipment, but I knew a great deal of effort was being expended, first to improve reliability, by modifications to both equipment and practice, and also to provide every spare possible. It was clear I was going to have to find a way of organising my reserve equipments and their crews so as to compensate quickly for any break-downs. At this stage I was not at all sure how this was to be done but I asked for, and after a lengthy debate was given, a battalion, whose task would be not only to organise and train my reserves but also to protect my headquarters and rear. This unit took a very long time to come because Ministers imposed an arbitrary cap[1] on the manpower being deployed. In the event it was employed slightly differently. My major concern at this stage was who commanded Brigadier Martin White and the FMA.

Command and Control

To my surprise I found on being briefed at Headquarters British Forces Middle East (BFME) that the FMA was to be under my command. The Headquarters was of this view because the FMA was not in fact supporting all the UK forces but only the Division. I believed then, and now, that such an arrangement was wrong in principle; it leads to a lack of economy of logistic effort and competition for scarce transport resources into theatre. However, I had a more pressing concern. I could not see how I, as a tactical commander, charged with attacking deep into Iraq or Kuwait, could be responsible for the command of an essentially static organisation based on the port of Jubail. In my view the FMA was a Theatre responsibility. It was located in the Communication Zone, holding third line or theatre stocks and should be commanded by the Theatre Headquarters, HQ British Forces Middle East. After some debate this was agreed, but it was to take until the middle of January before the communications were available to allow this to happen. Of course Martin White was directed by HQ BFME to support the Division and he and I maintained a very close liaison. Furthermore, when elements of the FMA came forward within the Divisional Area they came under my tactical control.

The logistic units that I commanded held the formation stocks (second line) for the Division, carried out our second line repairs and were mobile. My principal logistic commanders were Lieutenant Colonel Gavin Haig, Commander Transport; Lieutenant Colonel Andy Ashley, Commander Maintenance and Lieutenant Colonel Tim Cross, Commander Supply. They were directed by me through my Divisional Rear Headquarters which was most ably run by my Deputy Chief of Staff, Colonel Graham Ewer. My Senior Medical Officer (SMO) or Commander Medical was Colonel Louis Lillywhite. A commander's relationship with his logistic and medical commanders and staff is a critical factor in the exercise of command. His logistic staff and commanders are usually some distance from him, for more often than not he will be forward with his Intelligence and Operational staff planning or conducting a battle. The medical commander is more difficult to place but in my experience he is usually found more forward than back for reasons I will discuss later. Because of this separation, the commander must have complete confidence in his logisticians and they in him. In particular he must give, by working out in good time how he wants to fight, clear direction as to his requirements. Without this confident direction, it is very difficult for the logistician to obey at least two of the Principles of Administration: Foresight and Economy.

Logistic and Medical Planning

Without direction the logistician will tend to play safe by covering all the options, each with sufficient resources for the worst case. This over-insurance violates the principle of Economy, it also tends to conceal logistic inefficiency. Failure to provide is evident, over-insurance gives a false impression of efficiency. The reverse is, of course the truth, since the waste of manpower, materiel, transport and time resulting in over-insurance may seriously handicap the development of operations. Largely because of the UK's incremental involvement in the campaign and the ad hoc groupings we deployed, this direction was lacking and over-insurance occurred. I think the lesson to draw from this is to deploy commanders from the outset. The logistics of an enterprise invariably take the longest to arrange and commanders should concentrate their efforts on these matters rather than the tactical detail in the early stages of planning.

The medical arrangements to support one's plan are managed by much the same staff as logistic matters, but one must guard against thinking that the medical and logistic plans are one and the same thing. Of course, the movement of casualties and the re-supply of medical stores are logistic matters, but the arrangements for the deployment and employment of your medical units is a separate and distinct plan. I think this because the medical plan deals with the treatment of men over time, rather than the repair of an equipment. And, unlike the repair of a broken down vehicle at first line by its crew, those in contact at first line must not become involved with more than initial first aid for their casualties, unless it is their designated task to do so. If this occurs the enemy is taking a bonus, men are starting to cooperate with their opponent's actions and the will to take offensive action is being corroded by concern for their wounded comrades. Because of this, there must always be a plan for the treatment and evacuation of casualties to match every tactical plan. The lack or failure of such a plan has an immediate adverse effect on morale. It is for this reason that, when engaged, I like to have my Commander Medical forward. After all, his problems are being caused, in part at least, by me and they lie, literally, forward. Additionally, he has the pulse of your command and it is from him that you can receive early indications of slipping morale, stress, laxness in discipline and so on.

Initial Preparation

We started to deploy to Saudi Arabia soon after my reconnaissance and I arrived on 11 December. I was directed to have the Division trained and ready for operations by 31 January, while also playing my part in the planning of those operations. Apart from getting to know those in my command that had deployed with 7 Armoured Brigade, and gleaning as much as I could from their experience, almost all the issues I was dealing with involved logistics. In particular, three matters affected my ability to form and train the Division: the maintenance of equipments, visibility and identification of stores, and movement into and within theatre.

The need to preserve the engines and major assemblies of our Armoured Fighting Vehicles (AFVs), our aircraft engines and to some extent the replacement black boxes (LRUs) for the tank turret systems, limited, sometimes severely, the amount of training that could be carried out on these equipments. I found myself having to strike a fine balance on a number of occasions between having the equipment available for the battle and training to ensure that the crews and commanders had confidence in their ability to fight the equipment in the battle. I usually came down on the side of the crew's confidence, on the ground that my spares-to-equipment ratio would improve once we lost a few equipments in battle, always assuming the enemy didn't attack the rear areas first! The worst period lasted for some two weeks, in late December and early January, when 7 Brigade had a track mileage allowance of only 15 kms per tank per week and the Warriors were not allowed to move for about seven days of that period. The situation improved during January but it was never satisfactory.

The lack of visibility of spares and the difficulty of identification exacerbated the maintenance problem. It was aggravated further by the tendency to over-insure and the plethora of different equipments, ranging from Centurion to Challenger, from Ferret Scout Car to Fuchs (German chemical recce vehicle). Again much was done to improve matters but the system was never satisfactory and, as we attacked into Iraq, we were still searching the FMA for tank dozer blades for some of the armoured squadrons. Fortunately, the enemy did not cause us to need them. Even so, one was left thinking that if we could not find something like a bulldozer blade for a tank, what hope was there of finding the essential widget for some obscure but vital piece of equipment?

The move from Germany and the United Kingdom to Saudi Arabia was conducted as an administrative move. That is to say making the best use of transport available and thus at least cost. To do this means fitting loads to the available ships and airplanes, accepting that men will be separated from their equipments and that units will lose their integrity. The commander may well stipulate his desired order of arrival for his units but this is not guaranteed. While I am sure this was the correct decision, the disadvantages of this type of move were increased by the need to enter the market for the necessary shipping with the result that the 'mover' only knew what could be embarked once the contract was let. Some of the ships were unreliable and broke down en route and others were slow. And, not for the first time in our history, storms in the Western Approaches disrupted our plans. The result was that during January the move of guns, gun ammunition and armoured engineer equipment became delayed. In some cases training either did not begin on time or was delayed, but to explain the full impact of this I must return to the planning process.

Subordination

After much debate during December, it was decided that the Division was to be subordinated to 7 (US) Corps. On Christmas Eve, I met Lieutenant General Fred Franks, the Commanding General of 7 (US) Corps, for the first time. He explained his plan and the part he wanted me to play in it. When the Corps attacked, we were to destroy the enemy's tactical reserves, so that the Corps could reach and destroy the Republican Guard without wasting time and combat power getting there. I thought this mission was well within our capabilities and we could fulfil it. The first thing we discussed after he had explained the plan was logistics. I was keen to make the point that my logistic problem was of the same order as his, rather than that of his other divisional commanders, the reason for this being that we were both supported by our nations from Theatre stocks in the Communications Zone. I had to have logistic information and knowledge of Corps level intentions in the Corps time frame. He understood my need at once and agreed to my placing logistic staff officers in his headquarters. Within days, a comprehensive, liaison, covering all the branches of an headquarters, was established but the first, and the only one discussed commander to commander, was the logistic liaison. The Corps commander went on to say he would like the UK Division in its Concentration Area ready for operations by 31 January. This proved a bit of a problem.

Forward Deployment

You will recall that the plan was to be ready in the area of Jubail by 31 January. We were now faced with the need to move the Division some 350 kms and by that same date to outload a considerable tonnage in order to establish a Forward Force Maintenance Area (FFMA). All this while units and formations were arriving, formed up, trained and acclimatised. After some most detailed staff work, I reckoned we could do it but I would have to take some risks. The move up to the Concentration Area would have to be administrative rather than tactical. Logistic unit and formation collective training and divisional formation training would have to be abandoned and I would have to see what could be done once we had joined 7 Corps. We would have to start by stocking the FFMA and building at least one Field Hospital, these would be on or close to an enemy axis if he attacked, and although elements of 7 Corps were deployed already, I would have no protection for them until I could get my brigades into the Concentration Area. The forward movement of stocks demanded that second line transport should be moved to reinforce the third line, which reduced the speed with which the brigades could react to an enemy attack. Because of their unreliability, we could not afford to drive the tracked vehicles, so they would have to be transported. Apart from placing even greater demands on our logistic vehicles, to complete this move in time called for expedient measures. Finally, and as a result of the delays caused by the sea move, my artillery units, which I wanted to fight as a formation and needed to train as one, would be the last to move up the route. Moving one's formations without their supporting artillery close to the enemy does not give one a comfortable feeling.

The move and the stocking of the FFMA started on 3 January and for much of the month I remained uncomfortable. Particularly when the air offensive began and all the indicators began to show an Iraqi attack in preparation. This attack, very largely defeated by air attacks as it moved to its start lines, resulted in the Iraqi seizure of Khafji, which was retaken by the Coalition some 24 hours later. By 29 January, we were complete in the Concentration Area and at last I had the Division under my hand.

Battle Preparation

While we concentrated, planning continued and had reached a stage that allowed me to hold an 'O Group' on 29 January explain the plan to all my commanders including Martin White and his immediate subordinates. During late December and early January, I had conducted a series of Map Exercises for all my commanders down to and including the Commanding Officers. The purpose of these was to show my commanders the part they would have to play and the way I wanted it played in my concept of operations. They had another effect. This was to bring the COs together and enable them to learn the interdependence of front and rear, supporter and supported in the forthcoming battle. Now we were together with the Americans, we could train together. We conducted a rehearsal with the US 1 Infantry Division of our passage through the breach that they were to drive through the enemy's Main Defensive Position. This exercise was the first time that the logistics units were able to deploy and practise moving as they would in battle.

By mid-February, 18 Airborne Corps completed its move west and it was 7 Corps' turn to move across the Wadi al Batin and into the Assembly Area from which it would attack. Once again second line transport was regrouped to third line and we rapidly built up a Divisional Maintenance Area (DMA) in our Assembly Area. The Tank Transporter Regiment moved the Divisional Artillery and that of the 1st Infantry Division up close to the enemy's Main Defensive Positions so that they could start the Artillery Raids which were to proceed the attack. I used the move of the Division to the assembly area as another exercise, practising the Headquarters in the control of movement and regrouping of units (see campaign map at Figure 1.4).

We were in the assembly area for several days. My attention was almost entirely devoted to the forthcoming fight but I still had two logistic matters which needed attention. The first was to ensure that we had some fresh rations for everybody before they attacked, many of us had been on an almost unrelieved diet of 'compo' for at least a month. The other matter concerned the arrangements for my reserve equipment. I had decided to form an Armoured Delivery Battle Group (ADBG) under the command of the CO of the Queen's Own Highlanders. This was the battalion that I had asked for at the end of my reconnaissance and at last its Commanding Officer had reached me. I also wished to form a Divisional Repair Group under the Commanding Officer of 7 Armoured Workshop. The ADBG was to consist of a fully manned tank squadron, an armoured infantry company, platoons and troops and fully manned single vehicles. These were to travel on tank transporters. The idea was that after an engagement I would direct the two COs to join the brigade that had been involved with instructions to bring it up to a certain level of fighting effectiveness. With the Brigade Commander they would make a plan to deal with what could be repaired and what must be replaced. If a Battle Group had suffered a number of casualties to men and equipment, it might receive a complete new sub-unit, allowing the CO of the ADBG to rest and reorganise the survivors. The COs would then call up from the Workshops and the Delivery Group the necessary replacement vehicles, either as formed sub-units or singletons, together with the necessary equipment, tools and so on, to carry out the repairs of that which could be repaired, so as to reconstitute the ADBG as much as possible, making it ready for the next battle. In the event, we did not have a proper opportunity to use this concept but I believe it would have served us well.

On 24th February the attack started. As we rolled forward to start our approach march to the breach, I was confident that our logistic arrangements were as well established as it was possible to make them. I will not rehearse the story of the actual attack except to record that all our arrangements appeared to work well. When we halted, having cut the Kuwait–Basra Road and the cease fire was called, it was not long before everybody was ready to continue the attack into Basra, if that had been required of us. All our preparations and all the hard work of the logistic units and their commanders had paid off, although I have to say that the enemy were a poor lot and things might not have gone as well for us if they had given a better account of themselves.

Chapter Three

The Force Maintenance Area

Part One

The Logistic Structure

Lieutenant Colonel W R Harber MBE Queens
(Deputy Chief of Staff Logistics, HQ FMA Gulf)

The Task Unfolds

Following the decision to send 7 Brigade to the Gulf, the Deputy Chief of Staff (DCOS) 1 (UK) Armoured Division Colonel Graham Ewer directed that there should be a logistic 'audit' to identify manpower and equipment shortfalls both against war establishment[1] and our Operation GRANBY aspirations. The weekend meeting included staff from all three of the BAOR divisional brigades (7, 12 and 22) and their respective units. The G1 and G3[2] staffs worked out the personnel requirements and the G4 staff identified the equipment demands. Against the restrictions of peacetime training, the demand to get to the normal war establishment would be large. To go beyond that to a tailored Operation GRANBY organisation would be a tremendous burden on the rest of BAOR. From this important meeting came the basic 'shopping list', initially passed from our brigades, subsequently to Corps Headquarters in Bielefeld, for a host of items to make 7 Brigade ready for war. The effects of this requirement should not be underestimated. Ultimately, no unit in Germany would be left untouched in the search for spares and equipment, principally to get the armour ready for battle.

Coincidentally, a number of events had occurred in BAOR to assist the planning and preparation for operations. Both the Challenger tank and Warrior infantry vehicle had had mechanical problems during the preceding twelve months. These were understandable, normal, 'teething' problems for relatively new equipment and the remedial action left the vehicles in good condition. However, that summer (1990) had also identified a problem of dust ingestion into the Challenger air filtration system whilst 7 Brigade were training at Soltau, the principal local training area. A timely problem to identify before deploying to the desert! 1990 had also seen a reassessment of our operational logistic concepts due to the introduction of the new Demountable Rack Off Loading and Pick-Up System (DROPS). This transport system meant that complete loads could be dropped from trucks with greater speed and flexibility than ever before. This 'conveyor belt' of supply was suited to manoeuvre warfare, with units in the advance and the artillery to support them.

The tempo of life in Verden[3] increased dramatically. The Headquarters went onto 24 hour manning, which for the principal operations staff officers, both G3 and G1/G4, meant snatching a few hours sleep as and when possible. Most of the problems were familiar, particularly as the staffs were generally nearing the end of their tours of duty in Verden and were therefore very experienced. However, when asked by DCOS 7 Armoured Brigade, we were all at a loss to know the type, name, part number and quantity available of sand-coloured paint! What was more worrying was the silence that was forthcoming when the question of desert combat kit was raised at higher headquarters. Someone joked that we had sold it all to the Iraqis some years before. Some joke. But the demands for items was immense and the supply organisation needed assistance. It was at such a time that the support services came into their own. A Movement Control Centre (MCC) was established in order to coordinate supply and distribution, if only to ensure that the right units got the right equipment and stores in the shortest possible time.

The Logistic Headquarters

The Headquarters was in full swing with its transition to war operations. Behind the scenes the Divisional Commander, Major General Roger Wheeler (shortly to become Major General Rupert Smith), was making sure that he placed a number of his staff into positions to support 7 Armoured Brigade in Saudi Arabia. After much debate it was announced that I would be going to the third line headquarters, with the SO2[4] G1, Major Steve Howe, Royal Army Medical Corps (RAMC). Shortly afterwards I was contacted by a friend from Corps Headquarters, Major Peter Cross, Royal Regiment of Fusiliers (RRF), who informed me that he was putting the detail together as the Chief of Staff (COS) and that with a blank sheet of paper in front of him, what about a few suggestions? Basing the layout on that of divisional rear headquarters, we discussed, in outline, the posts required to fill all of the staff functions for a logistic headquarters, including its signals and administrative support, and with the same ability to provide local defence. It was at this stage that HQ FMA began to take shape. Peter Cross was already at Rheindahlen, working in Headquarters BAOR for Colonel Martin White who was to command the formation and it was clear that an early visit to this embryonic gathering was necessary.

Major Steve Howe and I travelled to Rheindahlen to be met by Peter Cross. We were shown to the G4 Logistic Operations branch in HQ BAOR and were introduced to the Deputy Commander, Lieutenant Colonel 'Tug' Wilson, Royal Army Ordnance Corps (RAOC) (sadly, 'casevaced' from Saudi Arabia in November 1990) and the officer helping to gather the staff together, Major Ernie Beck. Having met the personalities and with Colonel White still on his initial recce of Saudi Arabia, discussion began on the layout and structure of the Headquarters as well as the priorities at that early stage. We confirmed the posts required: the staff, including the important aspect of G5 (civil and military cooperation); the Services; and our own support, including communications, vehicles, administration and defence. At this stage the title Headquarters Rear Maintenance Area was being used and HQ RMA was the official abbreviation.

That evening we dined in the Officers' Mess and had a few glasses of German beer at the bar. For those of us who had managed little sleep in the preceding fortnight, we discovered the attraction of sleeping whilst at the bar! During the next day, we flew to England to discuss the establishment of our Headquarters with Joint Headquarters (JHQ) at High Wycombe.[5] Brigadier Simon Firth was setting up the Land Logistics cell and they were not much further into the task than we were in Germany. The main points of contact were Major Nigel Lloyd RAOC and Major David Arthur, Royal Artillery (RA). Fortunately, those in the logistics organisation were able, and willing, to discuss our requirements. Principally our command, control and communications (C^3) needs had to be organised (see Figure 3.1). It was agreed between ourselves that, initially, HQ RMA should report back direct to JHQ on logistic matters, only informing HQ BFME in Riyadh of the details. Much heated discussion was involved in getting this decision accepted, as some of the operations staff felt strongly that everything needed to go through Riyadh, although later this changed. It was sometimes difficult to explain to the staff in JHQ that the nucleus of the Headquarters under General de la Billière did not yet contain sufficient breadth of army operational logistics staff officers with experience of armoured warfare. In the end, it was agreed that operational G4 matters, reports and returns would be sent from HQ RMA through HQ BFME to JHQ and then on to MOD. Priority requirements could, of course, be passed direct to High Wycombe, if necessary. Functional matters were on a direct link to the

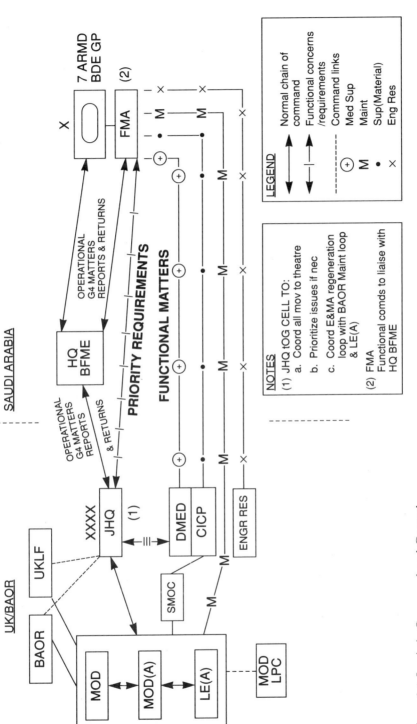

Figure 3.1 Logistic Command and Control

UK. This meant that medical supplies, maintenance (Equipment Management), material supplies and engineer resources could be dealt with quickly. At the same time, we discussed the requirements for regular reports and returns back to the UK. This was done using the revised Army Standing Operational Procedures (SOP) pamphlet but without any real knowledge of what detailed information would be required from Saudi Arabia. Using our judgement and some best guesses, we agreed on 29 report and return formats which would form the basis of the detailed information required at JHQ, as and when the operation was up and running.

At this time, Steve Howe was not having the most successful visit. G1 matters not only cover operational details relating to personnel but also welfare. It seemed that welfare was easily discussed but the most difficult operational ones were not – and would not be for some considerable time to come. The policy on repatriation of the dead, for example, had to be raised early on, as we anticipated the need for some ministerial direction. The reaction to the question of a prisoner of war guard force was also fairly inconclusive at this stage. It was explained that any sizeable number of prisoners needed a large force to guard and administer them. If the prisoners were to be extracted from the battlefield and detained under national arrangements, any-thing up to a brigade sized force could be needed. As only a reinforced brigade was deploying to Saudi Arabia, this was not the sort of advice that was likely to be militarily or politically popular at this stage of planning.

We returned to Rheindahlen and thence to Verden the following day. Life was hectic and now there were matters to be discussed and handed on before departing for HQ RMA. My SO3 G1/G4 (Operations) in 1(UK) Armoured Division was Captain Angus MacDonald, Black Watch. Another logistic infanteer and good friend, I had tried to get him included in the RMA, but this was unacceptable to Colonel Ewer as so much work remained to be done in Verden. He never did thank me for leaving him in the lurch, but I knew he would do a good job in my absence!

After a few more days in the Headquarters it was time to leave. There was a strong mixture of emotions as farewells were said, but happily we were to meet again in a few months' time. A short break at home and then we travelled to Rheindahlen, carrying as much useful stationery and pamphlets as we could from the Division, as well as our personal equipment. Arriving in Rheindahlen, I met Colonel Martin White for the first time. An early decision was to drop any reference to Rear Maintenance Area and adapt the Force Maintenance Area (FMA) as our title. We believed that it reflected a greater degree of flexibility and more accurately reflected our role. The following day we flew to Fallingbostel to attend a briefing by Commander 7 Armoured Brigade at the barracks of the Queen's Royal Irish Hussars. It included a briefing by the US Marine Corps (USMC) from Saudi Arabia and the deployment began to take shape in our minds. As this was the first time we had attended any meeting as Commander and DCOS HQ FMA, there was some confusion as to our role and structure. It was just this sort of teething problem that could be overcome by knowing and understanding the personalities within the Brigade Headquarters.

Preparation for Saudi Arabia

The next few days were a confirmatory period and our order of battle was agreed with the Headquarters and units. Our operating procedures were discussed in detail and, again, in simple terms, procedures used within Divisional Rear Headquarters were adopted. The Headquarters, when deployed out of the reception area in Jubail, would operate from staff vehicles which were soft skinned, but had an effective defence against chemical or biological attack. Our small headquarters was growing and we were bulking out in HQ BAOR. We decanted ourselves into temporary accommodation in Rheindahlen, which allowed us to work and plan for the reception of the staff in a couple of weeks time. Our new home was known as 10 Rillington Place,[6] and from there the effort was concentrated into producing the first HQ FMA Logistics Operation Order (Log Op O), but to do this required a second visit to JHQ and High Wycombe. Our major problem was to try and obtain confirmation of the medical support plan and for this reason Major Tim Pitcher RAMC (SO2 Medical) accompanied me. The medical support was being planned on a tri-service basis and the coordination of so much medical input was proving difficult and some crucial decisions were yet to be made. But at this late stage, any information was useful. The Land Logistics cell was well-established by now, but an important decision had to be made concerning the preferred computer system for communication between UK and Saudi Arabia. The RAF ASMA network (Air Staff Management Aid) had already been identified as the prime medium but the preferred Army system (MAPPER) seemed far more user-friendly and meant that chat-lines could be established which complemented voice links over such large distances. After a very hard sell, it was obvious that, if possible, both systems were required by us.

Having agreed our final input for the JHQ Administrative Instruction for the mounting of 7 Brigade, we returned to Germany to put together our own logistic operation order. This took a considerable amount of time, as it involved all of the BAOR service branches in completing their own detailed Annexes and then the compilation of the finished document. The basic concept had been agreed, for 30 days worth of ammunition at normal rates to be held on land and another 12 days

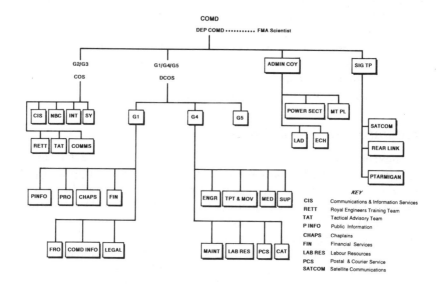

Figure 3.2 Headquarters Force Maintenance Area – Organisation

strategic reserve to be held at sea. Around this basic logistic plot went the detail for transport, supply including food, spares, clothing, and maintenance, with the latter's long regeneration loops back to the UK base and Germany for engines and major assemblies.

HQ FMA was formally established on Sunday 7 October 1990 (see Fig. 3.2). A conveyor belt reception system had been put together to receive and allocate all the new staff and soldiers. There was also a central briefing which was just about the only gathering of all members of the Headquarters during its existence. But time was running short and Colonel White and Peter Cross, the COS, left on 8 October on a pre-advance party flight in order to be in Jubail as soon as possible. I took the rest of the staff to Sennelager for a short two-day training package, designed to check personal equipment, including Nuclear Biological and Chemical (NBC) kit and to get the benefit of some briefings on operating in desert conditions. Most importantly, we were able to use the facilities of the Brigade and Battle Group Trainer under the guidance of Colonel Colin Groves. With his assistance, personal support and enthusiasm, the Headquarters was able to go through the only operational staff training available prior to deployment. In essence, it was possible to produce a graphical layout of the 7 Armoured Brigade deployment by echelons and to talk through how the third line support might work and how the staff would operate. This period was invaluable in starting to bring this ad hoc group together as a functioning headquarters.

Early Days

On the last night prior to deployment I stayed with close friends from The Queen's Regiment. The greatest personal challenge was to fit all one's kit into a bergen, a kit bag and a briefcase. After some hours (and quite a few glasses of beer) this last hurdle was overcome!

On 11 October, we departed for the airport at Gutersloh, where a number of senior officers, including GOC 1 (UK) Armoured Division appeared to say farewell. When we arrived in Jubail via Riyadh it was late at night. Even so, the wall of heat that hit you on leaving the RAF VCIO (strategic transport aircraft) was a surprise. We were shepherded onto local buses, handed a litre of the ubiquitous bottled water, and driven to the port area. There we were led into one of the large sheds which were to become a familiar feature as transit accommodation to brigade and divisional units prior to moving to the desert with their vehicles. In the shed we were given an introductory brief on the operational situation, followed by a short brief on the deployment within the port area. Most personnel were then taken away to Baldrick Lines, whilst Peter Cross, who I was glad to see, and I went to HQ FMA. This was lodged in the Port Clearance building, and home was a camp bed on one of the office floors. Amenities were basic but adequate, although the smell took some getting used to!

Within the Port Clearance building, offices were allocated by function. Each service (transport, medical and so on) had an office, including a detachment of 50 Movement Control Squadron. G1/G4 had its own operations room, with G2/G3 in an adjoining room. This allowed a reasonable level of information to pass between cells and also emphasised the leading operational role of G1/G4 in this logistic headquarters. Communications were in their early stages, based on line using the insecure civilian port telephone system or by personal liaison. The VDUs of both satellite systems and word processors came later, as did the secure trunk network (Ptarmigan). One 'briefcase' secure telephone was established as a voice link back to High Wycombe, but this was not easy to use. Running down either side of the building, on the outside, were the staff vehicles after they had arrived by sea. They provided extra meeting or planning space, as well as some security from NBC attacks should this prove necessary. The only problem was that access was by a thin window which defeated the larger members of the Headmasters and caused numerous cracked heads on the low ceiling. An early priority was for liaison with the USMC, our neighbours in the Port, whose control we were under and who were therefore giving us overall logistic as direction. It was a slow process to meet all those personnel who were involved in logistic operations, as their staff functions were not arranged in a similar fashion to our own. Nevertheless, the US Marines could not have been more helpful, spending hours explaining their procedures and also

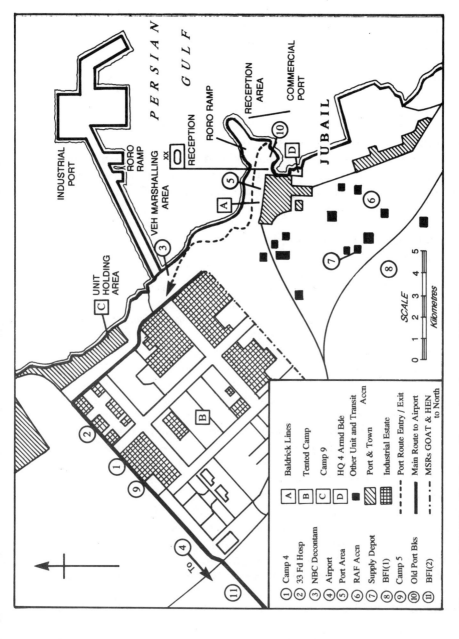

Figure 3.3 JUBAIL. The Port, Reception Area and FMA

listening to ours. The most immediate problem was getting sufficient real estate for the reception of 7 Armoured Brigade and this needed a protracted period of negotiation by Peter Cross, if only because the US operation dwarfed ours, even at this stage, and they needed facilities as well. Although there was frequent contact with 7 Brigade, this was essentially a period of getting organised for the reception of men and equipment. Whilst the real estate problem was left to the COS, a myriad of minor G4 problems began to emerge and these were my responsibility.

We were all into the basics of life. HQ 7 Brigade had offices in one of the transit sheds. The sheds themselves were to house units prior to moving to the desert. In addition, there were also the tented Baldrick Lines. But the tented camp needed expansion and negotiations continued with JHQ about available tentage from Depots in UK. Used mostly for medical units, the canvas had never been in such demand and there was some difficulty in identifying and assembling the necessary items. In Jubail, the FMA Headquarters also needed a larger location and other sites were considered, in competition with the Americans, of course. Our FMA units were also looking for more suitable accommodation in order that their work would not be hindered as reception started. (See Figure 3.3.)

Probably our most difficult task at this time was to ensure a sufficient supply of portable lavatories and showers for Brigade units. The toilets locally manufactured by our Engineers were not of a high standard, but were better than nothing when that was the only option. They were visited daily by a tanker which emptied their contents, usually in the early hours of the morning. The 'honeysucker', as it was nicknamed, was a useful ploy to get visitors used to the trials and tribulations of Jubail. In one corner of Baldrick Lines was the visitors tent. Situated conveniently by the main row of lavatories, visitors would be woken in the early hours by the noise of the lorry and the smell. Eventually, the aim was to build wooden 'two seaters' (partitioned only from the Mark II versions) allowing a strengthening of the social contact between all ranks. The other challenge was showers. Initially a basic system was acceptable, but soon numbers demanded a more sophisticated method. The Sappers adopted an American design and rows of wooden-based showers could be seen sprouting up around the port area. But demand always outstripped supply and the strategic importance of 'showers and s....s' was a constant headache and required frequent resiting by our Quartermaster to suit the movement of units in and around the Port area.

Water was proving a difficult commodity to get to the customers. Drinking water was not a problem, being supplied by the bottle and locally purchased. But other potable and washing water needed tankers taken up from local sources or military equivalents. Early on, we relied on the USMC to fill up our showers and water storage containers, but this was not satisfactory in the long run and prior to our own system being operable we borrowed a USMC modular container system (the SIXCON) which allowed some independence, with 10,000 litres being available on a DROPS flatrack. Eventually our own containers arrived. The 'beancan' held some 14,000 litres but, with a high centre of gravity, tended to be unstable. At this time, with resources under some strain, gifts were always welcomed. The US Marines accepted a large quantity of bags of water as a gift from our hosts. Regrettably, the water was contaminated and stomach upsets on a very large scale were the result.

Food is always close to a soldier's heart. Again the USMC were of assistance and their supply of field rations was essential. Meals Ready to Eat (or MRE) were retitled 'Meals Really Exciting' and 'Meals Rejected by Everyone'. They were in fact very palatable and the tuna pasta dish with Tabasco sauce was a favourite. Other menus tasted rather like reconstituted sawdust and were best offered to the honeysucker!

The Brigade Arrives

The first ship arrived on 18 October and from then on the aim was to marry up men and vehicles and get them to the desert without delay. Delays in shipping often meant that men were accommodated for up to three weeks in the sheds. In addition, quayside (principally up-armouring) modifications to the Challenger tanks and Warrior infantry combat vehicles meant further delays. Our first reports and returns were sent back to JHQ as the first units deployed to the desert. The Brigade Headquarters also deployed forward to its initial location and everyone began to discover the problems of working in the desert. The sand on the eastern seaboard was fine, even dusty, when churned up by armoured vehicles. Logistic support with many vehicles having low mobility only was likely to be a problem. Reduced tyre pressures helped but there was some concern that this might not be enough to reach some gun positions. There was also discussion on the logistic chain of command with 7 Brigade. Whilst it was understood who commanded what, it was never really clear how logistic direction might work in detail. At each logistic line of support the lead time for decision-making by staff and action by units became longer. At brigade, this would mean that the staff would have to direct the requirement for third and second line support whilst also preparing for and then fighting the contact battle forward. Whilst not an insurmountable problem, the key was for the Commander to give broad direction to the rear and then to trust that the framework was sufficiently flexible to carry out the detail. The last thing Brigade Headquarters needed was to have to worry about what was happening behind them. Regrettably, this was never practised with 7 Brigade on exercise, as events overtook us.

As the Brigade was declared operationally ready on 14 November 1990, we were in close discussion with the USMC over establishing a joint logistic headquarters for any future option that might involve a direct assault into Kuwait from the south. The Marines were able to build prefabricated wooden offices for use as a mobile headquarters which we thought might also house an element of HQ FMA. However, after some discussion, the idea was dropped, mainly because other operational options were being considered for us. Nevertheless, in November, Brigadier Martin White and I went North to Ras A1 Mishab on the East Coast to recce suitable logistic locations for a forward FMA (FFMA) should this prove necessary. The small naval port was an attractive location, and it was obvious that the US Marines also had plans for the area. After a short drive up to Ras Al Kafji (made famous later), we then headed West across the desert, paralleling the border. Driving through lines of Arab troops, we identified two locations for a move either direct into Kuwait from the south or from a south/south east direction moving into a salient that was created by the border line. Our discussions with the Marines continued, refining our option to support their intended move into Kuwait. They were desperately short of third line transport and there was no doubt that both our resources and those taken up from local Host Nation contract would be essential for the operation if it ever took place.

Change of Plan

At this time, the Commander FMA was warned of a further resubordination of the UK forces. In private he invited me to consider a move to the west in our line of attack to Kuwait. Naturally I assumed he meant the north eastern approach that we had previously recced. I pointed to the rough area on the map that we had considered. 'Further west' was his reply and after several attempts at this operational guessing game my finger stopped around the small town of Hafr Al Batin. He further explained that two officers were arriving from JHQ to talk through the logistic support required for a move north-east into Iraq/Kuwait, roughly along the line of the Wadi Al Batin. This was a challenge in all senses. Importantly, the only maps available were on 1:250,000 scale! Hence any detailed consideration of suitable locations for a forward logistic site from the map was limited. Lots more questions were raised but the information was highly classified and few knew of this latest proposal. Lieutenant Colonel Phillip Taylorson and Major Peter Sharpe arrived to talk through their calculations for a move to the west. Figures showing tonnages of ammunition and materiel, litres of fuel, water and rations and also the available transport for such a move were revealed in late November. Some possible locations had been chosen and we were invited to consider their calculations and to confirm quickly the feasibility of the operation. This was difficult as the detailed calculations were normally done by our Service branches, principally

Transport and Supply, but, of course, they were not yet allowed to know the new plan. Taking the information provided, I confirmed to the Commander that I believed we could inload a new forward site at best in two weeks but certainly within four weeks, allowing for problems. These problems were, of course, not insignificant. Even our large scale maps told us that there was only one road from Jubail to Hafr Al Batin. Choosing the Main Supply Route (or MSR) was not a problem but it was going to be a popular and crowded road which might delay the movement of stocks.

The Commander was in frequent contact with both Riyadh and JHQ and gradually the option to sweep west with a reinforced order of battle became clearer. Our Service Heads were briefed on the latest position including the identification of Headquarters 1 (UK) Armoured Division, with probably 4 Armoured Brigade as the other subordinate formation. We were still in close liaison with the US Marines, but now our main effort was in trying to identify the bill for the western option, which would also mean a resubordination of the UK Division to a US Army Corps, yet to be identified. My own reaction to this new option initially was one of disappointment. A very strong relationship had been built up with the US Marines and we were very keen to fight alongside them. This was mixed with the enthusiasm we all felt for the imminent arrival of Headquarters 1 (UK) Division. There was no doubt that this rein-forcement would be invaluable and was a clear indication that the political will was behind a Coalition offensive.

Looking at our own organisation, we were going to need reinforce-ment in most of the Service and Support areas, with more transport an urgent requirement. Additionally, our own headquarters needed a substantial increase in personnel and, most importantly, to be able to split, to create a forward and a rear element, and to run both parts on a 24-hour basis. We had also confirmed the move of the Headquarters into new accommodation. The Port Clearance building was too small and the whole operation was getting cramped. Colonel Martin had seen some accommodation on his initial recce and the Marines confirmed that old Port Barracks, in the southern part of the port area, could be used by us (rather than the US Army). The accommodation was being used by itinerant workers but, apart from the kitchen and drains, the complex provided comfortable sleeping accommodation with four or five to a room, good working facilities, an excellent kitchen and dining area (once refurbished) and most important of all, a large operations complex that allowed all the staff and service branches to be within the same general area. This was an exciting period of planning and was another great step forward for our logistic operations.

Before we left the Port Clearance building, it became obvious that a recce to the intended operational area was essential. A small recce party of the Commander, myself and the OC of 3 Field Squadron Royal

Engineers, Major Hamish Rollo, set off to look at Hafr Al Batin and the Wadi Al Batin for the first time. The Tapline road (MSR DODGE) was as difficult as we thought it might be, being single lane for over half its length and already suffering from large amounts of military traffic. Setting off from Jubail late in the evening, the plan was to camp en route at a convenient site. Having driven far enough, we turned off the road in the dark and drove, rather cautiously, onto the desert. After a few hundred metres, we stopped, cooked a meal and set up our American camp cots and slept. The sight that greeted us the next morning was a surprise. Nothing. There was simply nothing around us except flat, hard desert. After the soft sandy terrain on the eastern seaboard this was a surprise. Naive this may have been, but the sheer scale of this vast sandy car park needed time to comprehend. Manoeuvrability of all our vehicles seemed not to be a problem. We packed up and moved on up the road, including a stretch that was dual carriageway, approximately half way to Hafr Al Batin. American Army units were everywhere and we identified the general area of their Logistic Base Alpha to the south east of Hafr. Beyond this area was the small town of Al Quaysumah. This offered some useful facilities, principally it had a very modern, small airfield. Moving on to Hafr Al Batin itself, this was a sprouting town on a crossroad which led south to King Kahled Military City (KKMC) and further down to Riyadh, whilst north was Iraq. We drove around the town in a sand-coloured Japanese 4-wheel-drive jeep.

Going north, we stopped on high ground and surveyed the town below. Some trucks with Syrian soldiers on board passed and waved and smiled, not really knowing who we were. We drove around the environs of the town and discerned a football stadium that was another attractive, potential logistic location. We then drove into the Wadi Al Batin. At this end it was so wide, with gently sloping sides, that it was nothing more than an easy valley to cross. This in itself was important to note. This recce had at least put the area into our minds, we knew the main centres of population and the ideal locations for a logistic base. Most importantly we knew the terrain. All in all a very useful trip. The information gleaned from this recce was passed back to JHQ and also to 1 (UK) Armoured Division in Germany.

The Division Arrives

Upon return to Jubail, we prepared for the recce of 1 (UK) Armoured Division. The initial briefing was held at the forward location of HQ 7 Armoured Brigade in the desert and they then toured unit locations, travelling by helicopter. This was an important visit and we were able to pass on logistic information to the Divisional team, mainly to Colonel Graham Ewer; the visit ended with a brain-storming session held at the Jubail Holiday Inn where we could discuss and confirm their initial thoughts. Personally, it meant a great deal, meeting friends and colleagues from Verden after three months away. This was also the first time we had met the new GOC, Major General Rupert Smith.

Having spoken at length with the Division, our own chain of command was becoming clearer. Whilst we were to work forward to the Division, the rearward link would be to HQ BFME in Riyadh. This meant that our direct link to the UK and JHQ would be severed and that we would be under command of BFME, not the Division. This was an important distinction in our minds, having experienced the working relationship with 7 Armoured Brigade. We only existed to support the Division, but it was important to be able to work to them, rather than for them. The Division needed to be able to look forward during operations and trust the organisation working to support it. Our independence meant that they had no direct responsibility for us. JHQ in High Wycombe did not look forward to this new arrangement as they had benefited from direct access to information from Saudi Arabia and were able to speak to the Ministry of Defence without the delay of an intermediate headquarters in Riyadh. This would change, particularly as BFME was also expanding to take on responsibility for the larger Force and a G4 staff was already beginning to arrive from the United Kingdom.

At the beginning of December, the Advance Party from the Division arrived. Lots of friendly faces and lots to talk about over a can of alcohol-free beer. They were all quickly settled into Baldrick Lines and the following day involved touring the Port area and briefings. There was a great deal for them all to take in, quickly. Fairly soon, they established themselves in their own accommodation on the outskirts of Jubail (Camp 9), outside the immediate area of the Port. At about the same time, our own Headquarters moved into Old Port Barracks (see Figure 3.3). This was an ideal moment as arrangements for the reception of the Division were being settled, including the arrival of extra ammunition and stores and we were untying from both the USMC and 7 Armoured Brigade.

The new FMA operations complex allowed a greater and more rapid dissemination of information between cells and there was also space for a briefing room and a large area for the Division to establish its own discreet reception cell, to control the arrival and movement of their own personnel and equipment. Up to the arrival of the Division, the FMA had been involved in reception, getting the right support to 7 Armoured Brigade in order that it might deploy into the desert for training, and also establishing its own infrastructure and operational procedures. The arrival of 1 (UK) Armoured Division felt something like a repeat of this process. The framework for an efficient system of reception had been established and all our support was now required to ensure that the Division was received and moved to its locations as soon as possible.

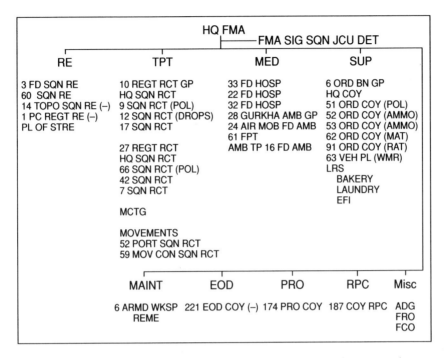

Figure 3.4 Expanded Order of Battle, Headquarters Force Maintenance Area –
January 1991

What HQ FMA failed to do was to get any period to train itself. It had
been operating since its arrival in early October but its cohesiveness on
operations had not seriously been tested. And now we were being reinforced, some personnel were moving back to Divisional Headquarters
and we were planning to split into forward and rear elements. The
expanded organisation is at Figure 3.4. Although it should not be
exaggerated, there was some concern that the new Headquarters FMA
was likely to be cumbersome. On a personal note, this was the critical
factor in my decision not to return to Divisional Rear Headquarters as
the SO2 G1/G4 Ops but to remain in HQ FMA as DCOS. It would
mean that the staff could at least have a known point of contact and
the essential interface between second and third line at staff level should
work smoothly.

As the Division arrived, squeezing into the port area amongst the huge
American reinforcement operation, the Divisional Headquarters planned
for future operations. The GOC led a divisional liaison team, including
Commander FMA and myself, on an initial visit to 7 (US) Corps, then
based in Dahran. Here we were able to meet the principal personalities
but we were also given the first brief on Operation DESERT SABRE
and its outline concepts. Time was spent subsequently with G1 and G4

staff, discussing various aspects of future operations, but mainly the problem of prisoners of war and how each national organisation might interface. After this visit to 7 Corps, the Division wrote its own plans and held a series of map exercises to develop concepts and talk through problem areas. At the same time we were in discussion with HQ BFME on the proposals for third line support. Our main concern was a continuing lack of transport. In our view, our lift capacity was not sufficient when extended over the planned lines of communication (LofC); and there was a desperate need for further contracts to be placed for Host Nation vehicles.

The Move West

As the Division moved into the desert to train, in weather that was to become very similar to a normal British winter, we were informed that our forward logistic base would probably have to be collocated with the US Log Base Alpha, some 60 kms to the south-east of Hafr Al Batin. This was not an ideal location as it meant a further leg to the west to support the proposed line of attack for the Division. However, it was still some 350 kms north-west of Jubail and represented a considerable task, moving the requisite stocks forward.

A recce to the proposed area was put together quickly. Loaded into some five vehicles, a group representing the FMA staff and Services, HQ BFME, and the RAF helicopter force, departed for Hafr Al Batin under the new Deputy Commander FMA, Lieutenant Colonel Chris Bradley RAOC. Following the general line of the earlier recce with Commander FMA, the recce team headed for Log Base Alpha. The main change since that earlier recce was the increase in activity. American troops were everywhere along the Tapline Road and there seemed to be no gap between unit areas, but rather a solid deployment, side-by-side up and down the road. The road itself was dangerous. The density of traffic was bound to be a problem in itself but when mixed with erratic local driving it was a potentially lethal combination. After the first night in the desert we arrived at Log Base Alpha. It was another large patch of desert with various tented areas, makeshift roads and a great many stores and vehicles. We were hosted that night by US National Guardsmen who were very friendly and helpful and allowed us to use a couple of tents to discuss plans and sleep. The next day we checked on Al Quaysumah and the airfield. This was already filling up with American units but still offered the most favourable site for casualty evacuation. We continued on to Hafr Al Batin, where we saw Arab troops already established in 'our' football stadium, and then south to King Kahled Military City (KKMC), which in addition to Saudi Arabian troops was full of French soldiers and their Puma helicopters. There was a need for the RAF to see more but we were conscious that the recce was now too far west and in order that we were not identified as British no contact was allowed at this stage.

As part of this recce the new SO2 G4 Ops from HQ BFME accompanied us. Major Andrew Burch, Royal Electrical and Mechanical Engineers (REME), and I had known each other for some years, attending both the Junior Division Staff College and subsequently the Staff College at Camberley together. At KKMC he left the group and headed towards Riyadh. Sadly, he was killed in a road accident on the way.

Following the recce, there was a ban imposed on movement west as the Division prepared its detailed plans. Operational security was crucial and any regular movement of British troops to the west might indicate the thrust of new plans. Our own plans confirmed the feasibility of the move to the forward location and that the inload would take 21 days, to the levels agreed with DCOS 1 Division. In order to 'sell' the outline logistic concept (see Figure 1.5), including the need for further Host Nation transport, Brigadier White and I flew to Riyadh, to HQ BFME, in order that General de la Billière and the Americans could be convinced of our plans. Brigadier Rob McAfee, the land Assistant Chief of Staff (ACOS), and Colonel Tony Welch listened to the detail and then they all left to brief Commander BFME. It was at this stage that we later heard that Brigadier Simon Firth from JHQ had also briefed General Schwarzkopf. Spending the night in the luxury of the Sheraton Hotel felt most odd. The next day we returned to Jubail and I called a planning conference of the Staff and Services in order to produce a logistic operations order to support the outline plan. The concept was explained and the 21 day time frame. L Day was to be the start of the operation and this looked likely to be early in the New Year. Christmas had come and gone and the Staff and Services concentrated their efforts into putting the detail together to make the plan work. The Operations Order was published near the end of December and detailed the move of stocks forward to a level of 15 days Artillery and 8 days tank and infantry ammunition and 10 days fuel. In addition there was a great deal of materiel, rations and water, as well as the equipment to establish a field hospital.

In preparation for the forward move, we had practised the establishment of a forward headquarters, using the box body staff vehicles. It was clear that, theoretically, we could establish a forward element but we were limited in any further movement, if required, as no real step-up[7] capability existed. This was not critical as it was unlikely that any further element would be required for any length of time. It was agreed that the Deputy commander would establish the FFMA with a skeleton staff, with L Day (the start of the forward move of stock) being 3 January 1991. There would be a replenishment facility for our units half way along the Tapline Road in the area of the dual carriageway. In the run up to the start of the inload, vehicles were prepared and loads put together in order that the start time was achieved. Everything went according to plan and the inload of the FFMA started on time. The

Deputy Commander had been allocated real estate and he established the HQ FFMA in an area already surrounded by sand banks, or berms. Although we were concerned at the signature this might present from the air there was a real danger of vehicles driving into and over a position that lacked such protection.

Preparing for War

It was decided that the Staff and Services, as well as unit headquarters would move forward at a time of their own choosing, when their own main point of effort had effectively moved from Jubail to the FFMA. We stayed long enough in Jubail to see the start of the air war (15 January 1991) and shortly afterwards we moved to our new home. The weather was bad. It was cold, wet and windy and we trudged around in puddles and mud, just like an exercise in England or Germany. HQ FFMA broadly consisted of a diamond shaped area, cut into two halves. In one was the administration, with a mess tent and sleeping area. The other had the G4 Ops grouping, including the principal services of Transport, Supply, Maintenance (Equipment Management) and Medical, the G3 Ops grouping including Intelligence and NBC and finally the communications complex. All three of these 'diamonds' were dug in, but lacked overhead protection other than camouflage nets (see Figure 3.5).

With the assistance of divisional second line transport, the inload of the FFMA was achieved as planned on L+21, 24 January 1991. On 31 January we began an outload to create the Divisional Maintenance Area (DMA) 30 kms north west of Hafr Al Batin in Forward Assembly Area (FAA) Ray using divisional transport. The DMA was planned to hold around 10 days of all natures and the reserve of fuel and materiel. While this second line inload took place, drawing stocks from the FFMA, the inload continued from Jubail to top up the FFMA stock to 12 days artillery ammunition and eight days of other combat supplies and materiel.

In developing the interface between ourselves and the Division, two study days were held. The first was organised by Colonel Graham Ewer and held at Regimental Headquarters of 4 Armoured Division Transport Regiment in Tactical Assembly Army (TAA) Keyes, where the Division had moved by early February. The purpose was to discuss Exchange Points (XPs). This was to be the method of transferring commodity loads between third and second line transport at pre-designated locations, maximising the efficiency of each transport 'loop' and thereby minimising the amount of stock that needed to be dumped on the ground. Divisional staff, FMA staff, as well as other second and third line transport regiments attended. Following this period, operating procedures for XPs were agreed and the concept would be successfully incorporated into the divisional plan for its logistic support once it had entered Iraq through the breach created by 1(US) Infantry Division (The Big Red One).

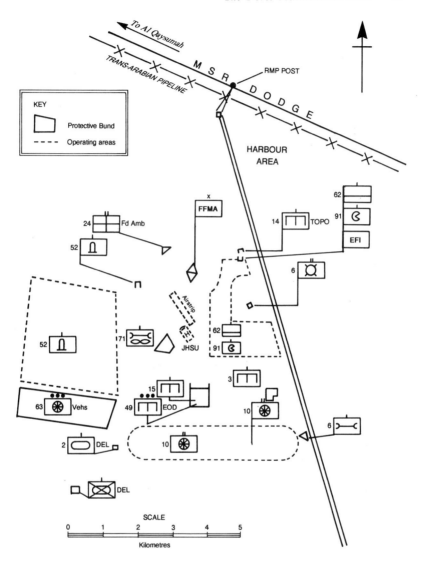

Figure 3.5 Forward Force Maintenance Area – Location of Units

Another study day was subsequently arranged, hosted by us, to discuss third line operations. This explained to both second and third line units, and staff, including some from HQ BFME, the forward movement of artillery and Battle Group ammunition, fuel, rations and water either to the XPs or by through-running to units as necessary and as agreed between HQ FFMA and Divisional Rear Headquarters. The key was to use transport efficiently and this meant putting vehicles under tactical control of the Division when in their area.

The outline logistic concept allowed for third line support of the

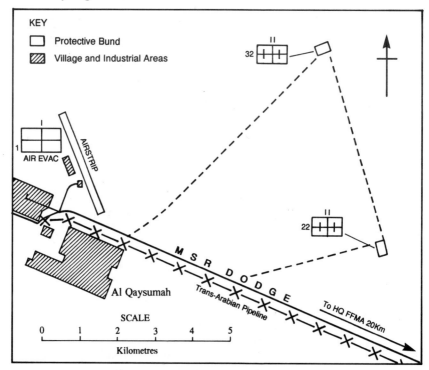

Figure 3.6 Al Qaysumah – Medical Deployment

Division direct from the FFMA to the DMA and to their staging areas. It also provided for support into Iraq, across the Wadi Al Batin, once the Division was in contact and moving North. In order to ensure Brigadier Martin White was able to move nearer to his logistic point of main effort as the LOC became extended, a Tactical Headquarters, or Tac HQ, was created from FFMA resources. Based on two staff box body vehicles, it was planned to collocate with the Headquarters of 10 Transport Regiment RCT. This would allow the Commander and his principal staff from G4 Ops, Transport and Supply to move forward, with the necessary communications to retain command of the third line logistic operation.

On 16 February, the DMA inload was complete and on 18 February, the FFMA top-up inload was also complete. On 21 February, our two transport regiments were called forward to prepare and train for the third line support of the Division in the forthcoming operation. From the blank sheet of paper in Rheindahlen, the ad hoc HQ FMA had developed into a workable logistic headquarters that managed initially to see a brigade, and subsequently a Division, into theatre and prepare for war. It had never succeeded in training itself and yet it had managed to achieve a balance of stocks in support that would have been enough to let the Division push on much further into Iraq had that been required.

Part Two

Rear Area Operations

Major P Cross RRF
(Chief of Staff HQ FMA, Gulf)

Although HQ FMA was formed in Germany, principally from logistic experts throughout the BAOR, it was evident that, despite an important focus on logistic matters, there would be a vital need for a G2/G3 element to the Headquarters. This was led by the Chief of Staff, Major Peter Cross, who coordinated rear area Security, Intelligence, real estate, Explosive Ordnance Disposal (EOD), Nuclear Biological and Chemical (NBC) Defence and visits, of which there were dozens. He liaised in detail with the Americans and ensured that duplication of effort was minimised and, importantly, that British areas of expertise were used to best overall effect. The Intelligence Cell had no collection or collation facilities[1] but was responsible for the dissemination of an Intelligence summary produced elsewhere; this was an important function that ensured logistic units were aware of the latest situation and kept up to date with the battle. As it transpired, the potential threat to the rear area never materialised, despite the rhetoric of the 'Mother of all Battles'. Had circumstances been different, a strong G2/G3 team would have been crucial in the maintenance of logistic operations.[2]

NBC

Nuclear, Biological and Chemical (NBC) operations in the rear area were controlled by a dedicated team of specialists trained at the Defence NBC School, Winterbourne Gunner, and led by Major Philip Mould. Their responsibilities were two-fold. First, they advised units on NBC training and equipment deployment; secondly, they were the focus for air raid and NBC warning and reporting.

Liaison with US Forces and the Host Nation

From the outset, it was vital to establish a close relationship with US forces in Jubail. The USMC ran the port and airfield, both of which were vital for our deployment into Saudi Arabia. The Marines were tremendously helpful, giving us food, water and transport, and helped make scarce resources such as Camp 4,[3] a modern construction workers camp outside Jubail, and Sheds 4, 5 and 6 in the Port Area available for our exclusive use.

There were differences of both opinion and method but to everyone's credit there were never any serious disagreements between 7 Armoured Brigade Group and the USMC. Major Kip Brueland was their 'Port Manager' who provided excellent service with a great degree of good humour. Several operations were conducted jointly. From an early stage, joint police patrols were to be seen in the Port. EOD procedures (bomb disposal), using our Company based in the port, were discussed and then practised during a number of short, rear area exercises. In retrospect, it was fortuitous that the proposed joint rear headquarters was never formed because we were to leave the US Marine Corps and work under 7 (US) Corps.

Relations with the locals in Jubail were generally good. They bore the arrival of an enormous military presence in their Port with good humour. Military discipline of the British soldiers was for the most part exemplary and rarely were explanations required for local irritations. On occasions there were complaints about seemingly unimportant issues such as the removal of kerb stones to allow fuel tankers to park on wasteland at the Port's exit, and yet the laying of two acres of tarmac within the fishing port without permission was never mentioned!

Liaison was significantly improved when the Saudi authorities provided a young Army captain as our Liaison Officer. His significance was enhanced when it was learned that he was a Prince! He was a valuable asset and it was very sad that the Saudis chose to replace him just before the war started.

On deployment of the FFMA, it was necessary to establish new relations with elements of 7(US) Corps and some reservist logistic units. These units were manned by National Guardsmen (and many women!) who were very different to the Marines in Jubail. In terms of Rear Area Operations, there was a shift in terms of leadership from the Marines to the FFMA in Log Base ALFA. This was due to our communications being significantly better (ASMA was a unique facility) and we had a fully worked up team who had been in theatre for some months. We were now at the stage that many Americans were moving forward in support of 7 Corps and their focus was definitely further west and north.

War Maintenance Reserves and Battle Casualty Replacements

Whilst the Armoured Delivery Group, based upon the Headquarters of 1st Battalion The Queen's Own Highlanders (see Chapters 2 and 10), had responsibility for much of the immediate reserves of men and equipment available to 1(UK) Armoured Division, both the Force Maintenance Area and Forward Force Maintenance Area held a proportion of these assets. Initially, the bulk of the personnel had been held in Blackadder Lines, a purpose-built tented camp among the oil refineries on the outskirts of Jubail. In order that the Armoured Delivery Group could be formed, it was necessary for men and equipment to be married together and for some training to take place.

The Commanding Officer, 1st Battalion Scots Guards, was given the responsibility for running Blackadder Lines. This was not a particularly exciting task but nonetheless essential for the coordination of up to 3000 Battle Casualty Replacements who lived there was not easy and sometimes needed firm leadership. Given that 1 Scots Guards was providing Armoured Infantry companies to the Armoured Delivery Group and would not be required to fight as a unit, their Battalion Headquarters was the ideal choice for this task.

An element of the Armoured Delivery Group was established with the FFMA under Majors Brian Broadhurst and Tony Domeisen. By late January 1991, when they were training, the procedures for setting up temporary ranges was well established. As 1(UK) Armoured Division moved into the breach the rearmost elements of the Armoured Delivery Group also moved forward.

Remaining in the FFMA were two elements. First, there were Battle Casualty Replacements for the Armoured Reconnaissance Regiment from a squadron of the 9th/12th Lancers. They were commanded by Major Henry Robertson and equipped with ageing Ferret Scout Cars. The squadron did extremely well to keep these vehicles working. They conducted rear area security patrols between the Forward Force Maintenance Area and the Divisional Maintenance Area. As it transpired, the threat in the rear area was low but it was a vital task for their soldiers to perform; it kept them well trained and gave them a sense of purpose. On one occasion it became apparent that the guard force at the Prisoner of War (PW) Cage at Al Qaysumah was inadequate and they were despatched to supplement it.

The second unit deployed was an ad hoc Air Defence Battery commanded by Major Lindsey Wilson. This battery did an excellent job in maintaining air defence equipment which might have been required forward. They were unable to operate their launchers as effectively as they would have liked because they were unable to receive timely Air Space Control measures. Given the complete lack of offensive air by the Iraqis, they were not required to engage targets. Indeed their deployment at all was questioned because the area was initially under Patriot cover. It came as an unwelcome surprise that the Americans redeployed their Patriots without our knowledge, leaving our extensive Supply Area without any air defence cover whatsoever.

There is no doubt that the soldiers who were Battle Casualty Replacements lacked the morale of those in formed units. It was equally apparent that every effort had to be made to keep them training rather than waiting for the call to go forward. It would be advantageous in future deployments to maintain a dedicated training team in theatre for such an eventuality.

Communications and Information Systems

Within the FFMA, strategic computer systems provided instant communication via satellite between the two headquarters and to Riyadh, High Wycombe and London. ASMA (Air Staff Management Aid) allowed the Force Maintenance Area staff immediate access to information about the overall situation which would otherwise not have been easily available outside Divisional Headquarters. In particular, it provided invaluable early warning of SCUD launches in Iraq. The Army Command Support System (MAPPER) was widely used for passing transport and movement information and provided a key element of the casualty reporting system. MAPPER also provided valuable facilities for international electronic mail and interactive conversations. With ASMA, it reduced significantly the load on Ptarmigan (the army mobile trunk communications system) and the Defence Communications Network (DCN). Links to two other major computer systems, COFFER and OLIVER, were also deployed in the FMA. Army supply operations are geared to the availability of COFFER and its deployment was essential; to have reverted to manual systems would have been a severely retrograde step. Quite late in the operation, OLIVER (an unclassified electronic mail system) was deployed, allowing access to up-to-date information on stores and permitting the rapid passage of demands to depots in the UK. It is difficult to quantify the benefit of such systems but there is no doubt that they contributed greatly to the success of the operation.

In addition to large, networked systems, much of the British Army had been using desktop and laptop computers for some time before Operation GRANBY. Many elements, particularly logistic and engineer units, had become reliant on their use for administration and day to day operation. This was not widely understood, especially in some branches of the Ministry of Defence, and it was extremely difficult to obtain sufficient computers which were rugged and secure enough for the battlefield. Nonetheless, the necessary authority was eventually obtained and a hastily assembled team procured, programmed and fielded the Desert Interim Computer System (which quickly became known by its rather unappealing acronym: DICS). Initially comprising 144 computers of varying sizes, by the end of the war the total number had risen to about 450. DICS was designed to provide computer support to headquarters, units and logistic sub-units. Its primary purpose was to provide computers for asset tracking, resource management and the production and transmission of reports and returns, between which data could be passed on floppy discs via modems over the Ptarmigan trunk network.

The support of these systems in the field was an additional problem. There was no existing infrastructure to support a large number of computers for a long period out of barracks. Specialist and strategic systems were supported by the various joint communications detachments and a few seconded individuals, but they were more and more thinly spread as the area of operations increased. A system support team grew gradually in Jubail to provide training and programming support and to distribute and maintain DICS equipment, but it was very much an ad hoc organisation: for example, the two REME technicians who provided equipment support were borrowed from the Battle Casualty Replacement pool and neither had any previous experience of computer repair. Nonetheless, DICS was successfully fielded, enhancing the production and passage of orders in the forward area and significantly improving the visibility and management of stocks in the divisional rear area and, to a lesser extent (because of delays in the delivery of computers), in the Force Maintenance Area.

Part Three

FMA Engineer Operations

Lieutenant Colonel N Rollo RE

3 Field Squadron, from 22 Engineer Regiment, based at Tidworth in Hampshire and commanded by Major Hamish Rollo, flew into Jubail to take over the role of providing engineer support to the FMA from 39 Engineer Regiment on 14 November 1990, the latter having provided all the early support in establishing the FMA and the infrastructure of Jubail. This changeover of engineer units was necessary due principally to the requirement for 39 Regiment commanded by Lieutenant Colonel Bob Pridham to revert to its priority role of providing support to the RAF at their bases in Bahrain, Tabuk and Dahran. Ironically, the earliest support to the RAF in Bahrain had been provided by a reinforced troop of 3 Squadron, who had the honour of being the first field engineers into theatre, beginning their deployment on 28 September. The deployment of the Squadron was complete, including the Bahrain troop, by 12 December, when the ship carrying the Squadron's plant and equipment was unloaded. By any standards, it possessed a high level of engineer capability. The Squadron was manned well over its peace establishment, with over 250 personnel; it had a complete field squadron's worth of G1098[4] equipment, and effectively an additional plant troop. As things turned out, the Squadron was to need all this and more.

The time between the advance party arriving and the Squadron being complete had been well spent. 39 Regiment had done a first-class job of establishing the necessary levels of infrastructure, and of providing the majority of units with the support they needed. Inevitably, however, there was much still to be done. The Squadron set about establishing the additional requirement for engineer support whilst completing those jobs which 39 Regiment had been unable to finish. Inevitably, the majority of FMA units were not fully aware of the real capabilities of an engineer squadron. As the evidence of their work became ever more visible around Jubail and its environs, so the list of engineer tasks grew and grew. Priorities for engineer work were therefore quickly needed and established, and units soon realised that they could not all be at the top of the priority list. This settling in period, from early deployment up to Christmas, served the additional and essential function of establishing a good rapport and liaison between the Squadron and the rest of the FMA units which was to stand them all in good stead.

The Move Forward

The requirement to establish the FFMA posed an enormous challenge to HQ FMA. As far as the Engineer Squadron was concerned this challenge was compounded by the fact that the majority of the logistic units were unable to deploy forward at all without a considerable level of infrastructure support already in place; for example fuel bunds and access routes. To meet this requirement the whole Squadron deployed to the area of Al Quaysumah on New Year's Eve and were complete at their new location in time for the Officer Commanding and Squadron Sergeant Major to see the New Year in with non-alcoholic beer at a fleabitten roadside cafe. At that stage, the Squadron was the only British unit in the area and as a result were very well treated by the Americans who had been in the location for some time. In essence, the Squadron had four main tasks: to construct a field hospital from scratch on a desert site; to provide all FFMA units with their drinking water; to construct earthworks, bunds and field defences; and to provide support to the RAF support helicopter fleet as they deployed forward.

Resources

Whilst the Squadron was manned and equipped to perform these tasks, the engineer resources required to complete them were enormous. The Squadron was fortunate to have attached to it, for the majority of the period, an enhanced Royal Engineer Specialist Team. This team possessed all the highly specialised and technical skills needed to plan and resource these tasks and to provide the right level of technical supervision. A lot of the engineer planning, for water supply and for the construction of field hospitals for example, had already taken place in the UK before deployment and had continued during the Squadron's time in Jubail. The quantity of resources for the hospital alone required 40 ISO containers to transport them; a huge logistic bill. In addition to the Specialist Team the Squadron worked very closely with the engineer staff of HQ FMA. This staff, ably headed by an SO2 RE, Major Max McNamara, carried out the lion's share of the provision of resources and the planning of future operations. This entailed very extensive liaison within the headquarters, with the UK, and with local contractors and agencies who were supplying resources or equipment. With this considerable load off their shoulders the Squadron was free to get on with the work in hand which consumed all their capacity.

The Hospital

The construction of 32 Field Hospital (see Figure 3.6 and detail at Chapter 5) in full took nearly six weeks although medical capacity existed from 22 January and increased steadily thereafter. The hospital boasted a total of 200 beds, a fully equipped operating theatre with appropriate facilities for the preparation and recovery of patients, a fully equipped resuscitation unit and its own laundry. The whole was provided with NBC collective protection, running water, full electrical power systems with a standby facility, and an incinerator. Outside the hospital, the area was protected by a 6 metre high earth bund. A Helicopter Landing Site (HLS), capable of taking two Chinooks (medium lift helicopter), was also installed.

The construction of the hospital was a considerable feat. In particular, the requirements for electrical power were particularly demanding and consumed a high proportion of the available effort. The Squadron would not have been able to complete the task on time without the unstinting efforts of the Specialist Team who performed sterling work. Inevitably, there was a conflict between the requirement to complete the job on time and to achieve the high standard of technical excellence required. In addition to its requirement for electrical power, the hospital had an enormous requirement for fresh, potable (drinking) water which, at full capacity, would have run to 80,000 litres a day.

Water Supply

It is the responsibility of every Royal Engineer unit to supply its parent formation with water and therefore the Squadron set about this task in time to meet the ever growing needs of the FFMA. The equipment used had been specially manufactured in the United Kingdom and was permanently installed in ISO containers for ease of transportation and use. Each container held a complete Reverse Osmosis (RO) unit capable of filtering impure water to an acceptable standard for drinking. In addition to the RO unit, there was a requirement to store the water in bulk tanks with the pumps and pipework necessary to transfer it from tank to tank and to load the Royal Corps of Transport (RCT) water bowsers. The capacity of each plant varied according to the level of contamination of the input water, but typically it was in the order of 80,000 litres per day although when filtering sea water, this rate was reduced to around 40,000 litres.

The first water point established by the Squadron was based on a Bedouin well. The owner was a little reluctant to take part at first, but with the help of an Arab phrase book and endless cups of tea, we were able to persuade him that it was all in a good cause. When he realised that his pumping station would be regularly and expertly serviced and, on departure, the Squadron would leave him with a year's supply of diesel, he became positively enthusiastic about the idea!

It had been estimated that an individual's daily requirement for water in the desert was about 40 litres per day. As far as the FFMA was concerned this amounted to a total requirement of around 40,000 litres. However, as the Division moved forward into its staging areas in late January, it soon became clear that water supply would be most efficiently achieved as an FFMA responsibility and therefore the Squadron undertook the task of supplying all the forces deployed forward. This entailed a considerable increase in water quantity to what could be provided by the Bedouin well, and therefore the main source of production was moved forward to Hafr al Batin where the main water pipeline to King Khaled Military City was available. Here the Squadron increased its capacity to nearly a million litres per day of production and storage. As the Division continued to move forward to its Line of Departure, water storage sites were also established and unloaded by the RCT using water containers on DROPS.

Field Defences and Routes

Concurrent with these two tasks was the requirement for the Squadron to provide all round protection for the FFMA and to ensure that routes into the locations from MSR DODGE were available and in good repair. To achieve this required the deployment of not only all the Squadron's plant, but the local hire of several large dozers and excavators. Each unit's area was demarked by an earth bund about two metres high and some of the storage sites for individual weapons, MLRS rockets for example, were given specific protection. The headquarters of all the units were dug in and accommodation areas protected by bunds. The defence of each area, whilst the responsibility of the local commander, was enhanced through the provision of trenches, and sentry and fire positions. The protection of HQ FFMA itself was afforded a particular priority and extensive earthworks created; even the staff officers' toilets were subterranean! The maintenance and construction of routes was clearly a priority requirement throughout the deployment of the FFMA and this particular task was made considerably more difficult by the atrocious weather conditions. Fortunately, the sand dried out quickly and was normally trafficable even when completely flooded. Indeed, the best surface could be maintained by rolling the sand when it was still wet after rain. In all, it was calculated that, in providing this support to the FFMA, the Squadron dug 100 kms of ditching and moved well over a million tons of earth; about enough to fill most of Wembley Stadium.

Support to the RAF

In addition to supporting the FFMA, the Squadron also supported the RAF helicopter fleet when it was deployed in the FFMA area and at forward sites. The particular problem was the obvious one of sand ingress into the engines when aircraft were in the hover prior to landing. A number of systems for stabilising the sand were trialled but without particular success until a specialist piece of plant, designed to pressure spray a bitumen emulsion to a depth of about 30 mm into the surface, was discovered in Jubail just before Christmas. Knowing the potential worth of this plant, a contract was quickly placed for its indefinite hire; just in time, as it turned out, as it was the envy of the American engineers for the rest of the operation. Each Helicopter Landing Site (HLS) was constructed out of aluminium matting and then surrounded by an area of sand sprayed with bitumen out to a distance of 40 metres all round. The result was perfect and enabled much more efficient use of the SH fleet by FFMA units. It also saved a number of Chinook engines! The plant, known, not always affectionately, as the Beast, had a voracious appetite for bitumen, water, fuel and spare parts. It also consumed many hours of REME manpower to keep it on the road; but it proved its worth many times over.

In this way, a number of HLS were prepared and used regularly by the RAF. However, the jewel in the crown of the Squadron's support to the RAF was the construction of a desert airstrip, levelled to the finest tolerances, close to HQ FFMA. Regrettably it was not used by C130 as circumstances had changed, but General de la Billière used it for liaison visits on several occasions.

Recovery

Once ground operations were complete, work began to recover the FFMA and its stocks. The Squadron remained fully committed to stripping out installations and sites, and in providing support to those units who needed assistance. It is a point of considerable pride that as far as the FFMA was concerned, the desert was restored to the state in which it was found on New Year's Eve 1990.

Chapter Four

Transport and Movements

Lieutenant Colonel P S Reehal RLC
(Staff Officer Grade 1, Transport and Movements, HQ FMA)

When the lead elements of 1 (UK) Armoured Division reached Kuwait and turned off their engines, they did so knowing that, if ordered to continue the advance, their Challengers were fully fuelled and loaded with ammunition. They were logistically complete. To the professional transporter this is the ultimate mark of success and the fact that of all the Coalition forces in the Gulf, the British were the first to be operationally ready speaks volumes for the quiet and unassuming men and women of the logistic corps. The Gulf War taught many lessons and the familiar cries of flexibility, adaptability and dogged determination are all true and important. The real lesson for me was that for a force to be able to fight effectively and maintain momentum the logistic backup must be total. The sophisticated Challenger tank, with its multitude of high-tech systems and highly trained crew, is simply expensive battlefield scrap without the ammunition to fire, the fuel to move and the combat supplies to sustain the men.

The realisation that Operation GRANBY was not an exercise and that there was a very real chance of war, concentrated the mind as we formed up in Rheindahlen in September 1990. Prior to the formation of the Headquarters, I was included in a lead element which, with the Commander 7 Armoured Brigade, flew to Saudi Arabia to conduct a recce. Many hours of detailed staff work had been carried out in HQ BAOR and 1st (BR) Corps to thrust an armour-heavy brigade and its logistic slice from Europe to the Gulf. The FMA Transport and Movements (Tpt and Mov) Order of Battle (ORBAT) for Operation GRANBY was determined by the need to maintain a balanced organisation to receive and deploy the formation and sustain it from the main logistic base somewhere on the east coast of Saudi Arabia to Kuwait City and beyond, a Line of Communication of some 400 kms.

The recce was fraught with many difficulties. Hours were spent discussing the ORBAT to keep within the manpower totals. The need

for security necessitated a low profile and the half day visit to the coast
to look at real estate was totally inadequate. Nonetheless, whilst the
lack of time in Jubail was a bitter blow, a quick drive around the port
allowed a reasonable assessment of what could be achieved and importantly, contacts were made with USMC officers that were to pay
enormous dividends for the future. The USMC had much in common
with the British Army. They ran the port like a well oiled machine
and, whilst they promised nothing, they literally gave everything they
could.

The port of Jubail was magnificent, the centre of a vast industrial
complex which, when finished, would be the single largest public works
project of modern times. As the Brigade was to be under the tactical
control (TACON) of the USMC and they were using Jubail as their port
of debarkation it naturally followed that our Brigade should use the same
port. Later events demonstrated just how fortunate we were to be
TACON the Marines; if the decision to support the US Army had been
made from the start, then the overcrowded port of Dammam would have
seriously undermined the flow of ships and aircraft of the Brigade. The
only real concern was the lack of roll-on roll-off (RO-RO) facilities; the
port only had one RO-RO berth and any delay in unloading ships would
seriously hinder the operational readiness of the Brigade. Luckily most
of the US ships had their own stern and side ramps and the RO-RO
berth became an almost exclusively British asset.

A quick flight over Jubail International Airport on the return to Riyadh
convinced me that the air and sea reception of the Brigade through
Jubail was feasible within the time frame. During the many discussions
in Riyadh the advice that the lead ships should have a large transport
element to include tank transporters was heeded. Whilst it was generally accepted that for political reasons, the first British vehicle to leave
the first ship should be a Challenger tank, it was successfully argued
that it should be followed by the less glamorous but equally important
tank transporter. It was. Discussions with the USMC had focused on
the paucity of transport that was available in the area and as a result
renewed emphasis was placed on the need to get third line transport
high on the Desired Order of Arrival Staff Table (DOAST).[1] Thankfully,
all the pleas were listened to and third[2] line transport was tasked within
one hour of leaving the first ship to arrive in Jubail.

The Transport and Movement Organisation

The recce party returned from Saudi Arabia by Hercules (RAF transport aircraft) and the 15-hour flight gave us ample time to write the
recce report, draw the ORBAT and start work on the reception plan and
transport operations. The original RCT Gulf ORBAT shown at Figure
4.1 was drawn on the floor of the Hercules, the only subsequent changes

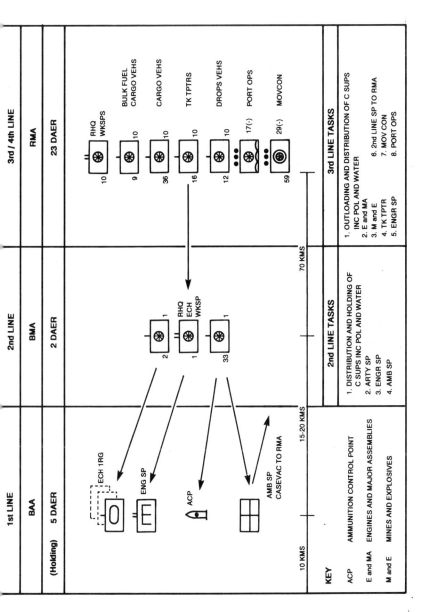

Figure 4.1 Transport: Initial Order of Battle and Concept

were 17 Squadron RCT not 36 Squadron of 10 (Corps) Transport Regiment RCT and 50 Movement Control (MC) Squadron and not 59 (MC) Squadron of 29 Transport and Movements Regiment RCT.

Third line transport was based upon 10 Corps Transport Regiment RCT and included general transport, fuel, water, tank transporter, port and maritime and movements squadrons. This unique group, with its multiplicity of types of transport and functions had an additional and novel aspect to contend with, the introduction of the DROPS not in its intended artillery resupply role but as a water replenishment vehicle. The 10 Regiment RCT Group ORBAT is shown at Figure 4.1. It was a powerful organisation comprising the 14 tonne Bedford's of 17 Squadron RCT, the 22.5 cubic metre Foden fuel tankers of 9 Squadron RCT, the Leyland DAF DROPS vehicles of 12 Squadron RCT and the Scammell Commander tank transporters of 16 Tank Transporter Squadron RCT. Add in the myriads of Land Rovers of various configurations, Can Am and Armstrong motorcycles and it is clear that not only did the Group have a wide ranging and diverse vehicle fleet with an enormous lift capability, but it had the makings of every mechanic's and storeman's nightmare. When it arrived in the Gulf, the Group was informed of the additional responsibility of the Host Nation transport fleet, which was in its infancy at that stage but growing fast. This ORBAT also includes 1 Armoured Division Transport Regiment who provided second line support to the Brigade.

With the ORBAT fine tuned and as complete as it ever would be, a small Transport and Movements (Tpt and Mov) headquarters of seven officers and soldiers was formed as part of the Headquarters FMA. This compact cell tasked the entire third line transport and movements effort throughout the whole campaign. It was at about this time, just before the pre-advance party deployment to Saudi Arabia, that a soon to be familiar phrase surfaced: 'Gentlemen, hold your nerve!' It took a lot of holding at times as the pressure to write the reception plan and the transport and movements concept became time sensitive and the size of the operation became all too clearly apparent. In essence, some 13,000 personnel, over 5,200 tracked and wheeled vehicles, 2,000 containers and 14,000 tonnes of ammunition were on their way and we really did not have a clue where to put it all. The only thing that was known was that it was coming and it was ours!

Reception

The Transport and Movements Annex to the FMA Logistic Operation Order was written and published. The concept of operations was based on Germany (BAOR) procedures, tailored to meet special-to-theatre requirements (Figure 4.1). Headquarters FMA, Transportation and Movement, would mirror the role of Corps Headquarters (Rear) with

Headquarters Brigade Maintenance Area (BMA) providing divisional second line responsibilities. The concept was simple: third line transport would offload all ships and aircraft and inload ammunition supply points (ASP) and depots, deploy personnel, equipment and materiel to the BMA and provide first line support to the FMA. All of this fell upon the 10 Regiment RCT Group with additional tasks of reception and the running and administration of Baldrick Lines. It was a tall order but one that was carried out with great efficiency and considerable style. No one will ever forget the CO, Lieutenant Colonel Philip Chaganis and RSM McLaughlin, 10 Regiment RCT Group at the reception shed when explaining the correct way to wear the less than stylish, 'Hats floppy ridiculous':

> Gentlemen, it is worn in a special way. On the head, with the brim all the way down, all the way round, all the time.

Whilst the sartorial elegance of the British Army was at times wanting, the hats floppy ridiculous, when worn properly, shielded the head and the eyes from the blazing sun and allowed the Australian Exchange Officer of 39 Engineer Regiment an element of exclusivity!

There was absolutely no reason to reinvent the wheel. The reception plan itself was designed to receive equipment by sea and air, marry it up with personnel arriving by air and deploy formed units to their operational locations in the desert to conduct training and await further orders.

The FMA pre-advance party deployed on 8 October 1990 and arrived at Jubail airport. The airhead was filled to capacity with transport and fighter aircraft of every conceivable type and illustrated perfectly the enormous scale of the Coalition effort. It was a frightening sight and was not lost on the FMA element as it trooped off the RAF Hercules. Reality was the blazing heat and an American staff sergeant in British Army uniform, telling us to get a move on. Staff Sergeant Berchey of 50 (MC) Squadron RCT, a US exchange SNCO, had been moved at short notice from the tranquillity of South Cerney in Wiltshire to Jubail. His ready brand of humour and unique situation amused the USMC (who ran the airport) and his liaison duties with his fellow countrymen proved vital over the coming weeks.

The Port Clearance building in Jubail Port was established as Headquarters FMA and was to become home and office for a few days whilst Baldrick Lines was built. The RCT had already established a presence with four movement controllers from 50 (MC) Squadron RCT. After a quick briefing and tour around the harbour in a Toyota Corolla which, together with a 4-ton Mercedes truck of dubious age and even more dubious mechanical condition, comprised the entire third line transport fleet, HQ FMA (Tpt and Mov) was established and open for business. Contact was made with JHQ High Wycombe and HQ BAOR

60   *Gulf Logistics*

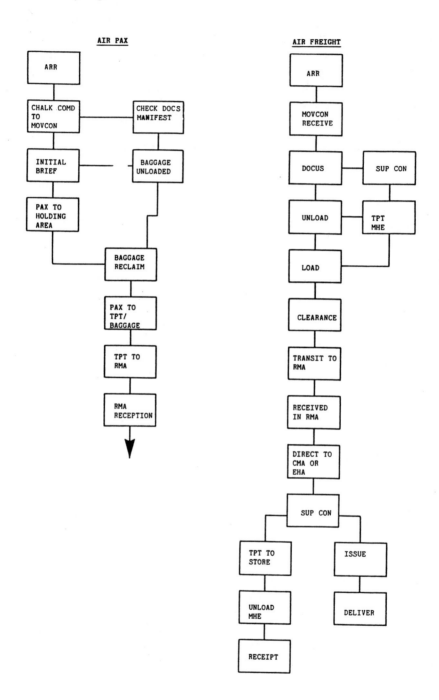

Figure 4.2 Reception Flow – Air

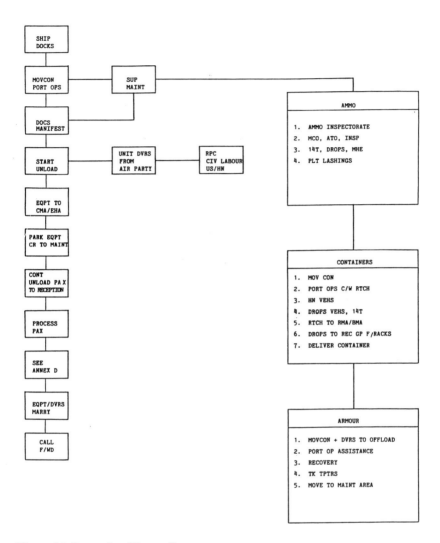

Figure 4.3 Reception Flow – Sea

(Tpt and Mov) and, armed with the knowledge that hard on our heels were the lead elements of the Brigade advance parties, the mechanics of the reception plan were put into place and practised. The first Tristar was due at Jubail airport on the 15 October, or six days away. Co-ordination with the port commanders (the USMC), the civilian Port Authority and liaison with local bus and transport contractors was swiftly done and within 24 hours, HQ FMA (Tpt and Mov) was ready to receive, account for and marshal the advance parties of the brigade. The reception flow is shown at Figures 4.2, 4.3 and 4.4.

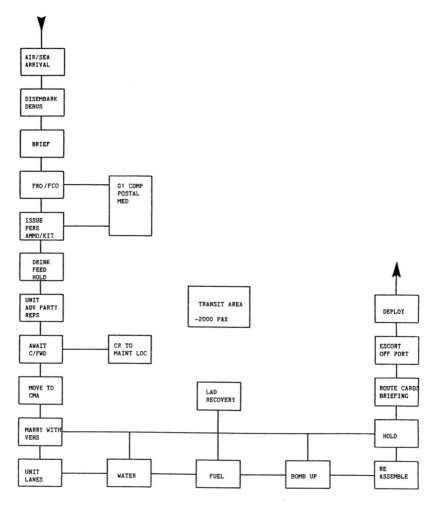

Figure 4.4 Reception Area Flow – Sequence of Events

At the same time, the remainder of the FMA staff had identified and been allocated the infamous sheds on the port jetty to receive, document and accommodate personnel while they waited for their equipment to arrive by sea and, once unloaded, for the Challenger and Warrior modification programme to start (see Chapter 7). It was not lost on the lead elements that Jubail presented a very attractive target to both strategic missile and terrorist attack. USMC patrols, our own security posts and the Patriot batteries adjacent to Baldrick Lines helped to reassure but the concern was very real even in the early days. The first Tristar arrived to the tumultuous clicking of the cameras of the world's press and on the 18 October the first ship arrived in Jubail.

By this time, the remaining 'movers' and port operators had arrived and were ready to receive the first of a daily flow of ships and aircraft.

*   *   *

The *Dana Cimbria*, with its hold full of Challenger tanks and Commander tank transporters, slowly reversed on to the RO-RO berth and lowered her stern ramp. As the ramp hit the concrete, the first Challenger tank noisily and menacingly deployed on to Saudi Arabian soil; the tangible and unequivocal evidence of the United Kingdom's commitment to the Coalition. You could almost hear the shouts of relief in High Wycombe and the glee of Lieutenant General Walter Boomer, the USMC Commander, as the Challengers roared off to the reception vehicle lanes. Relief because the seemingly endless voyage had ended and glee because the Challengers represented enhanced firepower when compared to the less modern M48 and M60 tanks of the USMC. Accusations of stage management hurt the port operators and movements staff! Rumours that the port squadron had sailed out to the *Dana Cimbria* in the pilot's launch and had prepared the vessel for immediate discharge were all true! It was an excellent start and the precursor to many ship arrivals with no less important cargoes. The reception plan worked.

Secretly the 'truckies' knew that the real cheers were for the tank transporters which at the time was an in-joke but which eventually became very real as far as the USMC and then the Brigade were concerned. The USMC had only three Heavy Equipment Transporters (HETs) to move all their tanks and all of these were off the road. The Commanders repaid much of the indebtedness owed to the USMC and their use in support of tank deployments to the Al Mishab region towards the Saudi/Kuwait border was much appreciated. The Commander tank transporter is an impressive beast at the best of times and the Marines were amazed that the British Army had HETs with Rolls Royce engines! 16 Squadron, with their 23 tractor units and 20 trailers, worked almost non-stop clearing ships, moving armoured vehicles around the port and deploying brigade units to their training areas and locations. With vehicle availability close to one hundred per cent, the Squadron experimented with double loads of Warriors (Infantry Combat Vehicles) and Scorpions (light tanks) by extending ramps over the trailer swan necks and even carried pallets of ammunition and containers. The USMC and US Army had few tank transporters at that stage and those they did have were unreliable and unable to carry fully loaded and substantially up-armoured tanks. The sound of tyres popping as the transporters laboured with their loads became common as did the congestion they caused while tyres were changed. The 20 British tank transporters soon became hot property and were tasked on numerous occasions in support of the

USMC and US Army. However, as the brigade massed and Challengers left the modification assembly line, tasking authority for the tank transporters was delegated to the brigade staff.

The reception of the Brigade gathered pace. Commercial aircraft operators were reluctant to fly in to Jubail airport not, it must be said, because of its proximity to the Kuwaiti border, but because of the lack of maintenance facilities should an aircraft suffer mechanical problems. The international airport of Dhahran, some three hours drive away was the only one available and an additional loop was added to the reception plan. An Air Transport Liaison Officer (ATLO) team was despatched to Dhahran to receive the aircraft and Host Nation (HN) buses and baggage trucks were contracted to bring the air parties to Jubail. Because of the terrorist threat, all convoys required armed guards and escort vehicles. Land Rovers were at a premium so a number of Toyota and Nissan pick-up trucks were hired and an escort organisation was formed.

Bad weather and mechanical problems delayed ships and resulted in overcrowding in the sheds on the port. It quickly became apparent that the air schedule would have to be altered to avoid a population explosion and some very quick staff work came up with a revised airflow which was blessed by Brigadier Cordingley and Commander FMA and presented to the movements staff in JHQ High Wycombe. They agreed, slowed the air flow and Shed 4 breathed a collective sigh of relief. It was the start of an excellent relationship with the staff at JHQ which held throughout the campaign and which smoothed many a heart-stopping problem.

Early Operations

Whilst receiving the Brigade, we were also inundated with third and second line transport requests. For some inexplicable reason, the second line transport group based on 1 Armoured Division Transport Regiment RCT was given a low priority on the DOAST and all transport details fell upon the still arriving vehicles and men of 10 Regiment RCT Group.

The transport organisation was swamped and the reluctance of units to release vehicles and drivers once they were under their control became critical. Whilst it was understandable, as everyone wanted transport, it was infuriating for the staff who had few assets, most of which were Host Nation (HN). In an effort to control the buses and flat bed trucks of numerous civilian contractors, a HN Transport Troop was formed and a subaltern of 10 Regiment 'chosen' to command. Despite many problems, the least of which was the fact that the drivers spoke little or no English, the troop performed well and released the few military vehicles available to more specialised tasks. Whilst holding vehicles and drivers hostage continued throughout the campaign, the allocation of HN troop vehicles or the threat of their exclusive use for future taskings, guaranteed a prompt release in the majority of cases!

As vehicles and units deployed to their operational locations, mobility trials and desert driving techniques were practised. The sand around Jubail was extremely soft and the going for wheeled vehicles was very difficult and almost impossible for the fuel tankers (TTF). As a result, several Urgent Operational Requirements (UOR) were written requesting all manner of vehicles and equipment. The delivery of ammunition and fuel and water became crucial and was elevated quite correctly to 'show stopper' status. It was clear that logistic wheeled vehicles would not be able to reach tracked vehicles or even keep pace with the advance. The UORs were immediately agreed and as a result large numbers of US M548 tracked cargo carriers were procured and sent to the Gulf as tracked ammunition limbers. Fuel and water in the necessary quantities could not be carried in the M548s and the only alternative was to order additional 20,000 litre AWD Multidrive tankers. This unique vehicle, which was already en route to the Gulf to carry water, consisted of a powerful tractor unit and a powered semi-trailer which promised improved mobility.

Whilst all this hectic activity was going on, the DROPS Squadron quietly conducted desert trials with dramatically reduced tyre pressures. The trials, with empty and loaded vehicles, were a revelation and DROPS proved to be a true ship of the desert, as it traversed over previously impassable sand dunes. When it did get stuck, intelligent use of the load system allowed it to self-extract and this, together with reversing out of trouble and checking routes, restored some wheeled vehicle mobility (and not a little credibility). Encouraged by the success of the DROPS Squadron, 17 Squadron conducted their own trials with their 14-tonne Bedfords and with deflated tyres, mirrored the results of the DROPS vehicles. It was very much trial and error and tyre pressures and mobility performance were constantly checked until the right balance was achieved; too little and there was a danger of the tyre coming off the rim; too much and mobility was reduced to an unacceptable degree. The major drawback to reduced tyre pressures was the inordinate amount of time it took to reflate tyres to road pressures. Unlike many US vehicles, which were equipped with a central tyre inflation and deflation device, the only aid to the British driver was the vehicle air line. In the midday sun the time it took was both uncomfortable and dangerous. Compressors were asked for as UORs and the DROPS Squadron even deployed the tyre changing flatrack which was fitted with a heavy duty compressor. The time to inflate 8 large tyres was still excessive and the waiting vehicles presented a superb target. Consideration was given to splitting units into road and off-road sections to minimise delays. This would have worked with DROPS but was a non-starter with conventional vehicles. The flexibility and adaptability of the DROPS was becoming more apparent.

As permission was granted for the Brigade to move out of the Jubail hinterland and recce additional locations further North, it became very clear that the sand around Jubail was amongst the worst in Saudi Arabia! The going further North, on the hard packed sand and gravel, was much easier. However the experience of driving on soft sand was not wasted, especially when mobility became a major factor again with the atrocious weather preceding and during the land war.

The outload of stocks from Jubail port continued unabated throughout November and the trucks were tasked at one hundred per cent of available vehicles. The introduction of DROPS proved a real test as we came to terms not only with the vehicle itself and its loading system but with the diverse roles it was able to perform. DROPS was undoubtedly one of the major successes of the campaign. Teething troubles did occur but prompt action by the drivers and the REME fitter sections minimised down time. Leyland DAF deployed a team of engineers to investigate several problems but, for a vehicle which had only just entered service and had been thrown in at the deep end, its reliability was truly impressive, as was the Multilift loading system which was virtually trouble free.

Although DROPS was intended for the resupply of the MLRS rocket system, water distribution became its major role in the Gulf, using 14,000 litre water tanks, the infamous 'bean cans', bought from Reynolds Boughton. The original concept called for 39 bean can tanks to be serviced by 26 DROPS vehicles; 13 on the ground, 13 loaded en-route and 13 returning to fill. Whilst the bean cans were on the high seas, water distribution was by courtesy of the USMC and palletised bottled water until the enterprising Officer Commanding the DROPS Squadron, Major John Wallace, 'happened by' the USMC transport pool and noticed some rather smart containerised tanks. Using native Yorkshire charm and the (very) generous offer of tank transporters for a task to move 53 USMC main battle tanks he secured the use of a number of SIXCON insulated water containers! The SIXCON, as its name suggests, is six small containers bolted together to form the dimensions of a 40 foot ISO container. As the DROPS flatrack was only 20 feet long, three SIXCON containers were bolted together and locked onto the DROPS flatrack. At a stroke the FMA had a robust water distribution system able to support several brigade unit exercises on the training areas.

Flatracks arrived with every ship, or so it seemed. Unfortunately the majority of them were artillery, or type 'A' instead of the general purpose, or type 'GP', flatracks. The GP flatracks had ISO locks which meant they could load containers. Containers were used for everything. From rather plush living quarters complete with fitted carpets and air conditioning to boring armouries, they became the answer to many an SQMS's prayer, particularly when mounted on a flatrack. Suddenly, RCT DROPS drivers were subjected to an amazing phenomenon as SQMS after SQMS said, 'Please leave the flatracks son and you can have five minutes in the store.' This was a phenomenon, as one had never heard an SQMS say 'please' before!

Unfortunately, there were only 237 'GP' flatracks and rather more than 237 containers in theatre. The type 'A' flatracks became an embarrassment and a constant enquiry from Commander FMA as to what to do with them was beyond the thoughts of a gentleman. They became a dinosaur until one day a unit, who shall remain nameless, played the 'possession is nine tenths of the law' game and occupied what was clear to all truckies of sound mind and good eyesight, a rattling good vehicle park. The type 'A' flatrack is heavy (especially so when stacked six deep), could only be moved by a heavy duty forklift or a DROPS truck, and there were lots (900) of them. It remains a mystery to this day how 10 Regiment RCT Group and follow-on RCT units managed to occupy some rather splendid real estate in and around Jubail with little or no problem excepting a few flatrack scratches on the tarmac!

As the first of many visitors descended on the FMA, the round of briefings and escorted tours took their toll. All the hard-working drivers, port operators and movers certainly appreciated the interest shown in what they were doing. However, what truly rankled many was the pristine desert combat kits that a number of high priced visitors wore at a time when many soldiers had been in the Gulf for some months and still had cold weather green combat suits.

Movement and Port Operations

It is often said that the difference between a movement controller and a terrorist is that terrorists have sympathisers. The 'movers' of 50 (MC) Squadron had a difficult task and few people to perform it. They coped with the incessant need for information from numerous headquarters with characteristic (and at times laconic) good humour noting that the same questions were being asked several times over. Information is knowledge but the Automated Data Processing (ADP) systems in the Gulf had one major failing; they did not interface or speak to each other. Manual information gathering using stubby pencil, T cards and the most famous RCT computer of all, FAGPACKET, became the day to day tool of the mover. The numerous changes to ship and air schedules, the need to deploy Air Transport Liaison Officers (ATLO) detachments to Riyadh and Bahrain and the reception of the armada of vessels with their diverse cargoes put a considerable strain on the young movers, who provided ample proof, if proof was ever needed, of their quality.

The 'worst job in the Gulf' title during the reception of the Brigade was not the hapless individual chosen from a cast of one to escort the infamous 'honeysucker'. The title was won with honour by the stevedores of 52 Port Squadron, who toiled in the holds of general cargo ships in temperatures of over 140 degrees Fahrenheit. The Battle Honour 'Al Jubail' should have been awarded to the men of the port squadron who unloaded RO-RO ships in less than six hours, ammunition ships in 24 hours and, on GRANBY 1.5, the *Atlantic Conveyor*, one of the largest RO-RO/container ships in the world, in less than 24 hours. Whilst the Port of Jubail was magnificent, the majority of the port handling equipment was unserviceable. Lack of use and poor ,naintenance meant that ships cranes had to be used, adding considerably to unload times. This, together with mechanical problems with the internal ramps of some RO-RO ships, lead to many improvisations with lifting gear. The sight of a Warrior suspended by one steel rope 30 feet above the jetty did not amuse the watching infantry battalion or SO1 Transportation and Movement, who quickly worked out that, even with NAAFI finance, monthly payments would exceed his annual salary.

Port operations required close liaison. Whilst the port was under the administrative command of the USMC, the US Navy controlled the flow of shipping into and out of the port. At the same time the Saudi Arabian Ports Authority exercised overall control of the Port and its facilities to include all marine services such as tug boats and pilots. Daily conferences quickly became hourly conferences as the port resources were divided between the British and US. The level of cooperation extended to stevedores from the 10th Transportation (Terminal) Battalion US Army working with 52 Port Squadron to discharge each nation's vessels on numerous occasions. From the very beginning of operation GRANBY, civilian managers from Hogg Robinson, the Government Freight Agents (GFA), worked alongside their military counterparts. They provided the essential liaison with the Saudi government freight agents, the shipping agents of the arriving vessels and the port's authorities. Their contribution, unrecognised for the most part, was total and the rapid discharge of the Brigade and the subsequent discharge of follow-on forces was due to their quiet professionalism and dedicated service.

The New Arrivals

In mid-November, depots and ammunition supply points (ASPs) were stocked and training began in earnest. The Port and the reception sheds were relatively quiet, although ammunition ships were still arriving. The transport and movements organisation had worked non-stop and batteries were recharged with some well deserved R&R[3] in Bahrain. Detailed plans to sustain the Brigade for its operations with the USMC were published and 10 Regiment RCT Group were well prepared to provide all the necessary third line support. The plan, which was not as cunning as later plans, called for the FFMA just south of the Kuwait/Saudi border and preparations were made to deploy a forward transportation operations cell. The LOC at this stage was about 170 kms.

The perceived long wait, whilst political pressure and sanctions were applied to Iraq, was rudely shattered by the announcement that the remainder of 1(UK) Armoured Division was to be sent to the Gulf. Plans were dusted off and the FMA prepared for the reception of 4 Armoured Brigade and the Divisional Headquarters. Operation Granby 1.5 details emerged to the joy of the movers and port operators; an additional 21,000 personnel and over 80 ships. It was a time to reflect on the enormity of the task and closely examine the resources necessary to receive, unload and deploy almost double the quantity of men and equipment of GRANBY 1.

Early discussions with headquarters in Germany and the United Kingdom focused on what transport was needed to support the division. Additional tank transporters, DROPS vehicles and their trailers, more bean cans, more 14-tonne vehicles and as many fuel vehicles as possible. With hindsight, it would have been simpler to have said 'Send everything'! The RCT cupboard was stripped, units reorganised, new vehicles issued or transferred and new roles given with what must have seemed at the time, a cavalier attitude. It wasn't, the transporters had shown amazing resilience during GRANBY 1 and there was absolutely no reason to doubt whether they could cope with the demands of GRANBY 1.5.

The RCT ORBAT, shown at Figure 3.4, included additional third and second line transport regiments, the remainder of the tank transporter fleet and a large ambulance squadron provided by the Gurkha Transport Regiment. In addition, a Host Nation transport squadron headquarter element, loosely based on the Mobile Civilian Transport Groups (MCTG)[4] in Germany, was requested along with a Transport Support Unit (TSU) for the FMA. The whole RCT was decimated to provide the necessary personnel and vehicles for GRANBY 1.5. Additional port operators and movement controllers were high on the list of essential personnel at a time when their very skills were needed to deploy the force. Trucks were taken away from units engaged on outloading UK and BAOR depots and the blinding realisation that to support one division, let alone four, required virtually every RCT soldier and vehicle in the British Army, was a salutary one. Later events were to highlight that even that seemingly excessive level of transport was insufficient. What was not lost on the Staff, especially those in the Gulf, was that GRANBY 1.5, unlike GRANBY 1, could not be relieved. There were no regular replacements left.

HQ FMA (Transportation and Movement) started the reception of 4 Armoured Brigade and HQ 1 (UK) Armoured Division and then handed over executive control of the air reception to the Divisional Staff. This allowed us to concentrate on ship arrivals, unloading and inloading of materiel and ammunition and the daily sustainment of 7 Armoured Brigade. The Port of Jubail not only received the additional UK ships of GRANBY 1.5 but USMC and US Army ships, which began to arrive in overwhelming numbers. The jetty, which was almost a mile long and half a mile wide, began to creak under the sheer numbers of tanks, helicopters, containers and ammunition. The sheds along the side of the jetty took on small town status as thousands of men and women were accommodated. Real estate and port resource management became crucial, as the sheer volume of people and ships threatened to choke the Port and the surrounding area. The one RO-RO berth again became a critical item and it was clear that alternative plans and arrangements were necessary. The industrial harbour, to the north of the commercial harbour was the only alternative. Dammam was saturated by the US Army and Kuwait Port had the wrong management (for the time being).

The majority of the expatriate harbour masters in Saudi Arabia were British which did, it has to be said, help get and retain much assistance, often to the annoyance of our US colleagues. One such expatriate was the harbour master of the industrial port and his two RO-RO berths and acres of prime marshalling area were potential life savers. The director of the Port, a charming Iraqi-born Saudi, was both gracious and welcoming but resolute that operations could not take place in his port. As for the marshalling areas, 'Of course you may use them', but the thought of ammunition coming ashore alongside the largest sulphur port in the world did not appeal to his patriotic sense of duty or personal safety. And who could have blamed him.

The marshalling area was vital. The USMC, under considerable pressure with enormous quantities of US Army equipment, could not be as generous with jetty space as they had been with 7 Armoured Brigade. Whilst the marshalling area was three miles from the port, it was a godsend and plans were quickly made to mark unit lanes, drive vehicles off the ship and return drivers in a round robin type operation. At the same time, one or two (actually 300) type 'A' flatracks were strategically placed on the marshalling area to ward off marauding US Army recce parties desperate for areas of their own. It was a shame that the Port Director had omitted to mention that the marshalling area so generously given was not his to give. The previously intransigent Saudi Royal Commission, who did own the area, saw the flatracks, relented and fortunately allowed its continued use.

Operational security (OPSEC) quickly put a stop to the rumours but planning continued for the move of the Division from the East coast inland to an area around the town of Hafr Al Batin. The LOC was extended from 170 kms to 350 kms and the only MSR available to the UK was the Tapline road (see Figure 2.5). The MSRs were named after car makers. There was AUDI, TOYOTA and the most aptly named one of the lot, DODGE. DODGE was the Tapline road and is a name indelibly etched in the minds of thousands of RCT drivers and anyone who had the misfortune to travel on it. DODGE began as a modern six lane highway from the Saudi Arabian coast and degenerated to a narrow ribbon of tarmac with (barely) two lanes. A colonel (late RCT) was heard to say after a Gulf War presentation to the Territorial Army (TA) at Grantham (the RCT TA Depot), 'If I hear another word on how awful DODGE was I shall bloody scream!' The good colonel fought his Gulf War in Andover, and never had the pleasure of driving up and down DODGE for weeks on end. If he had, he probably *would* have screamed.

The reception of GRANBY 1.5 continued with frightening speed. Units married up with their vehicles and deployed to their desert locations. The marshalling area never seemed to empty and as one unit left, another one took its place. The port area reverberated with the constant movement of military vehicles of all kinds and sizes. The arrival of 27 Regiment RCT[5] provided a very welcome relief to 10 Regiment RCT Group, whose drivers and vehicles had not stopped working from day one.

A detailed staff check[6] of available assets versus the known requirement confirmed our worst fears. To achieve the outload to the FFMA within the timeframe was going to take every single third line task vehicle in the ORBAT and more. The staff check was presented to Commander FMA:

1. To achieve the planned inload of FFMA by 25 Jan 91 and unload vessels and air freight arriving before the 26 Jan 91 to ASPs and Depots required the following:
   a. All of 10 Regiment RCT[7]
   b. All of 27 Regiment RCT
   c. 500 pallets of lift from 38 Squadron RCT (Div asset) plus 52 Host Nation (HN) flatbeds

2. If HN was not forthcoming, the time frame would be achieved with the following:
   a. All of 10 Regiment RCT
   b. All of 27 Regiment RCT
   c. All of 1 Armoured Division Transport Regiment RCT ⎫ both units
   d. 45% of 4 Armoured Division Transport Regiment RCT ⎬ belonging to 1 (UK) Armoured Division ⎭

3. If ordered to begin inloading additional stocks using third line military transport only, the time frame would be:

   a. FFMA   13 Feb 91
   b. FFMA and Port   6 Mar 91
4. The addition of 30 HN flatbeds (current fleet) reduced the time-frame to:
   a. FFMA   29 Jan 91
   b. FFMA and Port   8 Feb 91
5. The addition of the 50 HN flatbeds requested reduced the time-frame to:
   a. FFMA   25 Jan 91
   b. FFMA and Port   5 Feb 91

Even with the large numbers of RCT personnel and vehicles in the Gulf it was obvious that the requirement could not be met without augmentation. The USMC and US Army could not help. Previous dealings with the Saudi Army Liaison Officer and his generous, but un-fulfilled promises of military assistance, narrowed the field to additional HN transport. Contacts were made with several civilian contractors and detailed quotations supplied for the assets needed. The total transport requirement was 50 x forty foot flatbeds and 30 x lowboys (40–60 ton semi-trailers capable of carrying plant or armoured vehicles) identified as essential by Colonel Graham Ewer.

Prices were quoted and passed to the Civil Secretariat[8] in HQ BFME, who were engaged in detailed negotiations with the Saudi Government over payment for all manner of services to include transportation. A similar Memorandum of Understanding (MOU) between the US and Saudi Government resulted in the Saudis paying for all HN transport hired by the US and clearly the Civil Secretariat were not prepared to commit vast sums of taxpayers' money. In the end, they won that battle but, as we shall see, not before a misunderstanding on our part had unfortunate financial consequences!

Planning continued to meet the inload deadlines and the Division, who were planning their own move west as well as training and reorganising, agreed to commit whatever transport they could spare to third line. It was a selfless offer and characteristic of the true team effort that existed throughout the campaign. Troops to task had to be identified not only to meet the 21 day target but beyond in support of operations. 10 Regiment RCT Group continued as the third line regiment responsible for inloading the FFMA and 27 Regiment RCT were to relieve 10 Regiment RCT Group of all port duties to include unloading ships and the FMA refuelling point. The HN troop, which had grown to squadron size was renamed the Mobile Control Transport Group (MCTG) detached from 10 Regiment RCT Group together with the TSU, and tasked direct by HQ FMA. The TSU, formed from 68 Squadron RCT and almost exclusively female, was responsible for transport support within the FMA. When the Saudi rule which forbade women to drive on the public roads was rescinded (or at least interpreted so), the female drivers of the TSU were tasked up to the FFMA and beyond, driving the whole range of military and civilian vehicles except tank transporters.

When the FMA first arrived in theatre, a contract was let with the major oil companies to deliver fuel from the refineries in Dammam direct to the fuel farms in Jubail. The fuel was delivered in HN tankers saving considerable wear and tear on the military tankers of 9 Squadron RCT. Written into the contract was a clause which allowed the British Army to commandeer the HN tankers and use military drivers if hostilities proved too much for the civilian drivers. It did, and the establishment of a bulk fuel delivery squadron was planned within the overall transport concept.

The concept was simple yet robust with command and control at both ends of the MSR as well as an administration and rest area at the half way point. 10 Regiment RCT Group were responsible for the inload of Log Base ALPHA and command and control halfway along the MSR and at the forward end of the loop. 27 Regiment RCT would augment third line transport together with divisional assets and be responsible for command and control in Jubail. At the same time the regiment would unload ships, inload the ASPs and fuel farms in the FFMA and provide fourth line fuel support to the FMA. The MCTG would assist in unloading ships, clearing the airhead at Jubail and Dhahran airports of freight and deliver containers and ammunition forward to the FFMA. The TSU, renamed FMA Transport Troop, assisted with mail deliveries, escort duties and tasks to the FFMA. To capitalise on the HN fuel tankers and provide a robust third line fuel squadron, 66 Squadron of 27 Regiment RCT handed over their TTFs to 9 Squadron of 10 Regiment RCT Group and became the fourth line fuel squadron.

As the deadline to start operations came closer, the question of additional HN transport was still unresolved. The contractor who had promised the vehicles was under considerable pressure to hire to the US and the fleet, essential if the 21 day target was to be met, was slowly disappearing from our grasp. Then an extraordinary thing happened. A telephone call was received from BFME by Wayne Harber, the DCOS HQ FMA, with permission to hire the HN vehicles. It seemed that the cavalry had arrived in the nick of time, or so it appeared. The contract was signed in good faith and the flatbeds and lowboys were released to the MCTG and the Division. Obviously the MOU with the Saudi Arabian Government had been signed or so we thought. It transpired that it had not and that I had signed away six million pounds of taxpayers' money on transport which would have been free of charge in due course! The signal traffic between Jubail and Riyadh was intense and Commander FMA was asked to account for his staff's blatant disobedience to previous instructions not to hire HN transport. It was a bit of a shame but as someone once said, 'all's fair in love and transition to war'. It would be churlish to say that sales of small tape recorders boomed after this incident but relations with BFME were difficult at my level for some time.

The plan for the move of stocks to the FFMA was published at the end of December with the inload to start on L Day, 3 January 1991. The logistic concept is shown at Figure 1.5. Loading started on L-1, and at 0400hrs on L Day the first packet of 14 tonne vehicles of 17 Squadron RCT crossed the start line on MSR DODGE. Over the next 21 days, third and fourth line vehicles, assisted by divisional assets, travelled the 750kms of living hell that was DODGE. The round trip took, on average, 36 hours and the young drivers were subjected to bad roads, horrendous driving and an almost endless stream of military and civilian vehicles of several nations. Among these were vehicles with loads projected over their sides, which were not lit and which failed to observe even the most basic of driving skills. French Renault tank transporters jostled with US Oshkosh HETs, Egyptian and Omani four-tonners raced alongside each other and, amidst this military mayhem, Saudi civilians resplendent in immaculate white robes piloted their Cadillacs and Chevrolets in and out of the smallest of gaps safe in the knowledge that their maker would protect them. Sadly, he often didn't and MSR DODGE was littered with broken expensive cars. The weather, and some very bad sand storms, did not help matters and the rain, together with oil spillages from poorly maintained trucks, turned the road into a skating rink.

On L+21, the inload of the FFMA was met. It was a quite magnificent achievement and every unit took great pride in recounting all the tonnages they had carried, the millions of litres of fuel they had unloaded and the millions of miles they had travelled. No one could deny them their glory but everyone breathed a sigh of relief when the targets were met. The inload was a close run thing. Tight command and control, rigorous vehicle maintenance and proper administration of the drivers was the key to success. Luckily, the start of the air war on 17 January 1991 did not affect the inload. The MSR was a prime target for either aircraft or SCUD and any disruption over and above the numerous traffic accidents would have seriously delayed the operation. Transport operations were established in HQ FFMA on 17 January 91, with an SO2 and SO3 Transportation and a small movements element. This allowed closer control of arriving transport assets and a planning cell to prepare for the next stage in the operation.

27 Regiment RCT continued to unload ships in Jubail, assumed responsibility for the halfway admin area on MSR DODGE from 17 Squadron RCT and continued the inload of fuel from Dammam to the fuel farms in Log Base Alpha with the tankers of 66 Squadron. On

17 February 91, the Regimental Headquarters (RHQ) deployed to the FFMA and together with 10 Regiment RCT Group began training with the division. A troop of 42 Squadron RCT remained in Jubail to clear ammunition to the ASPs and the MCTG continued to clear airheads and deliver forward from the FMA, effectively providing fourth line transport. A detachment of 59 (MC) Squadron RCT established an Air Transport Liaison Officer (ATLO) at the forward airfield of Al Qaysumah ready to receive both passengers, freight and mail, and a small transport troop was provided to clear the airhead, using troop carrying vehicles (TCVs) and general transport (GT) trucks.

The rapid advance of the Coalition forces caught everyone by surprise and resulted in lower than planned fire rates. Consequently, ammunition expenditure was low but the speed of the advance dramatically increased fuel consumption. Whilst the AWD fuel tankers were able to (just) keep going, the muddy slime was a real obstacle to the low mobility TTFs of 9 Squadron RCT. As the division raced into Kuwait the fuel loop was too long for the TTFs to battle through, so an additional fuel XP was established close to the breach and the Mercedes HN tankers of 66 Squadron RCT were used to cross load into 9 Squadrons TTFs. The TTFs, suitably loaded, then returned to the second line XP and filled the AWD and 12,000 litre TTFs of 1 Armoured Division Transport Regiment and 4 Armoured Division Transport Regiment. In a perfect example of flexibility to meet a new situation, third line transport again showed considerable initiative to meet the unexpected.

The war was over in 100 hrs and third line transport was still loaded and ready. The division was fully stocked and could have continued through Basra and to all points north. The transport concept had worked. Drivers were exhausted but elated in the knowledge that they were not only alive but had done everything expected of them. It was a proud day to be in the British Army but an even prouder one to be in the RCT. However, all good things must surely end and the realisation that what was delivered up had to be delivered down dawned on many astute drivers and staff officers. Low fire rates meant lots of unused ammunition at various XPs, DMAs and the FFMA and of course sustainment of the division was still required. Fuel, water and materiel were all needed in Kuwait. The tortuous route from Hafr Al Batin, through the breach and on to Kuwait, was still the only way to resupply the division and a 48 hour round trip was the rule rather than the exception. Matters improved dramatically when our Engineers opened a new MSR up the Wadi Al Batin and soon after hostilities ceased, the coast road from Saudi to Kuwait was cleared of debris, rendered safe by Explosive Ordnance Disposal personnel and opened to traffic. Third line transport from the FMA began resupply direct from the fuel farms and cold stores of Jubail. It was over.

Subsequent analysis of the war and the conduct of transport operations has focused on many aspects. Notwithstanding the personal views of many who would naturally have done things a) different, and b) better; third and fourth line transport and movements and operations in the FMA were highly successful. The key to it all was the quality of the soldier and the unprecedented levels of vehicle availability. Professional, high quality leadership at all levels motivated the soldiers. It developed a momentum of immense pride that nothing could stop.

Everyone had given their all. Units competed to see who could carry the most or complete journeys quickest. MCTG personnel, who managed a regiment's worth of lift, comprised drivers from 11 nations, most of whom spoke no English. How they got to desert locations with no maps and only third or fourth hand translated instructions defied logic. Port operators who handled ships of all sizes in unprecedented turnaround times. The movers who received over 30,000 personnel and didn't lose one and who accounted for over 11,000 military vehicles, and the small staff of seven who ran HQ FMA Transport and Movements throughout the campaign. The civilian managers of the GFA and the countless, and nameless, third world civilians who contributed more than could reasonably be expected. And the female drivers who proved equal to, and in many cases better than, their male counterparts. The list is endless.

Chapter 5

Medical Support

Colonel L P Lillywhite MBE
(Commander Medical 1 (UK) Armoured Division)

Colonel R A Leitch MBE
(Staff Officer Grade 1, Medical, HQ FMA)

*The only certain result of your plan will be casualties – mainly the
enemy's if it's a good plan, yours if it's not. Either way, foremost in
your supporting plans must be your medical plan.*

Brigadier Rupert Smith
Deputy Commandant
Army Staff College 1990

The Medical Task

Over a period of three months the United Kingdom deployed to Saudi
Arabia a complete military health service comprising four hospitals of up
to 600 beds each, a hospital ship, five Field Ambulances (mobile medical
units) and numerous smaller doctor-manned medical posts. To evacuate
to, between and from these treatment facilities, a complex evacuation
organization was constructed, comprising over 40 medium helicopters
from the RN and RAF, two regiments of Land Rover ambulances, a
squadron of coaches converted to the ambulance role and armoured and
wheeled ambulances of the Field Ambulances[1] and combat units. For
lengthy evacuation, the RAF provided, on an as-required basis, C-130
Hercules, operating from desert airstrips and VC-10s and Tristars (long
range transport aircraft) operating from Riyadh. These moved the
wounded back to the United Kingdom often through the RAF hospital
at Akrotiri which was reinforced for the purpose.

A measure of the work-load can be appreciated from the number of sick
and injured seen by 1 (UK) Division medical resources alone. Over the
period 11 January to 28 February 1991 4,427 sick and injured had been
admitted, 1,175 evacuated, 3,232 returned to duty (manpower equivalent
to five infantry battalions) with 20 still being held with minor conditions.

To sustain these services, a large and complex medical supply operation, stretching from British industry to the forward fighting vehicles, was established. This covered a vast array of medical supplies, ranging from simple dressings to state of the art technology, capable of generating oxygen from air. This task was made more complex by the fact that almost half of the items demanded by the deployed medical units, and provided by the medical supply organization, were not even in the Defence Medical Services inventory at the outset of the conflict.

The medical planning staff at all levels had recognised, from the beginning, that in this conflict, as in every other since the Crimean War, the key to effective medical support would lie in preventive medicine. They were thus quickly off the mark, implementing essential prophylactic and preventive medical measures. The first priority was to manage the effects of the extreme climate, particularly the heat of a desert summer, and to prevent the outbreak of a major epidemic. Such epidemics are common in war and in areas where the basic public health infrastructure has either been destroyed or, as was the case in some locations in Saudi Arabia, were insufficient to cope with a sudden large influx of people. The measures designed to combat the climate are described later in the Chapter; at this early stage what was required was a Health Risk Assessment and clear policy guidance on such issues as education and vaccination. In addition, the Medical Services had to consider the special measures that would be required to counteract the known threat from Iraqi chemical weapons; soon after the initial deployment, this threat expanded to include biological weapons. All in all, this provided a considerable challenge to the organisation, which was tested long before the Coalition Forces fired their first shot in anger. A measure of the success in this most vital and fundamental aspect of combat medicine was the lowest disease and non-battle injury rate in the British Army's history.

Concurrently with the preventive medicine work, the MOD staff were considering the other most important step in the medical planning process. This was the construction of a Command, Control, Communications and Information (C^3I) system to enable the medical organization to mobilise, draw equipment, train, deploy and redeploy. It would also be required to regulate the evacuation of casualties and direct them to appropriate medical units, generate the movement of medical stores and equipment and monitor the numbers of sick and injured. The organization stretched from JHQ High Wycombe and extended down through the various HQs to the individual medical units and medical officers in the forward combat units. To complicate matters in theatre, everything had to be done in the context of a coalition operation in which each of the contributing nations had a different way of doing things and where, for example, the same medicine might be used by all but might be known by three different names.

From the beginning, the Gulf Conflict was, for the Defence Medical Services, a Joint Operation involving the resources of all three Medical Services. The involvement of the Army Medical Services actually began before the Army itself became involved, with the deployment in late August of a small medical group based on 22 Field Hospital to Bahrain in support of the RAF. This unit is the Army's only truly mobile hospital and forms the core of medical support to rapid reaction forces. Its early deployment to support the RAF was, although the best option at the time, a move which complicated the Army's medical plans right up to beginning of the land battle. Following the UK's decision to deploy ground forces, planning began in earnest to produce a logistic concept. The initial recce included an experienced medical officer from the staff of HQ 1 (BR) Corps, Lieutenant Colonel Louis Lillywhite. At first there were reservations about the need for a medic, because of limits on the size of the recce party. This reflected one view of the operational staffs with regard to medical issues, a view that had perhaps evolved from many years of stereotyped thinking in BAOR. In the end however the Medical Staff at DMSD and JHQ prevailed and after a period of uncertainty it was agreed to include the medical representative.

The first medical task that Colonel Lillywhite had was to consider what direct medical support was likely to be available from Saudi Arabia, so-called Host Nation Support (HNS), and what might be available from US Forces in theatre. It was obvious from the outset that Saudi Arabia although keen to provide whatever assistance it could, had only enough medical resources to meet the predicted needs of its own Armed Forces and civilian community. There appeared to be some potential in the major towns for providing vital logistic support for medical units, such as buildings, water and labour although the US Forces were, of course, looking for the same type of support. The US Forces were keen to help wherever possible but they also were short of mobile hospital beds, blood and helicopters for casualty evacuation. The only asset of which they had enough at this time was fixed-wing evacuation. The American representatives in theatre therefore recommended that the British should deploy with a full 'stand alone' medical support organization. A similar conclusion was being reached by the medical staff in the Ministry of Defence.

This need to provide stand alone medical support was a recurrent and dominant theme throughout the consequent expansion of the British forces. To achieve it would require a considerable increase in the size of the medical support first envisaged, causing considerable angst amongst the General Staff in the UK (who were working to an imposed maximum limit, known as rate capping on the size of the force which could be deployed), delaying vital and urgent decisions on the size and shape of the medical organization required in theatre. Thus whilst the rest of the Force had a clear idea of its shape, size and capability, the medical organisation was still fighting to justify to the General Staff, and then to the political masters, every individual medical post. This ponderous decision-making process was complicated by disagreement within the medical chain of command over the best approach to building up a balanced medical organization and a lack of clear direction from operational staffs as to what the casualty estimate would be. In total, this was a considerable handicap to the medical planning staffs and in particular to the land forces medical organisation. It continued to pose difficulties which were only finally resolved by the establishing of a one star Commander Medical Land Forces, in HQ FMA in late December 1990.

The Medical Structure

With the designation of 7 Armoured Brigade as the initial UK land force came the medical support structure, comprising the Regimental Aid Posts (RAPs)[2] of infantry, armour, artillery and engineer units and a complete Divisional Field Ambulance (1 Armoured Field Ambulance). The RAPs were reinforced by medical manpower, armoured vehicles and drivers (to a previously agreed establishment, which had never been financed) by robbing the RAPs of other combat units across BAOR as well as taking much of the Division's second armoured field ambulance. In addition to the wheeled ambulances integral to the field ambulance (used to evacuate from RAPs to Dressing Stations) a troop of ambulances from the Army's only Regular Army Ambulance Unit (54 Engineer Support and Ambulance Squadron RCT) was provided for evacuation out of the Brigade. By the time it was fully deployed, 1 Armoured Field Ambulance was more than double its peacetime size and well above its War Establishment (the element supporting 7 Armoured Brigade comprised 27 Officers, 254 men and 71 vehicles whilst the balance comprised 16 Officers, 171 men and 54 vehicles; these statistics exclude attachments). To achieve this without mobilizing the Reserves (the planned way of obtaining reinforcements) required the virtual disbandment of the 4th Armoured Division's field ambulance with its personnel posted to 1 Armoured Field Ambulance.

Even at this early stage, it was becoming clear that the Army Medical Services would soon exhaust their Regular manpower and that mobilisation of the Reserves would be the only option if the UK force was further increased. This produced additional staffing problems for the MOD medical staffs as ministers were naturally reluctant to mobilize the reserves. In order to overcome this reluctance, it was necessary to persuade ministers that although there were still regulars left to deploy, these did not have the specialist medical skills which were in short supply; it is not possible simply to substitute any old medic when a specialist is required.

The medical C³I plan required a Force Commander Medical and the newly appointed Commander Medical 1 Armoured Division, Colonel Louis Lillywhite, who, as we have seen, had carried out the initial recce and also had an Out of Area background was appointed. 7 Armoured Brigade's Senior Medical Officer was the Commanding Officer of 1 Armoured Field Ambulance, Lieutenant Colonel Malcolm Braithwaite.

As planning developed it, continued to be hampered by the lack of an agreed Casualty Rate from the Central Staff. This was despite the best efforts of the General Staff and the Director of Medical Operations in MOD, Brigadier Chris Ticehurst who, together with his staffs, had developed a sophisticated planning model using computer-generated casualty statistics. Consequently plans for reinforcement went ahead, based upon the best guess of the MOD medical staffs. A decision was made as a result of work after the recce, to deploy a field hospital to support land forces. As 22 Field Hospital was already committed to the RAF in Bahrain, the Cambridge Military Hospital in Aldershot was to be mobilized in its field role as 33 Field Hospital. It was at this stage that the complex and ad hoc nature of the resourcing of the medical plan became apparent. Despite closing the peacetime Service Hospital in Aldershot completely, it still was necessary to draw manpower in penny packages, from every other Army peacetime hospital in Britain and BAOR and to obtain specialist staff from RAF hospitals too. In addition, Combat Medical Technicians[3] were found from UK field ambulances. Dental Officers were tasked to assist with resuscitation and anaesthesia, coming from peacetime dental practices Army-wide, while bandsmen from three Army bands[4] provided vital stretcher-bearers.

33 Field Hospital's general equipment or camp stores were pre-stocked in a depot in Dulmen, Germany for its General War role. Its medical scales of equipment were in the Defence Medical Equipment Depot Bielefeld. Neither had even been seen by the unit, let alone checked and prepared for role. The Commanding Officer was required, in a very short time-frame, to accept the equipment and to allow its dispatch to the theatre of operations where it would have to be sorted out. The risk was that the equipment would not be suitable for the task and that there would not be time to prepare it for its role. As it turned out, much of it was less than suitable with some of it being so old that it had 1940's markings (not all that is old is necessarily inadequate. First prize for old but workable equipment must go to the hospital Matron who found amongst the cooking equipment a soup ladle still in its original wrappings, dated 1917!). However there would be time to correct deficiencies, albeit at great expense in both money and manpower. It was recognised that it would be very difficult to undertake this task with a group of individuals who had not trained together at all before. Thus the unit's command and administrative infrastructure, together with the

first tranche of manpower for a unit of about 400 general surgical beds, formed up in the UK at the AMS TA Training Centre at Chester. Here they undertook a vital period of training in basic military skills such as NBC as well as attempting to identify and address the potential problems which were to confront them.

Even as the unit deployed and began to establish itself, its precise role remained unclear. As a result it began as a unit configured for about 400 general surgical beds but ended up as a large immobile 600 bed (expandable to 800) General Hospital. In consequence, the unit's original War Establishment was exceeded by a considerable margin: and by the time the Ground War began, it was an incredible ad hocery of almost 800 personnel drawn from the Army and RAF, both Regular and Reserves, totalling about 25 different cap-badges from 65 parent units! Notwithstanding the problems it faced events would prove that in the role as a rear hospital (which it was eventually to adopt) it was a reasonably successful venture. That it succeeded at all is a reflection of the quality of the individual medical personnel who made up this temporary ensemble.

Medical Deployment

The one clear message from the recce was that the medical concept would be dictated by the huge distances involved and the potential speed and mobility of land operations. It was unfortunately difficult for those who had never operated or trained in the desert and who were now beginning to exert control from back in the UK, to appreciate the problems. The recce team's appreciation was that it would be vital to deploy expert resuscitation forward in the form of Field Surgical Teams. These would be based in Field Ambulance Dressing Stations to cope with the inevitable lengthy evacuation times that would result from distance and friction of battle. It would also be necessary to re-configure the traditional BAOR-style field hospitals into much smaller deployable units capable of moving rapidly to support the battle and to survive in the desert on a minimal logistic tail. The recommendations on Field Surgical Teams were not met with total enthusiasm in all quarters of the Defence Medical Services and that measure was not fully implemented until the one star Commander Medical, Brigadier Dick Hardie, an Airborne officer with considerable experience of Out of Area operations, endorsed the recommendation in January 1991. However, it was apparent from the outset that helicopters, in spite of the considerable logistic penalties, would be vital to the success of the medical plan and, after considerable work by JHQ and DMSD agreement was reached to deploy a number of RAF Support Helicopters (Pumas) for casualty evacuation.

The lead elements of the 7 Armoured Brigade Group which deployed by air and sea to Al Jubail in October included a field ambulance section, a hygiene element and a small medical cell of Colonel Louis Lillywhite, Major Tim Pitcher, Captain Joe Donahoe and WO2 Peter White. The major task at the outset was the prevention of heat casualties and prevention of the outbreak of the D & V types of illness ('having trouble') so common when large groups are living, cooking and eating in close proximity. This was no mean undertaking given the considerable physical activity required in temperatures in the high 30s, with high humidity and with very rudimentary field sanitation available.

The key to success lay in three simple measures. First, the implementation of a strict régime of enforced fluid intake, ensuring that water was drunk at regular intervals regardless of thirst; sunbathing was also strictly limited. Second, rigid food and water hygiene rules were implemented, fresh fruit and vegetables were carefully selected and prepared; for the first time in an operational setting, disposable cups, plates and cutlery were issued and their use enforced. Finally, the disposal of waste and the control of flies and other insects were carefully monitored and controlled. The construction of desert latrines, fly-proof wooden structures resembling telephone kiosks and nicknamed Turdises, became a minor industry. All solid waste was collected daily by the sanitary patrol and burnt in pits (a less than pleasant task!). Waste water was run off into deep soakage pits and Desert Roses (for urinating into) bloomed wherever we went. It may surprise readers with previous military experience up to the 1960s, to know that many of these fundamental field hygiene measures had to be taught or re-taught, even to quite senior personnel. As the scale and importance of the preventive medicine task grew, the medical cell was enhanced by a field hygiene team led by Major John Graham, a Consultant Public Health Physician, who later went on to fill a key role as the Force Preventive Medicine Adviser.

Not far behind the lead elements was the advance party of 33 Field Hospital, who had previously sent their own recce party and identified a site in a tyre factory. Unfortunately their agreement was with a sub-tenant (a fact unknown either to them or the true owner). It took some fast footwork and slick diplomacy by Colonels White and Lillywhite to secure the site from the proper owner, just hours before the main body of the hospital arrived to occupy it. It remains a mystery as to how they obtained it for half the asking price and double the time first offered! The Advance Party was in fact provided by personnel of a second wheeled field ambulance (which was smaller than 1 Armoured Field Ambulance) from Britain, 24 Airmobile Field Ambulance under the command of Lieutenant Colonel Paddy Magee. There was some degree of confusion, and disagreement, between the medical staff in theatre and at JHQ, as to what the exact role of this unit was to be. Initially, HQ FMA understood that the personnel were to be a constituent part of 33 Field Hospital but, as they came with their own equipment, this appeared not to be the case, and there was no clear task for it in theatre. However, the unit set to with enthusiasm and undertook a whole range of medical tasks in the rapidly expanding Force Maintenance Area, including assistance in building 33 Field Hospital. Eventually, as events unfolded, it became a vital element of the final medical plan, providing the Force medical reserve and undertaking a number of missions including the provision of medics for Support Helicopters in their casevac role and intimate medical support for 1 (UK) Armoured Division as it crossed the Line of Departure into Iraq.

33 Field Hospital's task included the provision of medical support to 7 Armoured Brigade as it arrived and it therefore started to deploy in advance of the 7 Armoured Brigade main body. However, the problems of building a hospital from scratch simply had not been appreciated. Luckily, the recce party had obtained the agreement of the US authorities to provide support from the US Fleet Hospital, already established in Al Jubail, to manage the UK's sick and injured, known as Disease and Non Battle Injuries or DNBI, during deployment. In the period before fighting started this proved a very successful option as the Fleet Hospital had state-of-the-art medical technology in abundance and was well able to cope with the numbers as well as the range of patient conditions. Meanwhile, it was becoming clear that 33 Field Hospital, designed for the management of trauma in a short, high-intensity conflict in BAOR, would need to expand its capability to manage the types of DNBI encountered in the Gulf.

The site chosen for the hospital had mains electrical power, mains water supply, sewerage, cover and hard standing, sufficient for only about 100 beds. As a result, a major engineering effort was required to lay in plumbing, power distribution, latrines and sluices. All this was complicated by the additional demands of providing NBC protection and air conditioning, which had to be designed into the structure. Once built, the hospital was totally immobile. Initial construction required a squadron of Royal Engineers working almost full-time for a month and considerable engineer support thereafter to maintain and expand it. In fact, the unit 'metamorphosed' so often from one shape to another to meet its changing roles in the period leading up to the ground war that the Sappers believed that it derived its name from the number of changes made to it! Moreover it was sited 20 km from the main operational airfield, a journey by road of over 30 minutes, which required the establishment of a separate ambulance troop to manage the evacuation loop. As a result, HQ FMA wished to plan to deploy a forward element of the hospital into the desert. However, disagreement in theatre between HQ FMA and HQ BFME, over whether its mission was to support 7 Armoured Brigade or to support the whole of the deployed UK force, prevented any plans from progressing far. The disagreement was never resolved as it was overtaken by events when the size of the British force eventually increased. Then, with the combat forces deploying north-west into the desert, the unit became marginalised, being 500 km from the force it was tasked to support and east of the evacuation route out of theatre. Notwithstanding its problems, when it opened in early November the unit was, in military terms, the best prepared amongst the coalition forces to treat chemical casualties and probably the best prepared to deal with high casualty rates. In summary, the management of 33 Field Hospital exemplified the problems of attempting to apply medical doctrine, designed for General War in BAOR, to a totally different operational scenario.

Meanwhile, 7 Armoured Brigade was deploying into theatre and had commenced training, first at sub-unit level, working up to brigade-level live firing exercises. These were designed to provide maximum realism and therefore a fairly high degree of risk, increasing the need for immediate medical support. Responsibility for the main part of the Brigade was devolved to Lieutenant Colonel Malcolm Braithwaite, commanding 1 Armoured Field Ambulance, who split his unit into the equivalent of two brigade field ambulances. He commanded from the forward one and acted as the Brigadier's medical adviser. The Clearing Squadron commander, Major Ewan Carmichael, a dental officer, commanded the second dressing station with responsibility for the Brigade Rear Area. Medical training also began to build up in intensity and sophistication, with the emphasis on using the considerable expertise of many of the senior medical officers to teach the Combat Medical Technicians and Bandsmen advanced first aid and resuscitation techniques.

In October 1990, Colonel John Tinsley, an experienced and senior medical officer, was deployed onto the staff of General Sir Peter de la Billière in HQ BFME at Riyadh. His task was to plan and coordinate the medical mission at the operational level, particularly Host Nation Support, coalition medical planning and evacuation out of theatre. His HQ's position in the C³ chain, between JHQ High Wycombe and the forward combat troops, was a vital and highly valued one, able to act as a filter for much of the unnecessary traffic that was beginning to flow in each direction and to take the heat out of the many moments of tension that were bound to occur in a mission of this type.

The story of deployment is not complete however without mention of the medical effort required to get the men and women of the force fit for deployment. In addition to the various vaccinations, the medical state of numerous individuals had to be reviewed; large numbers of individuals who wore glasses did not have the lenses for their respirators, and dental fitness within 7 Armoured Brigade was only between 65 and 70%.

The dental effort required to get the force fit was particularly great with six dental teams working in Fallingbostel in shifts from 0600 to

2200. Even though the force deployed with over a 90% dental fitness rate, there was still considerable work in theatre with a dental sickness rate of 0.17 per day. Up until March 1991, in the Gulf, some 650 teeth were extracted and 2,334 filled. The Dental Officers noticed that a much higher proportion reported early than was the case back in barracks – the thought of being stuck in the middle of the desert with toothache obviously overcame any inhibitions about seeing a dentist. In common with their doctor colleagues, the field dental equipment available to treat casualties left a lot to be desired. However, a number of modern equipments which were on trial found their way to the Gulf. These were enhanced by a mixture of local purchase, writing home to peacetime dental centres and various other techniques! Dentistry was undertaken by Dental Officers in Field Ambulances and Field Hospitals. However only 24 dentists were primarily employed as dentists or specialist hospital dental staff (nine); the balance of 75 were instead employed as Anaesthetic Support Officers or in a resuscitation role (34) and in command or staff roles. Of the Dental Other Ranks only 29 of the 78 were employed in their primary role with the balance acting as blood transfusion assistants, in charge of Chemical Decontamination Teams, or as Combat Medical Technicians. Unfortunately, all Dentists were found in field medical units, and as there were no Mobile Dental Teams left in existence to deploy, this had a penalty in time lost as patients from the front line made their way back to medical units for their dental treatment.

The Divisional Medical Plan

In late November, following 1 (UK) Armoured Division's recce, Major General Rupert Smith, the Commander, drew up a 'shopping list' of medical resources to complete the medical support for what was rapidly becoming a large and powerful land force, estimates of which were already in excess of 25,000 and growing. The medical organisation required comprised a field ambulance with one dressing station, to support 4 Armoured Brigade, 22 Field Hospital redeployed from Bahrain at 200 beds and a second deployable field hospital of no more than 200 beds able to move forward into the Desert as well as support helicopters and ambulances, a field hygiene team, a medical supply unit and four field surgical teams. Colonel John Tinsley, at JHFQ, believed it necessary to provide an additional hospital in Riyadh as the Force Evacuation Hospital.

Based on casualty estimates now emerging from Operational Analysis sources in Britain, JHQ developed a plan to provide a 400 bed field hospital (32 Field Hospital) drawn initially from British Military Hospital (BMH) Hannover; an Evacuation Hospital at Riyadh; and enhancement to 33 Field Hospital in Al Jubail. They also wished to provide a second, complete armoured field ambulance to support 4 Armoured Brigade. A compromise was eventually reached between the medical planning staffs in-theatre and those in JHQ and MOD. 5 Armoured Field Ambulance, at almost the same strength as 1 Armoured Field Ambulance, commanded by Lieutenant Colonel Bruce Reece–Russell, was nominated to provide second line support. 32 Field Hospital was re-configured to deploy at 200 beds and 22 Field Hospital was relieved in Bahrain by Number 1 RAF War Hospital and re-tasked to provide support to the Land Forces.

It was also recognised that additional ground ambulances would be needed to support the evacuation system. Within the Division they would increase evacuation capability from the second-line field ambulances to third-line hospitals. Behind the Division, in the Force Maintenance Area, they would provide evacuation between the evacuation airfields and third line hospitals. As the only Regular unit, 54 Squadron RCT had already been deployed and the major TA Ambulance Regiment could not be made available without mobilisation, MOD decided to create an all-regular Ambulance Group based upon the Gurkha Transport Regiment in Hong Kong. The preparation and deployment of this unit, 28 Gurkha Ambulance Group, was a major achievement, requiring the movement of the core of the unit from its base in Hong Kong to the UK, effectively re-roling it to an ambulance mission, providing the additional medical manpower and equipment for its new role and finally training it. There is no doubt that by the time the ground war started the unit was mission-ready but getting there was fraught. Among its major problems was a lack of equipment, particularly for communications. More importantly, it lacked relevant operating procedures and medical expertise within the unit to help create them. On a number of occasions, the unit questioned the paucity of medical training and general support given to them by the medical services, particularly that there was not one medical officer in the unit and the majority of the medical assistants deployed in the ambulances were inexperienced bandsmen. There is a major lesson to be learned here concerning the responsibilities of both the Royal Corps of Transport (or Royal Logistic Corps as it is now) and the RAMC in preparing ambulance units for operations. Despite its limitations however, it was considered to be another successful 'military ad hocery' and ambulances were always where they were required and when they were required. Its success was largely the result of the very high esprit de corps that typifies all Gurkha units and the flexible and determined approach of their Commanding Officer, Lieutenant Colonel Ian Gunn.

By now it was becoming even clearer that the evolving medical plan would not only require most of the Regular assets of all three medical services (RN, Army and RAF) but would also need considerable numbers of Reserves. It was to be some weeks before ministerial approval for the medical ORBAT and the calling out of the Reserves was to be obtained. Once again, medical planning was lagging behind the operational plan. It was also obvious that Colonel Louis Lillywhite's span of command as Commander Medical, which had increased to include the huge organisation in the Force Maintenance Area as well as the newly arriving Division, was quickly becoming too large for one medical headquarters. Colonel John Tinsley in Riyadh was now well established in a key role as the senior UK medical staff officer in HQ BFME and could not be redeployed easily nor take on responsibility for a growing Force medical ORBAT. Another medical HQ was thus required and the decision was taken to form a one star medical head-quarters led by Brigadier Dick Hardie, the Commander Medical 1st (British) Corps, based in Bielefeld. He relieved Colonel Lillywhite in HQ FMA in December, keeping all but one of the medical staff officers. In addition, a Chief Medical Plans, Lieutenant Colonel Bob Leitch, joined HQ FMA from Staff College Camberley. HQ FMA took over responsibility for medical planning rear of the Division. The medical plan could now be completed as the medical ORBAT was known and HQ FMA produced a medical Concept of Operations for Operation GRANBY LAND OPS which is shown in diagrammatic form at Figure 5.1. The complete medical C^3I was now in position and ready to go.

In the Desert, 1 (UK) Armoured Division was building up. It too had a Medical headquarters, part of the Division Rear HQ (although during the actual fighting part of it was to redeploy forward to Divisional Main HQ). In addition to Commander Medical, who joined the Division when Brigadier Dick Hardie arrived in the FMA, there were two SO2s, Major Sean Drysdale the SO2 Preventive Medicine and Major Alan Newcombe the SO2 Medical Operations, and a number of SO3s. The deployment of the Division, although a complex operation, was relatively trouble free thanks to the procedures developed by the 7 Armoured Brigade Group. In particular, the preventive medical measures were well established and proven and, in any case, temperatures had fallen and the threat to health now was from the cold and wet. The deployment into the Al Jubail area and subsequently North and then West was accompanied by a number of Map Exercises under the direction of GOC 1 (UK) Armoured Division (which were always followed by Medical Map Exercises under the direction of Commander Medical) and two major Field Training Exer-cises (FTX), which included intensive medical training and testing. These FTXs in particular, showed that the individual soldier was rapidly adjusting to his environment and becoming physically and mentally battle-hardened. The incidence of DNBI as result of training remained markedly low, though the number of injuries from road traffic accidents was an ominous indicator that the 'Tap-Line Road' (Route DODGE) was likely to be as dangerous a place as any in theatre.

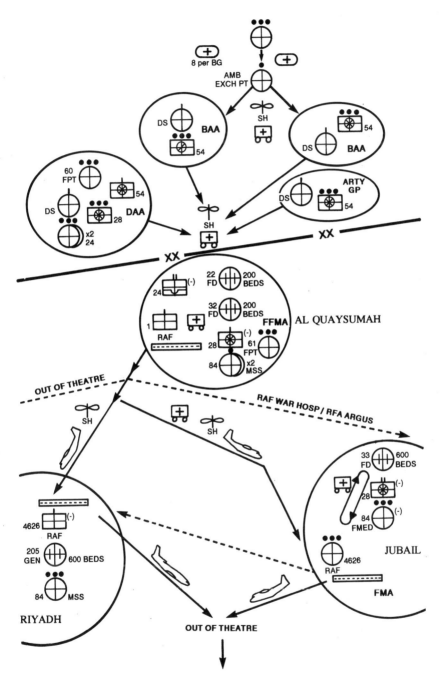

Figure 5.1 Operation GRANBY. The Medical Concept and Casualty Evacuation Plan

The effectiveness of the medical support in the Division, both during deployment, exercises and the eventual war, was in large part due to the inclusion of Commander Medical and the CO of the RAF Helicopters in the GOC's Command Cell. Inclusion of Commander Medical within this small cell, comprising only 11 officers in the Division who were fully briefed by the GOC on the developing Coalition plans, ensured that medical factors were taken into account early in the planning process and that medical planning reflected divisional needs.

Concurrent with the reception and deployment of the Division, plans were put into action to establish the FFMA. The medical plan was developed to construct a 'Forward Surgical Complex', comprising 22 Field Hospital and 32 Field Hospital (both at 200 beds); 24 Field Ambulance, less two sections deployed to 1 (UK) Armoured Division; 1 Aeromedical Evacuation Armoured Division Squadron of the RAF; elements of 28 Gurkha Ambulance Transport Group; forward elements of 84 Field Medical Equipment Depot and a Field Psychiatric Team, 61 FPT.

The establishment of this complex was not without drama. It was decided that the hospitals should be grouped together approximately five kilometres to the east of the airfield of the Forward Operational Base at Al Quasumah at the southern end of the Wadi Al Batin, which was to act as a forward air-evacuation site. The exact spot was decided using GPS and marked, using that universally recognised site-marker – an Army suitcase! Not surprisingly, the unit recce party had some difficulty in locating it as the weather was poor and they had no GPS.[5] However, within 48 hours the building of 32 Field Hospital was well under way when suddenly a major crisis developed. US intelligence sources detected what they thought was a major Iraqi attack, about to develop down the Wadi Al Batin. The first Coalition unit in its path was the hospital! Late at night, in the middle of a violent desert storm, Major Tim Pitcher was dispatched with the only available GPS to effect the evacuation of the entire advance party of 100 men and women. Despite his considerable experience and the fact that he was an Army-standard orienteer, he found the mission 'more than a little exciting; particularly leading the vehicles out of the danger area'. The scare lasted a few days but construction work continued with the Advance Party moving forward at first light and being evacuated as darkness fell.

The move up of '32's' Main Party also had its moment of drama when the leading coach failed to take the one and only turn off the North/South road. In consequence, the coaches headed north towards Kuwait, only realising what had happened when they stopped to confirm directions and were told, by a well-known National Newspaper correspondent, that the village, for which they were on the outskirts of was not Al Qasumah but Al Kafjih, some hours before a major battle for that town.

As the British were constructing their Forward Hospital Base, 332 (US) Medical Brigade, the Medical Organization supporting 7 (US) Corps was also establishing its centre of operations in an adjacent area. This very large organisation was in due course to include a number of state-of-the-art field hospitals (being re-equipped in-theatre with Deployable Medical Systems (DEPMEDS)) together with Medical Battalions, ground ambulance companies, a well stocked medical supply unit (which even had its own capability to supply prescription spectacles) and air ambulance companies with a total of almost 100 'Dust-off' CASEVAC helicopters. The whole organisation was commanded and controlled from HQ 332 Medical Brigade by a team of highly competent and experienced medical staff officers under the command of Brigadier Michael J Strong, a competent and very amiable General in the Reserve who in civilian life is a well known cardiac surgeons in the United States. His staff, made up of both Regular and Reserve officers had a large range of experience. The one who was most memorable to the Brits was unquestionably Colonel Jesse Fulfar. A Texan with almost 30 years service, including Vietnam, his calm down-to-earth approach to crises and 'powers of expression' were legendary. In one memorable and heated exchange, he was asked his opinion. His response was a long slow stretch, a long slow drag on a 'Marlboro' and in long slow drawl, 'we're pole-vaultin' over a mouse-turd here'.

Joint Medical Operations

Throughout the build-up to operations, both the British and US medical planning staff had recognized the vital need to cooperate at every level in medical matters. The British were most fortunate that at Riyadh the US Joint Staffs included Colonel 'Dee' Tsoulas, a US Army Physician who had recently completed a very successful tour as the US Medical Liaison Officer in MOD London. He not only knew 'the Brits' medical capability but also the individuals in the medical staffs and was well respected by all. Once planning in earnest began the advantages of the years of cooperation in NATO and the historical close links in the military medical world made inter-operability easier to achieve and minimized difficulties where full inter-operability was not possible. Arguably, it was in medical matters that the Coalition Forces worked most closely once the forces were deployed on the ground and preparations began in earnest to fight a land battle.

This working relationship was not a one-way process. The UK had expertise, experience and resources in areas that the US did not and the US had strengths which matched the UK's weaknesses. This co-operation expanded across the whole spectrum of medical support. Co-operation was perhaps closest from the outset in the area of Preventive Medicine as there were few organizational or doctrinal differences. The

US had a much larger organization and more sophisticated resources which they were happy to share. In areas of medical treatment, however, there were a number of doctrinal and organisational differences. The US had better facilities for the treatment of non-battle injury and disease, for instance, but their equivalent of field ambulance dressing stations,[6] in their Medical Battalions, had less capability for advanced resuscitation. The Americans had deployed with hospitals designed for north-west Europe (as had the British, except for 22 Field Hospital) but began a re-equipment programme with the new DEPMEDS deployable hospital system in late November. The effect was to slow down the establishment of the Forward Hospital Complexes but there were greater advantages in the very sophisticated equipments available. The UK's Field Ambulance Medical Sections gave them the capability of providing rapid medical reinforcement at First Line or unit level, which the US did not have.

Perhaps surprisingly the Americans sometimes had local shortfalls of 'Dust-off'[7] helicopters and ground ambulances, particularly the latter and were, on a number of occasions reinforced by British assets. The US Medical Supply organization was bigger and better than the UK's and frequently assisted in supply, particularly of drugs and material for the management of infectious diseases.

Organizational differences sometimes complicated inter-operability, particularly the establishment of liaison systems. In the British Army medical command in a Division is vested solely in the Divisional Commander Medical (and at Corps level in the Corps Commander Medical) whilst in the US system it is split in practice between the Divisional Surgeon and the DISCOM (Divisional Support Command) Surgeon (or, at Corps level, the Corps Surgeon and Corps Medical Brigade Commander). At Divisional level, liaison had to be with both levels but rear of the Division all liaison was effected through the Medical Brigade HQ, where a UK Liaison was permanently established and considered to be a very successful working relationship.

Plans formulated by HQ (US) Medical Brigade were designed to make best use of the forward hospital and evacuation assets of both nations. In particular the US had a very tight management of the main LofC, the 'Tap-Line Road', and provided medical support along its entire 300 km. CASEVAC (casualty evacuation) was managed by the US Military Police and a 'Dust-Off' helicopter system which was generally both prompt and efficient. However, the limitations of helicopters were highlighted in one incident where a British casualty from a Road Traffic Accident was rescued from the road by a helicopter flying in the most difficult weather and visibility. Sadly, the aircraft crashed just short of the US Hospital and a US Paramedic was killed. That the remainder of the crew and the casualty survived, relatively unharmed, is a measure of the survivability of the US Blackhawk helicopter they were flying.

The RCT Driver, who had luckily only received minor injuries, was nevertheless very shocked and, having survived both a road traffic accident and a flying accident within a couple of hours, declared his intention to leave the hospital only on foot. The incident, however, reinforced the view of those who had doubts that helicopters were the final answer to casualty care on the battlefield. Despite the high-tech navigation aids and night vision devices, flying at night on the type of battlefield envisaged is a highly dangerous occupation and best avoided if possible; it is even more dangerous in bad desert weather. The incident also led to the imposition, during deployment and training, of procedures to ensure that, in adverse flying conditions, helicopters were only tasked after a proper risk assessment.

Even if all helicopters were available (and there were almost 100 dedicated evacuation helicopters in support of 7 Corps alone) some US and UK medical planners believed that the type of operation envisaged would stretch their CASEVAC resources, particularly the helicopters, to the limit once combat began. A joint plan was therefore formulated aimed at limiting the amount of aero-medevac (aero-medevac is the evacuation of sick and injured by air using aircraft with on board medical staff) that would have to be carried out to empty the forward medical units and deployable hospitals, particularly during darkness. The plan involved a 'milk run' of US and UK medical units at dawn and dusk, using the big Chinook and Sea King helicopters, with the smaller US Blackhawk and Huey helicopters, together with the Pumas, concentrating on forward evacuation and intimate medical support. Although, in the event, this plan was not tested, it showed what could be achieved by a determined international medical planning staff working closely together. Similar planning was undertaken in the Division where a task of the Surgical Teams was to stabilize, if possible, casualties arriving at night thus restricting helicopter evacuation to those who would die if not evacuated. Close co-operation between Dressing Station staff, and medical and RAF staff at Divisional HQ made the policy successful for those Dressing Stations which had Surgical Teams.

Medical Supply

Medical supply caused considerable problems from pre-deployment until the day before the ground war. Items as simple as individual first aid kits (agreed as being necessary for operations outside Europe as a result of lessons learnt in the Falkland Islands) were only finally agreed in January and the final issue was effected the day before the ground war and then only by using helicopters to distribute in time. Scales were in some cases a decade out of date. Action, both official and unofficial, was quickly taken to rectify the situation. However, lack of any modern stock tracking or control measures made implementation of any enhancements difficult. Hospital equipment arriving from Depots was often incomplete, although this was not always evident until a box was opened and an 'IOU' discovered! As well as being deficient, equipments were not always correctly labelled and ISO containers easily got lost in the massive distribution complex surrounding the port area of Jubail. Much of the 'lost' equipment was discovered by the initiative of Captain Sean O'Mara, the Medical Logistics Staff officer, who patrolled the port area day and night and, like some long, forgotten biblical character, swooped upon medical containers marking them with a red cross! Many problems, however, rose from the sheer antiquity of that part of the medical stores called Pre-stocked Unit Equipment or PUE[8] of the deploying hospitals. As we have already seen they had left BAOR and collected their equipment in-theatre, much of it having been stored for years without detailed checking and review. It is however an ill wind ... and at least one hospital on opening some camp stores discovered a very nice silver service for the Officers Mess, circa 1942!

Another example was a particular Regimental Medical Officer (of a Cavalry Regiment) who wrote home to his mother to ask her to obtain a Red Cross flag for his ambulance, assuring her that 'he could not get one in Theatre'. His Mum duly obliged but was so incensed by what she perceived as shortfall of a vital piece of equipment, that she wrote to her MP. The result was predictable. In fact the medical planning staff had long recognised that there was a shortfall of Red Cross emblems (and equally importantly Red Crescent emblems used by Muslim countries) and had already put matters in hand to obtain them. A more important question to be addressed was why we had a shortfall in the first place. There is no doubt that attitudes developed in Germany during the Cold War had much to do with it. For many years the 'operational' staffs had argued that, in British Forces Germany (BFG), concealment and camouflage were tactically vital and the displaying of red crosses was counter to that ethos. They had also argued that displaying the red cross was a nugatory exercise anyway because the 'Soviets' were unlikely to recognise (they argued) the Geneva Conventions. This area of our responsibilities in international law and military/medical ethics has still not been fully resolved and is bound to become a major issue again in the future, particularly as the nature of conflict becomes increasingly complex.

Much as the medical supply system is criticised note has to be taken of the fact that by the time the Ground War started a medical supply system had been established which was delivering 9,000 different items, of which only 5,000 were on official scales at the beginning and which ranged from whole blood to pulse oximeters (to measure oxygen concentration in blood) and sophisticated X-Ray machines. Often this equipment was sent direct from manufacturers, down a supply chain 5,000 miles long and packed with equally 'vital' stores for war. It is a measure of the success of the system that almost every medical item, no matter how large or small, got through to the user in the end, even if some of it arrived at 'the eleventh hour'.

Chemical and Biological Warfare

Because of Saddam Hussein's previous track record the preventive medical aspects of Chemical and Biological Defence were very much a live issue in the build up period. The threat had been identified quite early and the UK had deployed with a scale of defensive equipment as sophisticated and capable as any in the modern world. Implementing these protective measures in such extremes of environment as the hot desert, though, was a different matter to exercises on the temperate plains of Germany or Salisbury!

The main decisions had to be taken in the area of individual medical protective procedures. Questions such as when NAPS (tablets used to protect against certain chemical agents) should be taken ie. whether it should be well in advance of an anticipated Iraqi use or not until the last moment, and whether there were any side effects from the drugs that constitute NAPS (there can be minor ones but they cease when the tablets are stopped) were frequently asked and had to be answered.

Measures proposed to combat Biological Warfare threats were particularly sensitive. Protection required vaccination against known threat agents. The decision from Britain was that vaccination was to be offered on the basis of voluntary informed consent, which gave us an immediate challenge as there were 40,000 individuals spread across the desert. Individuals naturally wanted to know about the advantages and disadvantages of vaccination. Its necessity, balanced against the risk, was assessed in theatre. There were further complications when, after the first vaccination, many individuals suffered the usual short term side effects which, whilst minor, were hardly welcome at a time of high activity and awful weather. In deciding how they should tender the advice to their subordinates, senior operational and medical commanders in theatre had to adjust the direction from JHQ in High Wycombe to meet local conditions. Plans had to be made for the distribution of the vaccine to individual medical officers, and medical officers had to arrange to visit the units, sub-units and detachments for which they were responsible. It was this last phase of the vaccination campaign which was most difficult owing to the dispersed nature of many units and the imminence of battle, and at a time when many were moving their locations. It is to the credit of individual medical officers that all who wanted the vaccine were given it.

At unit level, the Dressing Stations and Field Hospitals developed flexible procedures to allow casualties to be treated in conventional tents, but with the ability to quickly change to the safer but hotter and more inconvenient chemically protective Porton Liners in the event of a chemical attack.

For reasons which are not clearly understood, Iraq chose not to use chemical or biological weapons. However, it is likely that the knowledge that coalition forces were prepared to fight in a 'dirty' environment was one factor which inhibited its use of such weapons.

Reserves

Reserves were more important to the Medical Services to complete their ORBAT than any other Arm or Service. They were used at every level of medical support from the 'sharp end' of the Regimental Aid Post back to Riyadh. They were made up of two fundamentally different types. First, the so-called Individual Reservist (IR) who is an ex-Regular with reserve liability in his or her contract and who was 'called-up'. Second, the volunteer from the Territorial Army and the Royal Auxiliary Air Force. IRS provided manpower at every level. The Volunteers, whilst also providing vital specialist manpower in Regular units at second and third line, (including two Field Surgical Teams forward with the brigade field ambulances) also provided two key units to complete the medical ORBAT. These were 205 General Hospital from the TA, the key third line Evacuation Hospital in Riyadh and 4626 (County of Wiltshire) Air Evacuation Squadron from the Royal Auxiliary Air Force, for both intra-theatre and inter-theatre air evacuation.

There is no question that the Reserves, in general, were successfully employed. 205 General Hospital and 4626 Squadron, in particular, were not only vital to the plan but also performed extremely well. Despite the lateness of their deployment into theatre (late January) 205 General Hospital were up and running by the time the ground war started. Their achievements were a total vindication of the decision to use the TA and much was owed to the unit's first rate leadership and totally professional approach to their mission.

Individual reservists were more problematic. Whilst there is no question that some individuals were eager to 'return to duty' (both MOD and the AMS Training Group were besieged from the outset by ex-medics offering their services), there were problems which exposed a fundamental flaw in the existing IR system. First, some were called who simply did not wish to serve. Once convinced of their legal obligation most got on with the task and some even enjoyed it but some gave their units unwelcome administrative problems. Second, many of those called up were either physically unfit for their role or, more often, had forgotten their medical and military skills – many were following totally different professions in civilian life – requiring considerable time and effort to bring them up to scratch. This so-called 'skill-fade' (also recognised in the US Forces) must raise questions about the utility of a plan that envisages the deployment of IRs far forward to such vital roles as the RAPs of regular combat units which form the leading edge of the UK's Reaction Forces.

Prepared for Operations

Once the air war started, everyone realised that a ground war was inevitable and it served to concentrate the mind wonderfully. There was a marked increase in unit morale and the medical mission assumed a new level of importance to everyone. By now, a complete medical ORBAT had been finalised which reflected the deployment of units to support the original Concept of Operations. This is shown in Figure 5.2.

In the final days before the land battle started, a quick audit of medical assets showed just about everything in place. 33 Field Hospital, now up and running in Jubail, had already taken and treated a number of real casualties resulting from accidents and had tested their systems thoroughly. Number 1 RAF War Hospital had arrived and was now well established in Bahrain where it had replaced 22 Field Hospital.

205 General Hospital, mobilised from Glasgow and commanded by the redoubtable Colonel Glynn Jones (a Welshman!) was rapidly settling into its role in Riyadh. Although the core of the unit was '205' it too was made up of a mixture of Volunteer Reserves, Regulars and Individual Reservists, all-up some 750 all-ranks. The hospital was established in the unfinished Terminal 4 buildings of King Khalid International Airport and co-located with a French Military Hospital. Both units adapted readily to each other and a close rapport developed, particularly once the 'SCUD Alerts' began to test their systems and their nerves. On the 25th of January, both units combined to celebrate Burns Night. In the middle of the readings from the Immortal Bard, the proceedings were interrupted by a 'Red Alert' and the entire assembly donned full NBC protection and dived under the tables for the next half hour (complete with the amber 'antidote' no doubt). With the wisdom of hindsight it would be right to question whether the siting of hospitals within the perimeter of what must have been a key target for the SCUDs, or any other attack, was an unnecessarily risky option. It again raises issues of the protection of medical units and international law and what might have resulted had a missile hit the hospitals, particularly if they had contained Iraqi Prisoners of War.

Out in the desert, at Al Quasumah, 32 had become the key unit for the first phase of future operations. It was well established with 200 beds and a wealth of clinical capability drawn from all three Services. They had already treated a number of serious accidents and had a busy medical department dealing with the usual gamut of diseases. Being the last Regular medical unit to be deployed into theatre it really was an ad hoc formation. Although based on BMH Hannover, commanded by

BFME TPS:

FULL COMD
RFA Argus (2 × FST, 1 × SST, 100 beds)
205 Gen Hosp (V) (6 × St, 2 × SST, 600 beds)
No 1 War Hosp RAF (2 × ST, 100 beds)
4626 Air Evac Sqn R Aux AF[-]
MST Alfa (1 × FST, 25 beds)
MST Bravo (1 × FST, 25 beds)
MSS 84 FMED

FMA TROOPS

FULL COMD
28 Gurkha Amb Gp[-]
33 Gen Hosp (6 × ST, 2 × SST, 600 beds) (CMH Aldershot)
32 Fd Hosp (8 × ST, 200 beds) (BMH Hannover)
22 Fd Hosp (8 × ST, 200 beds)
24 (Airmob) Fd Amb
61 FPT
1 Air Evac Sqn RAF

OPCON
84 FMED[-]
Elms 4626 Air Evac Ssn R Aux AF

1 (UK) ARMD DIV

DIV TPS
54 Amb Sqn RCT[-]
DS 5 Bravo (DS of 3 Armd Fd Amb, 1 × Armd & 2 × Wh Sect, 4 × Armd &
10 × Wh Ambs)
60 FPT
Hygiene Det

4 ARMD BDE
5 Armd Fd Amb[-] (DS, 3 × Armd & one Wheeled Sect; 14 × Armd & 10
× Wheeled Ambs)
2×FST (one 23 Para Fd Amb, one 205 Gen Hosp (V))
Tp HQ, 28 Gurkha Amb Gp
MAOT
Hygiene Det

7 ARMD BDE
1 Armd Fd Amb[-] (DS; 3 × Armd & one Wheeled Sect; 14 × Armd & 12
× Wheeled Ambs)
2×FST (one 23 Para Fd Amb, one 205 Gen Hosp (V))
Tp HQ, 54 Amb Sqn RCT
MAOT
Hygiene Det

ARTY GP
DS 1 Bravo (DS of 4 Armd Fd Amb; one × Armd & one × Wheeled Sect;
4 × Armd & 10 × Wheeled Ambs)
Tp HQ, 54 Amb Sqn Rct
MAOT

Figure 5.2 The Medical Order of Battle

32 Field Hospital RAMC

Total strength (Regular, Reserves and TA)	529
RAMC	155
QARANC	108
RN	37
RM Commando	33
Bandsmen (RIR, Gordons and Cheshires)	63
RADC	6
WRAC/ACC	17
RA(BCRs) Guard Force	40
RAPC	3
RAOC	7
RE	8
Red Cross/St John	2
RAChD	2
Kuwaiti Interpreters	6
RAF	42
Total 'Cap Badges'	26
Units represented	56

Figure 5.3 Composition of 32 Field Hospital RAMC

Colonel Peter Lynch, it had of necessity to draw its additional manpower to bring it up to War Establishment from just about anyone available. The final establishment showed that from a total of 529 all ranks, a staggering 56 units with 26 different 'cap-badges', from all three Services, both Regular and Reserve, were represented! The detailed breakdown is shown at Figure 5.3. Despite the very real successes achieved by this unit (it treated over 100 battle casualties, more than any other UK medical unit) it raises questions about the flexibility of our planning, which had been orientated towards a general war scenario in Central Europe.

22 Field Hospital, under the command of Lieutenant Colonel Chris Town and the indefatigable matron Lieutenant Colonel Kathy Bland, was already the longest serving unit in the Gulf. After a period in Jubail for re-equipment and reinforcement to bring it to 200 beds, it was now well established some three kilometres across the sand from '32' and about four kilometres from the airfield at Al Quasumah. Although in many respects its role and configuration was similar to '32' it was designed towards greater mobility and had therefore been warned that when and if a hospital was to be deployed forward into Iraq or Kuwait, '22' would go. An element of two surgical teams and 50 beds worth of support was constantly at short notice to move. As a consequence, '22', despite its undoubted capability and expertise never really got in on the act. The final outcome of the land battles meant that there were few casualties, most of which went to '32' and there was no requirement for them to redeploy forward either. Notwithstanding the unit's dissatisfaction at the outcome, there is no question that it was the best prepared and trained medical unit we deployed, with the highest morale at all times. Much of what it achieved in terms of operational procedures has been used as the basis for the development of the future generation of more mobile deployable hospitals.

The other supporting medical units, 24 Field Ambulance, 1 Aeromedical Evacuation Squadron, 4626 Aeromedical Evacuation Squadron and 28 Ambulance Group were also well established and had trained and practised their support and evacuation roles. There were medical supply sections with both hospitals and an established resupply system functioning out of Jubail which included regular and constant supplies of whole blood. Both Field Psychiatric Teams had deployed, 60 FPT to the Division and 61 FPT to the FMA, and were actively involved in preparing units psychologically for the coming battles.

The Medical Cell at HQ FFMA had by now established and practised their operating and Command and Control procedures. Communications were restricted to secure means, Ptarmigan for intra-theatre and MAPPER/ASMA/OPCON between theatre and UK. Whilst there were real reservations about Ptarmigan – it constantly 'dropped out' under any heavy signal traffic load – the medical staff were much impressed by the 'real time' communications capability inter-theatre. The contrast between the Gulf Conflict and the Falklands War was never more stark than in this area. Having experienced the trials of trying to communicate vital information through such 'steam age' technology as 'D Triple S'[9] in the Falklands, the sheer power of MAPPER and its counterparts was almost magical, particularly when it was operated in the back of a truck in a hole in the sand. When signal traffic was low it could also be used for welfare purposes as for example on February 13th, when the FMA medical cell managed collectively to send flowers to their wives for Valentines Day, using the back end of a standard return, the

Plate 1 Major General Rupert Smith (GOC 1 (UK) Armoured Division) and Colonel Graham Ewer (Divisional Deputy Chief of Staff for Logistics)

Plate 2 Lieutenant General Sir Peter de la Billière (Commander British Forces Middle East) talks to the Prisoner of War Guard Force

Plate 3
Brigadier Martin White
(Commander Force
Maintenance Area)

Plate 4
Ammunition Supply Point 1.
Privates Culpin (left) and
Jeffrey of the 6th Ordnance
Battalion
(Photo: Soldier Magazine)

Plate 5 A 'Loggies' gathering (Left to Right) Colonel Graham Ewer, Major Wayne Harbor and Captain Angus Macdonald at Rear Divisional Headquarters, February 1991

Plate 6 Headquarters 1 (UK) Armoured Division, well camouflaged

Plate 7 Loads from *Atlantic Conveyor* and *Baltic Progress* on the dockside at Jubail

Plate 8 Baldrick Lines

Plate 9 DROPS. A new vehicle and an outstanding success. Here seen on mobility trials in theatre *(Photo: Lieutenant Colonel PS Reehal)*

Plate 10 Water 'Bean Cans' at the 7th Armoured Brigade Water Point

Plate 11 DODGE *(Photo: Lieutenant Colonel PS Reehal RLC)*

Plate 12 32 Field Hospital

Plate 13 In the reception shed at Jubail

Plate 14 The bulk fuel installation in the FFMA *(Photo: Soldier Magazine)*

Plate 15 Recovery – in the Convoy Marshalling Area
(Photo: Brigadier Noel Muddiman)

Plate 16 The last Battle Group (3 RRF) flies home. 13 April 1991
(Photo: Brigadier Noel Muddiman)

goodwill of a Southeast District Duty Officer and the credit card of one of the authors. The whole transaction was completed in 15 minutes from start to finish. The system also had its drawbacks. It allowed instant and almost permanent communications between HQ FFMA, HQ BFME, JHQ High Wycombe and MOD. There was a tendency, at times, to circumvent the Chain of Command both downwards and upwards. It also enabled and even encouraged over-direction from the UK, known colloquially as 'the long-distance screwdriver'. For instance, Commander Medical 1 (UK) Armoured Division had only just crossed into Iraq during the ground war when he stopped to answer his Ptarmigan. Did he have any comment on a few cases of diarrhoea reported in one unit two days before?

As a part of final preparations, the RAF decided that a Desert Airstrip should be built in case 'K-ZUMMAH' as it was known was put out of action. The Engineers, despite their massive work load, duly obliged and within a couple of days a perfect, fully-graded strip, almost a kilometre long and half a kilometre wide, surrounded by a metre high 'berm', appeared in the area between '32' and '22' hospitals. A day later the first C130 landed on it with the minimum of fuss and 'proved it'. Thereafter a number of landings were made and it became something of an article of faith to go along for what was an adrenalin-generator for the uninitiated. One such trip was a little more 'scary' than most as a company of infantry from the Prisoner of War Guard Force had decided to practise a little night navigation and had taken their unit, vehicles and all, in a diagonal march across the strip. Not as simple a task as it sounds as it required the berm to be broken down first! Thereafter, the strip was assumed proved until required!

Forward in the Division, the RAPs and Field Ambulances were undertaking final preparations and trying hard to reconcile the growing mountains of medical equipment they had received with the limited transport they had to carry it in. The RAPs were all of considerable size, much larger than their existing War Establishments and bearing absolutely no resemblance to their 'peacetime' organisations. They had been enlarged to bring them into line with recommendations made after the Falkland's conflict but never implemented. They comprised one or two medical officers together with 20 or more 'medics' – Regimental Medical Assistants, RAMC Combat Medical Technicians (some of whom were IRs) and Bandsmen – with an armoured ambulance troop of 10 tracked ambulances. In some units, the ambulance troop was even commanded by a regimental officer to improve tactical expertise (this innovation, too, was based on lessons learnt in the Falkland Islands campaign). All in all, a far cry from the 'flimsy' organisation normally seen in barracks and on training exercises. By the time the ground war started, they had been considerably enhanced with new scales of medical equipment and a great deal of medical training had been achieved. This was vital as there

was unquestionably considerable disparity in the levels of medical ability
of the various types of 'medics'. Critically, there was almost no experience at this level in the management of trauma in the wounds and
injuries expected in combat.

Whilst the driving force behind this 'First Line enhancement'
was undoubtedly the medical services, particularly Colonel Louis
Lillywhite's ability to draw on previous experience, the success was
clearly only achieved because the customer – the commanders at every
level, recognised the need, not just to be sure they could deal with the
casualties when they occurred, but also as a vital element of morale-
building and battle preparation. The question this raises is why, if this
was the medical organisation they (the commanders) believed they
needed for war, was this not highlighted in the subsequent 'lessons
learned', despite the fact that it was a key 'lesson' from the medical
post operational report. If it was recognised as 'over-insurance' and not
necessary for future conflict, then this should have been made clear by
the Operational staffs. If not, why have the combat and combat support
arms not included enhancements to their RAPs and First Line medical
organisations in their post-Options organisation to bring them into line
with the medical staff they deployed in the Gulf?

The Second Line medical organisation, the field ambulances together
with their supporting units from the Ambulance Group, had re-organised
into 4 smaller 'brigade' style units, each structured around a single dressing station (DS). DS1A ('DS one alpha') and DS5A ('DS five alpha')
supported 7 and 4 Armoured Brigades and DS 1B and DS 5B with the
Artillery Group and Divisional Administrative Area respectively. Each
Brigade Field Ambulance comprised a small headquarters, a Dressing
Station, a number of Medical Sections (some of which were armoured),
a hygiene section, and attached bandsmen. The Dressing Stations were
by now fully worked-up and re-equipped to provide the best possible
care, both in a conventional war environment and if necessary in a
chemical one as well. Each was now 250 strong whilst in addition they
had under command elements of the Ambulance Regiments, Pioneer
platoons to help decontaminate chemical casualties, and from time to
time Field Surgical Teams and RAF helicopter elements. In total these
comprised 400 individuals and when tactically dispersed covered a
minimum of four kilometres of desert. A statistic worth noting is that the
number of vehicles in a Brigade belonging to the Field Ambulance was
87, and this excludes Battle Group Medical vehicles belonging to the
various attachments to the Dressing Station. A dressing station lumber-
ing across the desert was beginning to look more like a caravan than a
convoy.

The field Ambulance Medical Sections were mainly deployed in
support of Battle-groups. They collected casualties from the Regimental
Aid Posts and evacuated to a Casualty Collection point with the Forward

Troop HQ where casualties were transferred to helicopters or other ambulances for evacuation to the Dressing Station. Other medical sections were deployed to the Brigade Maintenance Area whilst in the rear area of the Division, medical sections of 5B and 24 Airmobile Field Ambulance provided support to various logistic units, the Divisional Reinforcement Group and gave the commander Medical a small reserve.

In early February the Division finally gained the two pairs of Field Surgical Teams which Commander Medical felt were vital in ensuring the survival of the maximum number of casualties. Although they arrived rather late, they had the advantage of almost all being from 23 Parachute Field Ambulance or were Reservists who had served with 23 Parachute Field Ambulance. They were thus versed in both the theory and practice of forward resuscitation. The Division also had 60 Field Psychiatric Team based in the Divisional Administrative Area (DAA). It was planned that any Battleshock casualties would be returned to their own unit's B Echelon in the DAA. The B Echelons would look after their own Battleshock, eventually returning them to duty, once they had been cleared by the Field Psychiatric Team. Any that did not spontaneously recover would be evacuated via 5B in the DAA.

The COs of 1 and 5 Armoured Field Ambulance and the OC of 1B were responsible for medical support within their Brigades and the Artillery Group, using the resources allocated to them by Commander Medical at Division. Commander Medical considered that once the ground war began and the Division gained momentum, it would be difficult for him to influence matters. The Brigades and Artillery Group were thus to be given as many resources as possible and, once through the breach, only if they ran into difficulties would Commander Medical intervene. In the meantime, he would keep sending helicopters (and medical supplies and stretchers if required) forward to evacuate casualties. The Field Surgical Teams would be deployed to 1 and 5 Armoured Field Ambulance, except during the initial artillery raids which preceded the breach, when one pair was to be deployed to the Artillery Group. At all times the function of these Field Surgical Teams was to carry out the minimum treatment necessary to save life and no more; more definitive treatment would be carried out later in hospitals.

The Divisional Medical Cell, when it was not involved in medical supply, preventive medicine issues or planning or running exercises, spent most of its time planning the medical support for the breach operation and passage of lines with 1 (US) Infantry Division (Mechanised). Planning was complicated on the US side as the span of responsibility of Commander Medical 1 (UK) Armoured Division was the responsibility of three authorities: 1 (US) Infantry Division HQ, 1 Infantry Division DISCOM (Divisional Support Command) and forward units of 332 (US) Medical Brigade. Matters were further complicated as neither the US or UK had in the recent past considered in detail the problems of medical support for the type of operation envisaged. It was finally agreed that the UK would, if necessary, provide land and helicopter support to 1 (US) Infantry Division whilst they fought through the breach. The UK would be responsible for its own medical support whilst it moved up to the breach. Once in the breach, the US would provide medical support. When the UK units emerged through the far side of the breach, the UK was to evacuate via its own Regimental Aid Posts (and if possible its own Dressing Stations) to US facilities for onward evacuation by US forces. Finally, once 1 (UK) Armoured Division passed out of 1 (US) Infantry Division's area, each nation would once again become self sufficient. Problems were envisaged in the event that 1 Infantry Division failed to break through the breach and 1 (UK) Armoured Division had to take on the battle. There would then be difficulties controlling medical support in what would be a relatively small and congested area. Similar difficulties were envisaged if 1 (UK) Armoured Division were to find itself facing Iraqi armoured forces immediately it left the breach. To facilitate the solving of any problems which arose Colonel Lillywhite co-located with 1 (US) Infantry Division DISCOM HQ during the breach battle; an RAF helicopter liaison team was co-located with the US helicopters and UK medical liaison teams were used to provide communications at all levels. Thus the UK and US medical authorities were ready to co-ordinate their joint assets should the need arise. 24 Airmobile Field Ambulance was used to provide medical support for 1 (UK) Armoured Division's move up to the breach, so that the Division's medical assets could be reserved for use beyond the breach and a radio frequency was designated which could be used as a '999' call by units or individuals as they passed through the breach and subsequent form up point. This frequency was monitored by both the UK and US medical authorities.

This plan was necessarily complex. It was arrived at following numerous meetings with the US Divisional Medical authorities who were developing their medical concepts at the same time. So important was this co-operation recognized to be that final agreement had to be endorsed at a meeting chaired by 1 (US) Infantry Division's Chief of Staff, in addition to the various medical staff, by the US and UK Logistic Commanders. The concepts behind the plan were put across at a combined UK-US Study Day organized by 1 (UK) Armoured Division and attended down to Medical Officer/Senior NCO level. It was also practised on combined exercises and appeared to work well. Indeed, with the exception of some difficulties with helicopter evacuation, the only problems were to be encountered during exercises; the war itself, as a result, was to be almost problem free. Finally, all 1 (UK) Armoured Division sub-units were issued with an Aide Memoir (Figure 5.4).

Road evacuation was always available and extensively exercised.

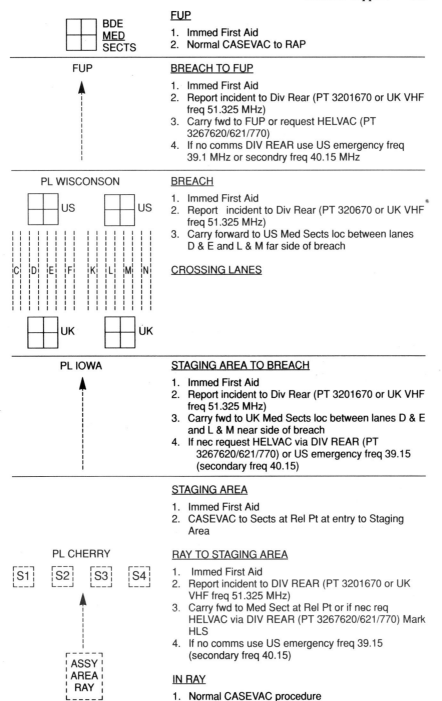

FUP

1. Immed First Aid
2. Normal CASEVAC to RAP

FUP

BREACH TO FUP

1. Immed First Aid
2. Report incident to Div Rear (PT 3201670 or UK VHF freq 51.325 MHz)
3. Carry fwd to FUP or request HELVAC (PT 3267620/621/770)
4. If no comms DIV REAR use US emergency freq 39.1 MHz or secondry freq 40.15 MHz

PL WISCONSON

BREACH

1. Immed First Aid
2. Report incident to Div Rear (PT 320670 or UK VHF freq 51.325 MHz)
3. Carry forward to US Med Sects loc between lanes D & E and L & M far side of breach

CROSSING LANES

PL IOWA

STAGING AREA TO BREACH

1. Immed First Aid
2. Report incident to Div Rear (PT 3201670 or UK VHF freq 51.325 MHz)
3. Carry fwd to UK Med Sects loc between lanes D & E and L & M near side of breach
4. If nec request HELVAC via DIV REAR (PT 3267620/621/770) or US emergency freq 39.15 (secondary freq 40.15)

STAGING AREA

1. Immed First Aid
2. CASEVAC to Sects at Rel Pt at entry to Staging Area

PL CHERRY

RAY TO STAGING AREA

1. Immed First Aid
2. Report incident to DIV REAR (PT 3201670 or UK VHF freq 51.325 MHz)
3. Carry fwd to Med Sect at Rel Pt or if nec req HELVAC via DIV REAR (PT 3267620/621/770) Mark HLS
4. If no comms use US emergency freq 39.15 (secondary freq 40.15)

IN RAY

1. Normal CASEVAC procedure

Figure 5.4 Casualty Evacuation Procedure Aide Memoire

However, even when 7 Armoured Brigade was deployed in Jubail, it was clear that evacuation even along the good North/South road from Kuwait would take in excess of five hours. In the desert it would have taken much longer and would have been more dangerous to the injured patient. The ambulances were old, lacked GPS and there were insufficient skilled medics to man every vehicle. One exercise showed that the average time from point of wounding back to the hospitals by road was likely to be about 12 hours, obviously unacceptable. Road evacuation was thus always considered only for local evacuation and a second option for journeys between the forward units and hospitals if air evacuation failed. Road ambulances were however vital to the function of evacuation between hospital and airhead and were used often. 1 (UK) Armoured Division procedures stated that if helicopters were grounded for what ever reason, casualties were to be held and treated at field ambulance level (a policy only possible through the deployment of Field Surgical Teams forward).

As a result, almost total reliance was placed on air evacuation, helicopters forward in the Divisional area and fixed-wing from the Forward Surgical Complex at A1 Quasumah, to Riyadh or Jubail and out of theatre. There was also an option to fly fixed-wing into the Divisional area using desert airstrips. Medical planners were allotted priority use of over 40 support helicopters (Puma, Sea King and Chinook) which in effect gave the UK greater assets than 7 (US) Corps. The Puma and Sea King were used almost exclusively for CASEVAC. The Helicopter Force HQ established itself forward with ASOC(SH) (Air Support Operations Centre Support Helicopters) deployed in Divisional HQ. MAOTs (Mobile Air Operation Teams)[10] were deployed to field ambulance Dressing Stations and at the Forward Hospital Complex, to control helicopters in their vicinity. As the ground war progressed, helicopters were allocated to each brigade medical organisation, along with supporting elements and were stationed at the dressing stations when not in use. As CASEVAC lines extended, the shorter range Pumas concentrated on the shorter forward loops with Sea Kings evacuating on the longer journeys rearward.

As predicted, helicopters were not the complete solution to CASEVAC problems and during the ground war there was no flying in the Divisional Area for approximately 10 hours. In addition coordination between the 'user' – the medical services – and the Support Helicopter Force proved difficult, owing to problems of communication over ever increasing distances and because of concerns by the RAF of letting the forward medical units have too much responsibility for what was a rare and expensive asset. It was only towards the end of the ground war that the difficulties were overcome and procedures refined to ensure the efficient and timely tasking from a specific forward medical unit to a specific rear hospital started to work.

Other Nations Medical Support

An examination of the medical support 'on the eve of the battle' would not be complete without mention of 'ONMA'. This acronym stood for Other Nations Medical Support and represented something radically different for the UK medical planners to come to terms with. It was the result of political initiatives taken early in the preparatory phase to elicit help from those nations who were unable to contribute combat troops but wished to assist the Coalition in some other way. A number of countries, including Canada, Norway, Sweden, Malaysia and Rumania, offered medical units. These offers were accepted and units eventually dispatched into theatre, arriving in mid to late January, late in the preparations for the ground war.

There is no question that in purely practical terms the concept worked. Canada deployed a very capable 100 bed Mobile Army Surgical Hospital (MASH) which was collocated with 32 Field Hospital. It dealt with amongst others the first UK combat casualty from the ground war and was, all in all, a highly professional and successful unit (although some visitors were a little overwhelmed by its security arrangements which comprised a company of heavily armed Royal Canadian Rifles, complete with armoured vehicles!). Norway too provided a highly professional and well equipped mobile hospital which deployed in Jubail and treated many wounded combatants, UK and Iraqi. However, as a medical plan, 'ONMA' created a number of administrative, supply and Command and Control difficulties which arguably outweighed the successes. Perhaps, if the casualty load had been higher and the ONMA units had been tasked specifically to manage, say, the definitive treatment of wounded Prisoners of War, clearer lessons could have been learned. It would be dangerous to assume that in future conflict a coherent and comprehensive medical plan could be put together using resources offered by our friends.

The Ground War and After

After all this build up, the actual events of the ground war seem almost incidental. The very success of the war stemmed from the meticulous preparation and Commander Medical 1 (UK) Armoured Division commented afterwards that it was the smoothest exercise he had ever been on. Prior to the start of the main attack, the US and UK artillery were used for artillery raids, moving up to and across the international border at night for a fire mission and then withdrawing. A slimmed down field ambulance (1B) supported these raids, moving up with the Artillery Group and setting up minimal facilities. The only casualties during these raids were accidents. It was reported at this time that back in High Wycombe a senior officer was passing the medical desk and saw the location of 1B, on the 'wrong' side of the border. It is alleged that he said that 1 Armoured Division was to be instructed to pull it back! Although the story is probably untrue, it did sometimes feel to those in the desert that individuals back in the UK were trying to fight the battle for them!

The breach operation went exactly according to plan. The elements of 24 Field Ambulance were in place as required. For the break-in battle, the US used UK helicopters in support of 1 (US) Infantry Division for casualty evacuation, and the US evacuated a number of UK casualties during the passage of lines.

The Field Ambulance Dressing Stations moved through the breach with the forward parts of their Brigades. On a previous training exercise, two Dressing Stations had been placed too far back by their Brigades and Commander Medical had had to provide cross-Brigade medical support when in consequence a Dressing Station was not available to support its Brigade. The lesson was learnt and for the war the Dressing Stations, with the all-important treatment elements, moved well forward, though they were forced to slim their size down by relegating some of their vehicles and equipment to the Brigade Maintenance Area (which travelled at the rear of the Brigade). Thus as soon as fighting began, the Dressing Stations were in a position to support it. Such a policy was not without its risk. Lieutenant Colonel Malcolm Braithwaite, CO 1 Armoured Field Ambulance, had the wheels of his Land Rover blown away by bomblets just across the breach and, on one occasion, the Dressing Station of 5 Armoured Field Ambulance accidentally got in front of its Brigade, to the consternation of the Brigade Commander! As Commander Medical commented to the GOC, it was better to be too far forward than too far rearward!

As the Brigades had a considerable amount of medical supply with them and a considerable number of ambulances, and teams to liaise with helicopters (plus tankers of helicopter fuel), there was little for the Divisional Medical Cell to do. The majority of the cell spent the war moving in the back of the Medical Cell's Armoured vehicle. Commander Medical deserted his cell at Divisional Rear HQ and, with a driver and radio operator, moved forward to Divisional Main HQ (Divisional Rear HQ was soon too far behind for medical command to be exercised from it) so that he could keep in touch with the battle and attempt to keep the forward medical units in touch with the helicopter support. Eventually it had to be agreed that helicopters should be pre-positioned with the forward Dressing Stations. Otherwise, there would be no evacuation.

It was only the availability of GPS (satellite navigation equipment) which allowed Commander Medical to move forward; not only were such moves navigated accurately but they were also done in comfort, as Commander Medical had retained his bright red Range Rover (with cassette player), now over-painted sand colour with the exception of areas left unpainted in the shape of a red cross! The Range Rover was in fact necessary as the communications Land Rover had an intermittent fault which meant it spent half the war been towed behind the Range Rover! As the heavily laden vehicle had spent most daylight hours and half the night preceding the ground war hurtling from brigade to division to FMA and back as well as visiting individual RAPs (frequently so well camouflaged that even with GPS they were difficult to find) that, by the time the ground war started, this most desirable of Yuppie status symbols was a dilapidated wreck. Colonel Lillywhite always regretted not seeing the face of the owner when the Range Rover was returned – it was a hired vehicle which was originally intended for use around the Port area!

Further to the rear, the hospitals had little work to do as casualties forward were light, although as the Division advanced the number of wounded Prisoners of War increased. However, as the Division advanced and the distance between the Dressing Stations and the Hospitals increased it became increasingly likely that 22 Field Hospital would be required to move forward. Its notice to move was thus reduced. At Divisional HQ on the last night of the war an operation which would have launched 1 (UK) Armoured Division towards Basra was planned. As part of the logistic support for the operation it was decided to form a forward logistic base which would include an airstrip, the headquarters of the Helicopter force and 22 Field Hospital. 22 Field Hospital was thus placed on five hours notice to move. Unfortunately, it proved too difficult to co-ordinate the movement of 1 (UK) Armoured Division, which would be moving North, with the movement of the US Divisions, which would be moving East and the operation was cancelled. However, 48 hours later, after the ground war had finished, surgical support in 1 (UK) Armoured Division was consolidated in the DAA at 5B and a nursing element of 22 Field Hospital was moved forward.

As the ground war progressed, Prisoners of War were collected behind the Division and evacuated rearwards. Injured PW, some of them with wounds a number of days old and not treated, were evacuated to the Forward Hospital Complex. Some Iraqi medical personnel were retained in the Field Ambulance Dressing Stations to help care for, and give confidence to, Iraqi injured. Many of the Iraqi medical personnel had had some training in the UK and became well integrated into the Dressing Stations. The total casualties (UK and PW) admitted during the ground war to the Dressing Stations were 342 casualties and of these 252 were evacuated and 87 were returned to duty. Only three died in the Dressing Stations. There were a few notable incidents such as the sad death of an ambulance driver who picked up a live bomblet which subsequently exploded, and the gallant attempt by a Light Infantry bandsman acting as a medic to rescue a fatally wounded US medical soldier. But in the main 'Medical' did not achieve the high profile that the Red and Green Life Machine had done in the Falklands War.

A first-rate plan well prepared and supported had achieved success with an almost incredibly low casualty rate – for the Coalition at least. As for the Iraqis, it is difficult to estimate how many were killed and wounded or how well their medical system worked. We, the Coalition medical planners, had expected a considerable number of sick and wounded Iraqi PWs, that they did not appear is still a mystery. Moreover, the aftermath of most wars is characterised by the re-appearance of the maimed and war-wounded in society. Post-war media coverage of Iraq has not shown the thousands of cripples that would be expected if 'Tens of thousands of Iraqi soldiers had died', whilst the retained Iraqi medical staff painted a picture of considerable equipment damage but a low casualty rate.

Emerging Medical Lessons

Even at this stage, five years after the event, much care needs to be taken in trying to draw clear medical 'lessons' from Operation GRANBY/DESERT STORM. That said, the Gulf War raised a number of fundamental issues which must be answered in order to decide the shape and size of operational medical support in the post-Cold War era.

* First and foremost have the very low casualty rates that were a feature of the war set the precedent for future conflict?
* Will future UK and NATO war-fighting doctrine be predicated upon much lower casualty rates than we have traditionally planned on?
* If so how much less medical support will we need?
* Can we expect the same sort of warning and preparation time?
* If so, how much can we rely on the mobilisation of Reserves and what size and capability do we require in our Regular medical organisation?
* Given that in future conflicts we are even more likely to be involved in Coalition warfare, how do we advance, in terms of medical interoperability, and how much 'stand alone' medical capability do we consider essential for future operations?

If we can produce clear answers to these questions and they confirm a need for operational medical support in the future, then there are a number of organisational concerns which must be addressed to improve on future medical capability.

Use of Reserves

First amongst these is the issue of the Regular/Reserve balance. The Army Medical Services has long relied on Reserves to complete its ORBAT – almost 70% of its operational total is made up of both IRs and Volunteer Reserves. Op GRANBY showed that this reliance on non-regular personnel caused difficulties. The Regular manpower was spread too thinly across the operational organisation and as a result there is a need for IRs to complete the War Establishments of every operational medical unit from RAP to field hospital. Moreover, IRs proved to be a hugely variable commodity. Although many gave excellent service many more were either 'unwilling volunteers', physically unfit for service or their medical skills so faded that they required considerable retraining. Of the total accessible, there was also a serious mis-match between the skills required and those available, particularly in nursing and para-medical areas. Volunteer Reserves had much greater utility, not least because they were enthusiastic volunteers in every sense. However, they were not without serious limitations. The one major TA unit, 205 General Hospital, had to be brought up to War Establishment using many individuals from other TA units as well as IRs. There was also a mis-match between medical skills needed and what was available, partic-ularly surgical staff. As operational medical support in the future is likely to continue to be dependent upon Reserves it is important to get the structure and balance right.

Preventive Medicine
Our preventive medical measures resulted in the lowest Disease and Non-Battle Injury rates in our military history. However, we found that there were areas such as vaccination policy, accident prevention and epidemiological study which were not done well. More importantly, perhaps, we found that much of the expertise in gathering medical intel-ligence, basic field hygiene and military health had taken second place to peacetime health and safety at work considerations. Not only did the combat troops lack experience and training in personal field hygiene but the medical services also had a lack of experts in this area to teach them. There is a need to go back to basics in this field.

Treatment at Point of Wounding
At first line there are a number of conflicting requirements to be adjusted. There is a balance to be struck between operational manoeuvrability, by minimizing the logistic burden, and providing effective care at first line. RAPs were augmented to incorporate enhancements previously recom-mended. An extra medical officer was deployed to each RAP and the number of Combat Medical Technicians doubled. This greatly increased casualty treatment capabilities and enabled the RAP to split so that it could provide care continuously to a battlegroup on the move. However, creating ad hoc organizations on operations is not the best way to develop medical structures. They should be developed in peace so that we are not having to 'rob Peter to pay Paul' when we deploy.

Furthermore, as regular medical organization reduces there will be less scope in future to build ad hoc structures. In recent years, regimental medical officers' training has been based on the BATLS (British Advanced Trauma and Life Support) model. This proved to be an invaluable asset and fully justifies its inclusion in the curriculum of all Army Medical Officers. Not only were RMOs trained to manage battle casualties appropriately, but they were all using the same treatment regimes. This ensured that patient management throughout the evacuation chain was consistent. Casualty treatment regimes, based on BATLS, formed a basis for medical supply enabling appropriate equipment scalings to be produced.

Second Line Support

The balances to be struck at first line apply equally at second line. Field Ambulances need reorganization and re-scaling to improve their C^3 and their capability to provide advanced resuscitation far forward. The concept of deploying FSTs at this level to enhance the Dressing Stations was successful. They undoubtedly saved some lives and they were also able to form the nucleus of a 25 bed hospital detachment towards the end of the ground war. They did not slow down casualty evacuation as it had been claimed they would, and their presence also allowed advanced teaching of resuscitation skills to paramedics and doctors. Their use must be expanded to include more than the specialist role units such as airborne units. The forward surgical teams must not be found from hospital surgical teams whose workload is in fact increased as forward surgical teams ensure the survival of a larger number of seriously injured casualties who will require further surgery once they arrive at the field hospital. There is clearly a need to create a 'seamless' CASEVAC system between first and second line and this will require much closer integration between the field ambulances and the combat units they support, in peace as well as on operations. There is also a need to re-examine the field ambulance role in evacuation between First and Third Line, particularly the interface with ambulance units which must be fully integrated into the operational medical support organisation at every level. However care must also be taken to ensure that the Field Ambulances are sufficiently light (or have a light element) to permit them to move with the forward elements of a Brigade. Having said that the concept of 'brigading' Field Ambulances was extremely successful, and arguably if this had not occurred, the brigades would have been without second line medical support for much of the ground war. They must still remain a Divisional asset so that, when necessary, they can be deployed across brigade boundaries.

Third Line

The field hospitals too must be closely re-examined and reorganised to exploit advances in medical technology, to improve the survivability of patients and to meet ever rising expectations of patient care, whilst at the same time avoiding becoming so 'high tech' that they cannot survive and work in the field without huge logistic support. On Op GRANBY it was recognized that hospitals needed to have a modular approach to deployment so that they could be tailored to suit different operational scenarios. This enables them to maximize clinical capability while remaining small and more mobile. Op GRANBY has forced us to concentrate on clinical capability rather than 'bed numbers'.

Evacuation

Op GRANBY showed that our ground ambulance fleet was old and worn. Armoured ambulances were not able to keep up with the faster, more modern fighting vehicles. The medical equipment in ambulances was rudimentary. Whilst these vehicles might have served over the short distances which would have been the case in a general deployment in Western Europe, when casualties would have received minimal medical care in transit, they were not adequate for evacuation over the extended distances and long periods. There are no overwhelming arguments to provide dedicated CASEVAC helicopters, but there is much room for improvement in managing those aircraft detailed to take on the task during operations. Command and control procedures must be enhanced and driven by the medical imperative. 'Medics' should be dedicated, resourced and trained to provide on-board medical management and medical planning staffs must learn to work with helicopters as yet another means of transport, rather than be in awe of them.

Equipment

There is much room for improvement in the selection of more state of the art technology. Much new medical equipment was bought during the war, and a great deal of it was leading edge technology. Medical scales must now be thoroughly reviewed, evaluating new apparatus to assess how it might enhance clinical capabilities without imposing unacceptable logistic penalties. Much new equipment being produced is computerised and provides information in electronic form. These need to be reconciled with each other and the hospital information networks to ensure that all outputs are compatible.

Command and Control

Many of the initial difficulties met by the Medical services resulted from a failure for medical factors to be adequately considered in the same time frame as the other military concerns. In Theatre much of the success was attributed to the full integration of the Medical Staff into the Command structure, examples being the inclusion of Commander Medical 1 (UK) Armoured Division in the GOC's Command Cell and the Brigade Commanders each having their own Medical Commander.

It is clear that for the medical services to be fully effective they must be fully involved at all levels and at all times so that medical factors can be taken into account and the medical plan can properly reflect the operational concept. There must then be the Commanders, in the right place and of the right rank and quality and with the necessary staff and communications, who can give effect to the medical plan. Casualties are often thought of as the reverse of ammunition. The difference between ammunition resupply and medical evacuation is that the amount of ammunition available is known and plans for its distribution can be made in peace. The number of casualties can never be known in advance; nor can it be known where they will occur or at what rate; and they cannot be 'stocked' up but must be evacuated as soon as possible. Medical Command and Control must therefore be much more responsive to battle so ensuring that treatment and evacuation are if necessary redeployed to meet the need.

And Finally

We will close the medical chapter of 'Blackadder's War' by reiterating a statement made in the immediate post-Gulf period and then answering it. The war was characterised by the very small numbers of Coalition casualties and some pundits, including a number of senior military officers believed that 'the medics had gold-plated the medical support'. Moreover, they concluded that such 'over-insurance' would not be needed in the future. The authors would argue that they were provided with the medical support to meet the operational staffs' predictions and no more. It is also worth pointing out that many other elements of the force were hardly used, such as Air Defence assets, and no-one suggests that these assets were gold plated. Returning to the quote at the beginning of the chapter, the majority of the casualties were the enemy's because it was a good plan. However plans do go wrong and 1 (UK) Armoured Division was able to go to war knowing that they were supported by a well organized and rehearsed medical organization. It is not unreasonable to suppose that it was in part this knowledge which sustained them during the ground war.

We must thank our military leaders (and providence) that we were not tested but this must not be used as a reason for reducing medical support for the future.

Chapter Six

Supply

Lieutenant Colonel S F Thornton RLC
(Staff Officer Grade 1, Supply Operations HQ FMA)

This chapter will describe the Order of Battle of supply units on Op GRANBY with particular emphasis on those units which were part of the FMA and supported 1 (UK) Armoured Division and the rest of the British Forces in the Gulf. Details of commodities and quantities which were received, stored and issued are shown, together with a range of specific factors which, hopefully, will give the reader a picture of the range and variety of subjects which were dealt with by the Royal Army Ordnance Corps (RAOC) officers and soldiers in the FMA.

Supply ORBAT

Clearly, the Supply ORBAT on Op GRANBY differed significantly from the well practised methods in BAOR. The often exercised and under-stood operational scenarios in Germany, within relatively confined and recognised geographical areas with a supply pipeline operating within a well developed infrastructure, was not to be found in Saudi Arabia. As can be seen from the ORBAT shown at Figure 6.1, 3 Ordnance Battalion, the divisional level unit and 6 Ordnance Battalion, the Corps (FMA) Battalion were enhanced by additional units and, perhaps more impor-tantly, the gaps originally to be filled by the RAOC Specialist Territorial Army (TA) personnel were predominantly found by regular soldiers from many other units throughout the RAOC. Without the necessary legislation being passed, we saw no prospect of receiving the TA soldiers, who knew the roles they were trained for, arriving in theatre. This partic-ular aspect will be discussed at a later stage.

It can be seen that the expansion of Supply Units to support the Division was relatively small; the majority were already in place to support 7 Brigade. This substantial quantity of units and manpower was significantly different from the concept of operations in Europe and a factor, which at times, was in danger of being forgotten by various external planners. To support a fully operational armoured brigade operating independently needed practically the same supply support as

3 Ordnance Battalion (7 Armoured Brigade and 1 (UK) Armoured Division)
HQ 3 Ordnance Battalion (including HQ Divisional Admin Area) (1)
11 Ordnance Company (Forward Ordnance Company) (1)
31 Ordnance Company (Forward Ordnance Company) (1)
90 Ordnance Company (Forward Ordnance Company)
43 Ordnance Company (Rear Ordnance Company) (1)
Additional:
Stores Platoons & Sections with Workshops (1)
Combat Supply Platoons with Transport Regiments (1)

6 Ordnance Battalion (FMA)
HQ 6 Ordnance Battalion (1)
51 Ordnance Company (POL) (1)
52 Ordnance Company (Ammunition)
53 Ordnance Company (Ammunition) (1)
62 Ordnance Company (Stores) (1)
623 Stores Platoon
624 Stores Platoon
91 Ordnance Company (Rations) (1)
63 Vehicle Platoon (1) (2)
Local Resources Section (LRS) (1)
Bakery (1)
Laundry (1)
Expeditionary Forces Institute (EFI) (1)

Figure 6.1 RAOC Order of Battle – OP GRANBY

Notes:
(1) Indicates units originally deployed in support of 7 Armoured Brigade Group.
(2) Originally, the Armoured Delivery Squadron (ADS), found from Royal Armoured Corps (RAC) personnel, was attached to 6 Ordnance Battalion. It was to move to the Armoured Delivery Group under command of 1 (UK) Armoured Division prior to operations.

that subsequently needed for 1 (UK) Armoured Division which had assigned to it almost all the 1 (BR) Corps Artillery assets.

FMA Organisation

The supply element in HQ FMA was, like the rest of that headquarters, an ad hoc grouping brought together to support the operation. From its original outline role, HQ FMA quickly took on the logistic support for many of the other British Forces in the Gulf Operational area. At a later stage, this even included many additional units provided by other nations.

With such an increasing range of responsibilities, it was decided that the Commanding Officer of 6 Ordnance Battalion, Lieutenant Colonel Tim Murray, who was also the supply adviser to the Commander FMA, should concentrate on the command of his unit which by now had increased to over 900 soldiers and was beginning to bulk out of some of the original locations due to the quantity of stores which continued to arrive by both sea and air.

To mirror the staffing arrangements of the other two main logistic support elements, each of which had a Grade One Staff Officer, I was appointed as SO1 Supply.

6 Ordnance Battalion deployed to the Gulf with its own operating equipment and established sites around Jubail. Within the Port Area, 62 Ordnance Company was allocated a 40,000 square metres area of fenced hardstanding which quickly became a fully fledged secondary depot, holding a wide range of stores covering much of the applicable inventory. The distance from the dockside to the Company's location was approximately 2 km over good roads.

The holding of fuels in flexible fuel tanks was clearly potentially dangerous and a site off the ring road to the north west of the town was chosen. Here 51 Ordnance Company deployed with a number of containers containing both their own equipment, including flexible fuel tanks, and a range of oils and lubricants as well as fuel which was to increase substantially as the inload continued (see Figure 3.3).

With the initial affiliation of 7 Armoured Brigade to the USMC one of 53 Company's Ammunition Supply Points (ASP) was located to the north of the airport with the Americans. An additional ASP was initially set up but this was to close as the situation changed.

91 Ordnance Company found itself located in an established Cold Store at Al Berri on the ring road. This location offered a refrigerated facility and accommodation for the unit which was substantially enhanced by the construction of an additional dry goods storehouse, an EFI (NAAFI)[1] store and decent hardstanding. It was also planned to use the cold store as a mortuary if required.

The Vehicle Platoon was located alongside 91 Company with sufficient ground area to accommodate the anticipated vehicle reserves.

It will be recalled that the original mission of 6 Ordnance Battalion was to hold and provide Combat Supplies and Materiel to fight a battle for 10 days on intense rates and that in consequence the plan was to inload into theatre 30 days at normal rates of all natures with a reserve of 12 days held in Jubail or afloat. This was to support some 13,000 personnel and their 5,000 vehicles. The target levels of 30 days stock for the Brigade was met and the formation declared Operationally Ready 27 days after the arrival of the first ship.

With the decision taken to deploy 1(UK) Armoured Division, there was obviously a need for a substantial increase in stocks and manpower. The additional units shown in the ORBAT (Figure 6.1) were sent to enhance 6 Ordnance Battalion and these began to arrive in theatre from December onwards. The decision taken by Tim Murray to confirm the contract to take on more land at the Al Berri complex for his ever expanding unit holdings proved correct and contractors were brought in to begin laying asphalt on the site in anticipation of the additional stocks of stores and vehicles which were expected. 62 Company relocated to this site and, despite the original plan of retreating to a larger single site operation, the quantities of stores arriving in theatre meant its original port location was retained for the duration of the operation.

The resubordination to 7 US Corps meant that, in reality, the supply focus of the FMA was directed away from a relatively short re-supply route up the coastal road to the area of Hafir Al Batin. It was decided that stocks from around Jubail would be moved to this new location. The actual operation is described in other chapters but to put the 21 day planned move in perspective, the following planning figures were used to establish the quantities of stores and vehicles to be moved.

Planning Figures

Assumptions:
One Pallet = One Tonne with the following exceptions:

a. Petrol, Oil and Lubricants (POL)/Oils, 2 pallets = 1 tonne.
b. MLRS Pod   = 2.375 tonnes.
c. Containers hold 12 tonnes of products but weigh 15 tonnes.
                                            = max for DROPS.

Daily Requirement of Combat Supplies:
a. *Ammunition*.

Artillery – mixed types + 86 MLRS Pods	= 1074.25 tonnes
Infantry and tank	220 tonnes
TOTAL AMMO:	**1294.25 tonnes**

b. *Fuel*. (Fuel Consumption Unit (FCU)).

F46 (Petrol) = 99 m^3	= 5 × tankers (22.5 m^3)
F54 (Dieso) = 450 m^3	= 23 × tankers (22.5 m^3)
F58 (Kero) = 2 pallets (500 cans)	= 1 tonne
Packed – 27450 cans = 1308 pallets	= 654 tonnes
1 × Oil Consumption Unit (OCU)	
2 Containers + 7 Pallets	= 28 tonnes

c. *Rations*. (Based on 25,000 feeding strength).

10 man pack × 13,000 = 22 pallets	= 22.22 tonnes
4 man pack × 12,000 = 25.2 pallets	= 25.2 tonnes
Tinned biscuits 8.6 pallets	= 5 tonnes

Total Lift for One Day's Combat Supplies:

Ammunition	1294.25 tonnes
Bulk Fuel	28 tankers (22.5 m^3)
Packed Fuel (cans)	654 tonnes (see Note)

OCU		28 tonnes	
RAT		52.42 tonnes	
	REQUIREMENT:	2029.67 tonnes and 28 tankers	

Note: This represents a one time lift of Back Up Fuel for the daily requirement of 28 tankers

The quantities to be moved forward over the 21 day period were:

Ammo.	Arty	15 days	16113.75 tonnes
	BG	8 days	1760 tonnes
Fuel.	FCU	10 days bulk	50 tankers F46
			230 tankers F54
		2 days packed	1308 tonnes
	30 OCU (56 containers + 195 pallets)		927.5 tonnes
Rations		10 days	542.2 tonnes
Total Combat Supplies Lift Required:			20651.45 tonnes
			$280 \times 22.5m^3$ tankers

Materiel Stocks for Outloading

Tank Track	300 tonnes
Road Wheels (for armoured vehicles)	350 tonnes
Issued Stores (already selected for units)	140 tonnes (daily requirement)
Engines & Major Assemblies	420 tonnes
Stock/Scalings	600 tonnes
TOTAL VEHICLE LIFT	127 (Based on lift provided by 14 tonne vehicles)

Stocks in ISO Containers

Defence Stores	80 containers/1200 tonnes
Engines & Major Assemblies	125 containers/1875 tonnes
Stock	41 containers/615 tonnes
TOTAL CONTAINERS/ VEHICLE LIFT	246 3690 tonnes

Vehicles (Some to be lifted and some driven.)

Light A Vehicles/C Vehicles[2]	170 (lowloader lift)
B Vehicles	211
Challenger – 2 Sqns)	
Warrior – 2 Coys)	60+

Elements of the HQ FMA supply staff had already deployed to the FFMA to set up the supply control element and gradually, throughout this period, the majority of the staff moved to the FFMA leaving a small control element under Major Digger Denholm behind in Old Port Barracks, Jubail.

To accept these stocks, elements of 6 Ordnance Battalion moved forward and created installations in the FFMA. The additional Ammunition Company (52) moved in its entirety (see Figure 3.5).

In late January, stocks began to be lifted from both FFMA and FMA locations to inload the Divisional Maintenance Area (DMA) with 10 days of Artillery, 10 days of Battle Group natures, 10 days of rations and water, 3 FCU[3] of Bulk Fuel, 1 FCU of Packed Fuel and an adequate stock of materiel items. Eventually, with the creation of the Divisional Maintenance Area (DMA), there was a need to send soldiers from 6 Ordnance Battalion forward to this location to supplement 3 Ordnance Battalion, as that unit prepared to support the Division in its battle for Iraq.

This has been a very brief resumé of the supply support in the FMA; in reality a substantial amount of sound planning, preparation and application ensured the success of the RAOC contribution to the operation. The basic framework and training were already well developed and in place: the successful formation of HQ FMA from a concept to a reality was due to the knowledge and experience of those who initially deployed and its instant familiarity for those who arrived later, proved that the basic elements of our logistic training were sound. From the original concept of supporting 7 Brigade, HQ FMA and its logistic units were eventually supporting some 40,000 personnel from all three Services together with other nations covering the whole of Saudi Arabia and Kuwait.

Before covering specific points, the following list of figures, show the quantities of Combat Supplies which were available to British Forces at the start of the ground war. It can be seen that with very few exceptions the Division enjoyed a range and depth of support which was to become the envy of our allies.

Lessons

A number of specific lessons will now be outlined. They are not in any order of priority and some, at such a length of time after the actual events, may appear relatively insignificant: at the time they were considered vital to the success of the operation. Other points will cover areas of operating which it is hoped will be relevant for the future and show the remarkable variety of topics with which the supply staff had to deal.

Containers

A mundane and unfashionable item but the commercial world cannot operate without them. The Army has been slow to recognise this and during Operation GRANBY soon came to realise that without adequate

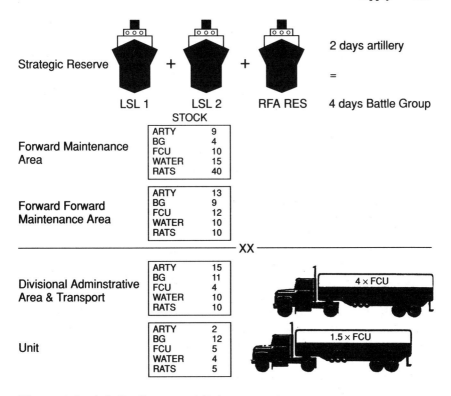

Figure 6.2 Logistic Profile as at 25 February 1995

and suitable lifting machinery containers are extremely difficult to move. The days of using recovery vehicle jibs must be a thing of the past; adequate and robust equipment at all points of the operation must be made available for future operations. The fact that we were extremely fortunate to operate in a well found and modern port must not be allowed to diminish the vital need for container handling equipment. 62 Ordnance Company were continually frustrated in their ability to move loaded containers around their sites and the hiring of old and mechanically unsound equipment from local sources was, at best, a dubious solution and at £700 hire charges per day a very expensive way to do business.

Equipment

All formed units in the British Army have an equipment table indicating what items it requires to fulfil its role. Items for equipment tables generally come from what are now called Base Ordnance Depots; second line supply units in the Gulf were not scaled for such items. The raising and equipping of various ad hoc units in the Gulf caused some difficulty. In order partly to overcome this the Local Resources Section

122   *Gulf Logistics*

(LRS) bought substantial quantities of beds, chairs, tables, cooking equipment and associated items so that the more static units could give up their military equipment those newly formed units which deployed forward. It was not unusual to see executive style highbacked chairs with castors being manoeuvred at speed around the FMA operations complex by exuberant staff officers!

Weapons
Another unshakeable tenet is that all service personnel entering a theatre of operations should be equipped with a personal weapon. It may be difficult to accept but there were a number of units and individuals arriving in the January and February airlift period who required weapons. The often heard cry of 'You'll get it in the Gulf' tended to wear thin when such a potentially disastrous act occurred, especially as our reserve stocks of small arms were extremely limited; particularly in the SA80 range, which was still being issued to the Services as part of a re-equipment programme.

'A' Vehicle Sustainability
The automotive sustainability of the Challenger and Warrior fleet was a critical issue affecting the operational capability of the force and it is described in detail in Chapter 7. Consequently a substantial quantity of replacement engines and major assemblies (E and MAs) were provisioned for the operation. So that failed E&MAs were repaired without delay, a regeneration loop between the Gulf and the UK/BAOR Workshops was introduced. The tracking of these equipments was a major part of my daily task. Inevitably there were delays built into the system; it was not unknown for the RAF to be understandably reluctant about carrying engines which showed a tendency to leak unidentifiable and therefore potentially dangerous oils into the aircraft. The carriage of our E&MAs was not the most popular task and it called for a great deal of tact, patience and persuasion to maintain the continuity of the repair loop.

'A' Vehicle Spares
With the complexity of modern armoured vehicles it is not surprising that critical spares shortages occurred. This was especially so with the filter systems suffering from sand ingress. Stocks of spare filters soon diminished and the whole range of filters was managed at the highest levels both in the Gulf and the United Kingdom to ensure that adequate stocks were procured. It didn't help when the only source of some charcoal products (for the filters) was from America. However, the liaison staffs in the States did a tremendous job in ensuring we received a fair share.

It was not only the complexity of 'A' Vehicles which caused concern. The range and age of our vehicles was remarkable. The Armoured

Vehicle Royal Engineer (AVRE) is based on the Centurion tank and is equipped with a Comet petrol engine of 1950's vintage. It had a tendency to catch fire, which resulted in the loss of at least two vehicles. This was not the only concern: the AVRE dozer equipments hadn't been used in anger for many years and were crucial for the building and breaching of sand barriers. A shortage of spares caused by very necessary training soon resulted. After a search around the world, spares were eventually located in Denmark and the Channel Islands to avert a potential crisis.

Spares Availability

The initial depth of spares held by all units in the Gulf was sufficient to ensure that the majority of demands were met in theatre. However, some spares were always in short supply and even the UK had difficulty obtaining them. The practice over the years of using funding earmarked for vehicle spares votes in Defence Estimates as a convenient method of immediate cash savings quickly showed deficiencies in some areas. For example, the new Landrover 90 and 110 series, the workhorses of the Army, were affected by this saving measure. For two years prior to Operation GRANBY little had been spent on spares for this vehicle group on the assumption that, as they were new, they wouldn't need so many spares. Unfortunately, the introduction of these vehicles into the Army was not an easy one and usage of some ranges of spares had been high enough to keep these vehicles off the road in both BAOR and the United Kingdom. With the deployment to the Gulf, where driving conditions exacted a heavy toll on vehicle availability, this shortage of spares soon became critical. The arrival of the local Landrover representative was met with some joy until he admitted that, as the domestic market in Saudi Arabia only used petrol Landrovers, the availability of diesel engined Landrover spares (for our vehicles) would be extremely difficult!

This is but one example of spares shortages caused by external factors. In general the supply of vehicle spares, together with the excellent engineering support in the Gulf, ensured the vehicle fleets, both armoured and soft skinned, retained a high state of operability.

NBC Equipment

Perhaps for the first and hopefully the last time we used our issued NBC equipments in anger. The alacrity which some people showed when suits and respirators were called for was remarkable as was the choosing of a volunteer to do the Sniff Test for the all clear!

For many years, on exercises, we had discussed the possibility of our civilian workforce needing NBC equipment. In Jubail, surrounded by the local population and the immigrant workers employed by the British Forces, the acquisition of the recently issued S10 Respirator and an

NBC Suit gained a great deal of street credibility as well as a certain level of confidence for a future. Unfortunately, we were not over-endowed with spare respirators and clothing and the control of such items caused much concern. Workers directly employed by us were issued adequate protection but all requests from elsewhere were politely declined. However, the civil authorities did issue protection to most of the population who were at risk from attack.

As with weapon issues, there were a significant number of personnel who arrived in the Gulf without such basic protection and the stocks of respirators became so critical that at one stage we held less than 10 in 62 Company. Clearly things had gone badly wrong somewhere in the chain.

Ammunition

Although our training had prepared us for the mechanics of ammunition accounting, storage and issue, the sheer volume was intimidating. Ammunition on exercises is simulated by using ammunition containers loaded with aggregate to give the correct weight and dimensions and is known as SIMMO (simulated ammunition). However, no stock of SIMMO could match the quantity of live ammunition received in the Gulf. Similarly, the complexity of the range and the need for detailed ammunition knowledge called for a high level of experience and aware-ness. The presence of sufficient ammunition-trained officers and warrant officers in any supply cell on future operations is an essential requirement.

Fuel

Perhaps more than any other commodity, the provision of adequate fuel, at the right place and at the right time, caused the most difficulty. In a country which is the largest producer of oil in the world, the difficulty in obtaining sufficient diesel (F54)[4] in the initial stages, caused surprise. Because most vehicles in Saudi Arabia use petrol (F46)[4] it took some time to switch domestic production to diesel. Our arrangement with a local contractor was subsumed by a centralised control system operated in Dahran by an Allied team on behalf of the government in Riyadh. The need from this point to forecast our usage, often days in advance, when we were unaware of consumption requirements, caused us numer-ous difficulties and frustratingly, many loaded tankers were retained in the fuel sites awaiting storage space because we had best guesstimated and got it wrong! Our storage ability was limited to our flexible fuel tanks which were of 45 m^3 or 136 m^3 capacity. To accommodate more, a local contractor was commissioned to build 42 metal tanks, each of 125 m^3 capacity and these were located in the Al Berri Bulk Fuel Installation (BFI) site so that all our flexible tanks could be emptied and moved forward to the FFMA and the Division. The availability of these fabric tanks was always a critical factor in our planning.

During the outload, the progress of the plan to locate 10 days of fuel in the FFMA was frustratingly slow. Because of the distances involved, the transport used to carry the stores, and perversely the fuel, needed to be refuelled at the FFMA thereby consuming our stocks. For a long period, the stored fuel levels remained very low, even though we committed as many tankers and fabric tanks to the task as possible.

Fuel Resupply Much has already been written elsewhere about the resupply of fuel and in particular the plan to pump fuel from a take-off point up a pipeline (PLOD) to a point as near to the Division as possible. Accordingly, the plan to lay some 100 km of pipeline, consisting of both rigid and layflat pipe, was conceived. To ensure that the fuel (diesel) moved along the pipeline, a series of pumping stations was required and three of these, manned by small groups of soldiers, mainly from 51 Company, found themselves isolated in the middle of the desert looking after a pump and hoping no-one could find them! The land war had finished before the pipe was completed but over its brief period of limited operation it certainly proved the worth of the project.

It was evident by this stage that we were suffering a severe shortage of trained petroleum personnel. This became so critical that soldiers undergoing training at the School of Petroleum at West Moors in Dorset were actually completing their course, on the job, in Saudi Arabia along with their instructors. This shortage was a continual problem which, hopefully, has now been rectified. Like some other specialised trades in the RAOC, because there are few calls for their skills in peace, it is a great temptation to make short term savings by reducing numbers; without wishing to sound too melodramatic, we do so at the risk of damaging our future operational logistic capability for some deployment options.

Food and Water

Whilst it was possible for the Army to live and operate on Composite Rations (COMPO)[5] there was only a finite number of COMPO rations available for consumption on operations. Apart from this consideration, there was the need to ensure that a balanced and varied diet was made available for as many members of the Force as possible. Accordingly, the decision to feed as many of us as possible with fresh rations was taken. Not knowing how the future operation would develop, the retention of as much COMPO as possible was also deemed to be operationally prudent. The availability of the cold store at Al Berri (Jubail) and the hiring of refrigerated rigid and articulated vehicles to carry the rations to user units allowed us to issue a full range of fresh food. It was not unknown for these vehicles, driven by local drivers, to be kidnapped by units and used as mobile freezers. The drivers were adopted and travelled with their units at least as far as the border. The

LRS Team entered into a number of contracts with wholesalers to provide fresh vegetables, fruit and dairy products. With the frozen and chilled stocks of meat and other products which were shipped out of the United Kingdom we soon built up a substantial depth of stock. By the end of the land war, we would have been capable of feeding the whole Force for a further 40 days on fresh rations.

Another aspect of rations supply was the need to provide water and eating equipment. Water in standard plastic bottles became very popular. During the outload, 2,445,534 one litre bottles were moved up to the FFMA. The competition to obtain stocks from suppliers was fierce and much of ours came from the Emirates or even as far as Oman. An early experience of the American Forces with food poisoning emphasised the need to regard health precautions as an absolute necessity (see Chapter 5). All food, whenever possible, was eaten from paper plates using plastic, disposable utensils. Where possible, prior to each meal everyone washed their hands in disinfected water and dried them on disposable paper towels. Yet again, the availability of such mundane domestic items caused difficulty and stocks were obtained from a variety of sources, including the UK. It did however help to eliminate food poisoning.

Throughout the operation, we were inundated with gifts from well-wishers in Britain. Many of these items were food parcels and came from individuals and were much appreciated. This idea was taken up by some of our national newspapers as a way of showing how they supported Our Lads in the Gulf. To our surprise, two of the more popular tabloids entered into a competition over the Christmas period to ensure we received appropriate gifts and so the great mince pie and Christmas pudding episode began. Both newspapers chartered air space to fly in their gifts with appropriate fanfare and publicity. Unfortunately, our own supply system had already anticipated Christmas and seen fit to order and have shipped out similar products in time for Christmas. To say that we had a surfeit of mince pies and Christmas puddings is an understatement and units receiving their normal ration issues in January were quite used to receiving compulsory issues of pies and pudding!

The ingenuity and generosity of senders was impressive and a real boost to morale. The range of gifts stretched from the expected knitted socks and balaclavas to real Christmas trees!

Stores Resupply

During the build-up in January and February, the realisation that our stores would take too long to arrive by sea prompted concentrated resupply by air. Apart from those cargoes already committed to shipping, such as ammunition, every item required in the Gulf was sent by air. Practically the only address which everyone knew was 62 Ordnance Company, Jubail. In consequence, during January and February the skies opened and practically every conceivable item arrived in that unit. The

Standard Priority System (SPS) used by demanding units to indicate the urgency of the requirement was put aside and every item treated in the same manner as if it was a Priority 1. This resulted in a mass of issues and stock arriving continually without any chance of identifying those stores which were genuinely battle winning or vital for the forthcoming operation. So many stores were arriving by this method that it was difficult to offload the air cargo pallets, which carried four standard pallets, and return them on empty aircraft returning to Europe. Eventually, the RAF put in a team to assist and our turnaround time improved but at the enormous expense of stores being misplaced and unidentified for days at a time. This was a herculean task and many Battle Casualty Replacements (BCRs) who would have spent their time waiting in the reinforcement camp at Blackadder were drafted in to help sort the stores into some semblance of order.

To overcome the problem of tracing vital stores, two systems were developed. First, small RAOC teams, called Priority Air Freight Sections (PAFS), were located in RAF stations to track high priority items and ensure that they received the most attention when passing through UK and BAOR airheads. Secondly, to identify these items a new priority classification was initiated and called Operationally Vital Items (OVI). We were informed by computer of the OVI details, the aircraft and airweight bill so that our own PAF Warrant Officer could isolate the item on its arrival at 62 Company. He was helped by the use of a large, distinctive label showing the legend OVI in red and three very large red stars.

Examples of some OVI items are shown below:

a. Warrior Uparmouring.
b. Warrior Power Packs.
c. Challenger Uparmouring.
d. Lynx Engines.
e. Reverse Osmosis Plants,

and tracked High Priority 1 Freight:

a. Global Positioning Systems.
b. KL43 secure communications equipment.
c. Lynx helicopter sand filters.
d. AARDVARK (engineer mine flail).
e. Mine Plough.
f. NAIAD/CAM (NBC detection).
g. Armoured vehicle NBC filters.
h. Body Armour.

From a daily low of 26 tonnes by air on 3 January 1991 the quantities increased to a daily average of 160 tonnes during the period 15–30 January with a peak on the 24th of 270 tonnes, comparable to the Berlin airlift of 1948.

Another problem was that when assigned stores, i.e. those already demanded and issued to a unit, reached them many of the items were no longer required because by now units were, for the first time, experiencing the fact that when ammunition and other warlike stores are being carried quantities of other stores have to be reduced. Inevitably these stores were recovered and returned to 62 Ordnance Company, often without any paperwork causing a further 'logjam' in reverse.

Laundry Units

Laundry units manned by a small number of TA volunteers were vital to provide support to the hospitals. They were not, as some people thought, established to wash everyone's dirty socks!

Manning

With the decision taken not to deploy TA personnel to fill the gaps in many of the RAOC and other units to which they were assigned on mobilisation, it was necessary to take regular officers and soldiers from practically every unit in the RAOC to ensure our units were up to strength. Some reinforcement was by individual personnel but one unit, 52 Ordnance Company (Ammunition) was made up entirely of individual reinforcements and even its number was 'borrowed' from the real 52 Company still in Germany. Even with the manning of the units to their war establishments there were still areas which needed additional manpower. We were fortunate to find just over 100 RAOC personnel in Blackadder, the reinforcement camp. These were quickly removed and assigned to both 3 and 6 Ordnance Battalion where their presence greatly enhanced the capability of all the units. From the HQ FMA position the finding of such suitable additional staff ensured the supply staff could be effectively split between the FFMA and FMA.

Clothing

Many varied emotive subjects arose during the operation. Operationally Vital Items were demanded and obtained, critical shortages rectified and generally the Force supported as well as possible for the forthcoming operation. However, there was no commodity which generated more emotion and involvement at high level than desert clothing and its ancillaries. If any television feature in the UK showed troops not wearing desert clothing we were guaranteed a phone call or computer message from the MOD demanding to know why they weren't wearing appropriate clothing! The facts were that 7 Brigade had been issued a 'one time buy' and by the time that 1 Armoured Division had deployed and numbers built up to the 40,000 mark there were no stocks in the Gulf. The sad fact was that the British clothing industry seemed to be unable to produce what we required and they sub-contracted the orders to Morocco and Turkey. Readers may remember that at this stage the emotions in Arab countries were running particularly high and riots in Morocco did not help production in that country. Eventually the first stocks became available and were shipped from Tangiers to Algeciras where the Spanish customs promptly impounded them. The RAF Hercules spent a couple of days waiting at Gibraltar during the Christmas period until they were released and flown out. On receipt the labelling and sizing left much to be desired. Every jacket and one pair of trousers had to be hand sorted as sizes had been loaded into large cardboard boxes without segregation. When the Turkish suits arrived they were of a slightly different colour and many of our more sartorially elegant friends found it difficult to suffer a colour clashing desert combat suit! Some refused to wear the items preferring instead their tropical (dark green) lightweight clothing which was comfortable, easy to wash and dry.

With the majority expecting hot dry weather the advent of the heaviest rains in living memory soon had demands arriving for parkas, waterproof clothing, Wellington boots and heaters. Kerosene for heaters became a very popular fuel and consumption had to be strictly monitored.

One final aspect of clothing was the saga of the shamagh, the substantial scarf which, when wrapped around the head, makes you look like Lawrence of Arabia. The initial stock was arranged by one of our own officers in HQFMA, using his own money and sent out by a contact in the UK. These were made, very quickly, from tablecloths, dyed sand coloured and made in Darlington. When we ran out of stocks we were ordered to re-demand through the 'channels' and this meant many weeks delay because of the insistence that the order had to go through the MOD tendering process. It was far cheaper and quicker to go to Darlington but others knew better. We finally received the replacements many weeks later, as the Division moved into Iraq.

Accounting

During peacetime the Army rightly insists on a high standard of equipment and stores accounting. Military items are invariably expensive and the MOD rightly takes a dim view of wastage. With the start of hostilities grew the myth of wartime accounting. To some this meant no recording of demands, receipts or usage. Our advice was to maintain the accounts whenever possible; the basic controls must be retained and all consumption would need to be proved after hostilities. Fortunately, the number of Quartermasters who disregarded our advice was very small and on return to BAOR and the UK the reconstitution and write-off action for stores, whilst involving a lengthy and laborious process, was possible.

Miscellaneous

Before concluding, a run through my field notebook for the period December 1990 to March 1991 reveals a remarkable mixture of subjects.

Many are the result of briefings, order groups and conversations. Others, which will be briefly touched on will, it is hoped, give the reader an idea of the range of subjects which arose within the supply operations cell.

Paint   Black for painting coalition recognition signs.

M548 Spares   The decision to obtain 150 M548 tracked cargo carriers from the Americans. Unfortunately, we didn't get the equivalent spares backing.

Batteries   The British Army uses a most comprehensive range of batteries. Many are mirrored commercially but others are 'one offs', difficult to obtain, identify and issue.

Cook Sets   Prone to exploding; an RAF cook was badly injured at King Khaled Military City. The caterers were continually on the lookout for potential disasters and we were always asking for more spares.

Haggis   Where, in dozens of refrigerated containers, were the haggis for Burns Night? Happily they were found and flown to the Scottish units. (I make no attempt at the plural of haggis!)

PW Guard Force   The arrival of an unplanned additional infantry brigade, who, quite correctly, expected full support, including ammunition, meant that their demands would have reduced some of our small arms ammunition holdings by over 50 per cent. To meet this unexpected requirement, we had to fly in additional quantities, including the total stock of UK-held 9 mm ammunition. We were told to be careful and not to use too much!

Body Bags   Not a subject anyone enjoyed talking about but nevertheless we had to ensure we had sufficient and they were held in the appropriate locations.

Bath Units   As ever, one of the most popular and morale boosting facilities, the presence of a bath unit was always appreciated. Unfortunately, the equipment was subject to breakdown and, despite the dedication of the soldiers manning them, were often inoperative whilst spares were awaited or repairs carried out. Yet again, the machinery had become worn out and, because there were so few equipments, spares support was minimal. Amongst our visitors to the bath unit in the FFMA were Kate Adie and her film crew.

Hire Vehicles   With so many units having inadequate numbers of administrative vehicles, the hiring of vehicles was a substantial part of the vehicle management system. Normal saloon cars were hired, so that Landrovers could go forward to field units and additional 4 × 4 vehicles, such as Range Rovers and Landcruisers, were obtained to meet the additional distances which were common in the desert. A round trip of 500 kms was not uncommon and on roads which were often atrocious, so additional reliable and robust vehicles were required. Needless to say, there were never enough vehicles available for all the bids received and a waiting list was maintained throughout the campaign. There were some cases of 'extended borrowing' and one aggrieved officer who had reached the top of the waiting list actually went 'up country' and liberated his vehicle! Others disappeared for a long time and a Senior Officer's missing Range Rover was discovered, with its markings removed, resprayed and plateless, hidden behind some containers. I wonder why!

Bakery   We were fortunate that commercial stocks of bread were available for distribution through 91 Ordnance Company. This supply system was maintained for as many units as possible but eventually the only Field Bakery operating in the Regular Army was deployed to the FFMA to produce bread and rolls for forward units. Anyone fortunate enough to have tasted their products, knows what a boost fresh bread can be and the bakery was a very popular stopping point for many units.

EFI   The Expeditionary Forces Institute (EFI), a part of NAAFI, was operated by uniformed members of that organisation who wore RAOC badges. The main storage location was with 91 Ordnance Company in Jubail where they also had a shop and mobile canteens which supplied units around the FMA area. A container shop was established at the FFMA and vehicles, carrying a range of confectionery and soft drinks, were collocated with brigades, so that units could buy such items for their soldiers. They provided a very necessary service and were a very popular facility throughout the Theatre.

Command and Control   Without doubt, the levels of control imposed on HQ FMA were many and varied. There were, at times, different levels of higher control dealing with the same subject at the same time with the same officer. Subjects which were being satisfactorily dealt with were often picked up by other agencies and confusion occurred. No doubt everyone's intentions were for the best but many of the pressures and tensions experienced by the supply staff at HQ FMA were caused by the diversity of the agencies trying to influence its work!

Conclusion

What you have read in this Chapter is not a detailed historical account of the RAOC in the FMA. However, it has been written by someone who was there for most of the operation and who was in contact with external agencies as well as dealing with those forward who saw the Supply Branch in HQ FMA as the place to go to get what they wanted. It was a tremendous experience and, even with some of the shortcomings mentioned, proved that the robust systems that have been developed over the years were still responsive to the needs of the soldier in modern warfare. We neglect them in peace at our peril.

Chapter Seven

Equipment Support

Lieutenant Colonel A M Campbell REME
(Staff Officer Grade 1, Equipment Management/Maintenance Operations, HQ FMA)

In August 1990, at the height of my serious summer leave season in HQ BAOR I was tasked to estimate roughly the quantities of spare engines and major assemblies (E & MA) and turret system line replaceable units (LRU) required to support two regiments of Challenger (CR) and 1 battalion of Warrior (WR) for 30 standard battlefield days usage in a possible Out of Area Operation. This calculation required some original thought and took several days to complete. It involved some imaginative assumptions based on the recent historical evidence of the British armoured regimental firing camps in Germany and the relative usage of spares on Chieftain tanks and armoured personnel carriers on the Alberta prairie at the British Army Training Unit, Suffield, compared with BAOR usage. These figures then had to be extrapolated to cater for Challenger and Warrior.

The bill arrived at was broadly 2½ times the BAOR spares usage, which at that time was rather high. Curious as to whether this bill would be deemed acceptable, the 'number cruncher' set off on his well earned leave. I was recalled from yacht racing in the Baltic at midday on Saturday 15 September 1990 to a briefing by Commander Maintenance BAOR, Brigadier Mike Heath at 11 p.m. that night in Rheindahlen. The MOD view was that the formation could be supported with fewer spares than the BAOR estimate. The recce party would be flying out to Saudi Arabia leaving in 15 hours. It would carry out an appreciation and make the operational plan which would include all logistic considerations. A Royal Electrical and Mechanical Engineer (REME) representative would be joining the recce party. Suitably armed, inoculated and weighed down with NBC equipment (and hip flask), I made the flight.

The Recce

The Brigade Commander and Commander FMA and staff were particularly interested in equipment support matters as they affected the operational plan. The effects of climate and terrain on equipment availability and sustainability were to be assessed. A base was to be established for carrying out key 'desertisation' modifications. A recovery plan was required to support armoured and wheeled vehicles using the Main Supply Routes (MSRs) and moving between the training area and the base. What would be the optimum REME organisation to support the formation and how best could second and limited third line repair be completed?

The recce lasted seven days of which four were spent holed up in the Intercontinental Hotel in Riyadh whilst the political issues were settled. The recce report and plan was typed out by Commander Medical on his lap top computer in the canvas seat of an RAF Hercules C130! The flight back to the United Kingdom lasted 15 hours with a short but memorable stop-over at RAF Akrotiri in Cyprus where the team was hosted by the Station Commander in the VIP lounge whilst waiting in vain for the promised upgrade to a VC 10! The onward flight was punctuated by the C 130 loadmaster serving quite acceptable Cyprus wine in plastic cups. The recce report was delivered the next day to the Joint Commander at High Wycombe. The REME support recommended was two Main Repair Groups (MRGs)[1] each with its associated Forward Repair Group[2] (FRG). All were to be familiar with Challenger and Warrior. One MRG would support 7 Armoured Brigade. The other would support the FMA and be tasked by Equipment Management (E Man). A small REME cell was to be incorporated within the FMA to be headed by a Lieutenant Colonel who would be the REME advisor to Commander FMA and on his behalf would co-ordinate first line and command second line REME support for FMA units. In addition he would be the in-theatre equipment manager.

Preparation

The REME team had to be formed and integrated within the FMA structure. A set of instructions had to be compiled and a system of reports and returns agreed with the Brigade Headquarters, the MRGs, HQ BAOR, and UK agencies. The five man team included two specialist E Man S02s, one for armoured vehicles, and the other for electronic equipment. A third major was responsible for logistic vehicles and was to act as advisor to units in the FMA. The final team member was a Sergeant clerk.

Our preparations focused on equipment management and concentrated on Challenger and Warrior, particularly what desertisation modifications and improvements would be required and were available. Links were established with defence contractors and all the MOD agencies involved in designing and manufacturing the modifications. It was clear, even at this early stage, that there could be spares shortages. The decision was taken to deploy 7 Armoured Workshop REME from Fallingbostel commanded by Lieutenant Colonel Rod Croucher to provide second line support for the operation; it had 2 MRGs and a composite FRG. One MRG which provided peacetime support to 7 Armoured Brigade was Challenger and Warrior experienced. The Commanding Officer would also deploy with a 25–strong headquarters team. The offer of a liaison flight in a Lynx helicopter of the Army Air Corps – painted yellow, somewhat prematurely at that stage – was accepted by me in order that he could discuss detailed support with the Brigade Commander and staff and the Workshop. A check on the throughput time and the predicted workload made it clear that the workshop power pack[3] repair facility was going to be busy. Failed E & MAS from Challenger and Warrior would require rapid processing to Europe for repair and return to theatre. This regeneration loop would have to be set up and streamlined to ensure acceptable levels of equipment sustainability. Support for logistic vehicles – and here we learned that Dismountable Rack Offloading and Pickup System (DROPS) vehicles would deploy with little visible means of support – looked like becoming a key support requirement.

On 8 October 1990, I deployed with the pre-advance party to Jubail. Liaison with the USMC repair and supply staffs already established revealed that with so little equipment commonality – only M 109s (self propelled 155mm artillery) – there would be little rationalisation of spares or repair support. Real estate was at a premium but a plan was quickly devised which would allow us the use of one of the large dock-side warehouses for our desertisation programme and an MRG location within the dock area.

REME Support

REME support was along traditional lines in three specific categories. First, the Maintenance Operations (Maint Ops) function: The senior REME officer in the formation was responsible for the deployment and tactical control of all second line repair and recovery support, for the technical control of all first line REME units, and the setting of repair priorities.

The engineering support function was carried out by commanders of REME units at all levels. Most of this activity would take place at second line in the REME MRGs. All fighting units had their integral Light Aid Detachments (LADs) which were restricted to quick and relatively simple repair recovery and equipment maintenance tasks.

Equipment Management responsibilities included the provision of equipment which was fit to fight in the desert environment and the means to sustain that equipment. The in-theatre E Man also had to ensure that the REME units had sufficient expertise, tools, test equipment, repair facilities and spare parts to carry out their tasks.

In BAOR, the E Man function was carried out only at Theatre Headquarters level. There was no E Man presence at brigade or division. At corps level there was a solitary S02 E Man briefer. This meant that G4 and Maint staffs forward of Theatre Headquarters were unfamiliar with the detail of E Man functions. The Maint Ops staff at brigade comprised the Brigade Electrical and Mechanical Engineer (BEME) and his Artificer, driver, clerks, and watchkeepers. The BEME was advisor to the Brigade Commander and his staff. He controlled the regimental LADs and tasked the FRG in accordance with his commander's priorities. When 1 (UK) Armoured Division deployed, it included a divisional Commander Maintenance (Comd Maint), Lieutenant Colonel Andy Ashley, who advised the GOC on all Maintenance matters and had a BEME from each brigade reporting to him for functional matters. Comd Maint also deployed and controlled all divisional MRGs. He was concerned with availability of vehicles. The identification of major technical problems on equipments was initially a Maint Ops matter before being passed back to E Man for quantification and solution. The divisional and Corps Troops elements in the brigade group and subsequently the Division itself were much larger and more complex than was the norm in Germany. Comd Maint and BEME staffs working from the back of a 432 (British Armoured Command vehicle) found the span of equipment types and depths of problems difficult to cope with. An S02 Maint and staffs for Artillery and Engineer groupings would have been useful additions to the REME ORBAT, especially if the operation had been protracted.

E Man support for logistic wheeled vehicles, certain specialist Engineer, and common user communications equipment was not formally structured but evolved in time as a joint effort by E Man, engineering support and equipment sponsor staffs

Command and Control

For maintenance this was not defined or clearly resolved until the arrival in Riyadh at Headquarters British Forces Middle East (HQ BFME) of a dedicated Comd Maint, Colonel Peter Gibson, in late December 1990.

There were many different headquarters involved in the recce, the operational plan and the manning, mounting and movement of soldiers and equipment to Saudi Arabia. This served to complicate command and control issues.

The recce report recommendations for REME support were not as I recommended in that only one of the 7 Armoured Workshop MRGs was familiar with both Challenger and Warrior. Also there was a single composite FRG rather than two independent ones and, of course, the Commanding Officer and his headquarters were also deployed.

For GRANBY 1 the Brigade Commander had his BEME, an S02; one

Lieutenant Colonel as CO of a large armoured workshop, and another double-hatted as the FMA Commander Maintenance and Theatre Equipment Manager. No decision was made as to which would act as the Maint Commander or to whom the Formation Commander would turn for specific advice. The personalities involved quickly agreed that BEME would carry out his traditional tasks, the CO would deploy and control the second line resources to support on the one hand formation training and on the other both the FMA units and the engineering requirements of the Equipment Manager. There was some overlapping of responsibilities but the system worked effectively. It was interesting for the Theatre E Man to work out his relationship with the Brigade DCOS in the early stages.

On the arrival of the second Brigade and a divisional HQ for GRANBY 1.5 things became more familiar. 7 Armoured Workshop (complete) and 11 Armoured Workshop were deployed and controlled by the Divisional Commander Maintenance. The 4th MRG (6 Armoured Workshop minus FRG) on the deployment of the division to the desert was placed under command of the FMA to provide second line support to FMA units and engineering support for E Man tasks.

Maintenance command and control issues in theatre were now clear. The Divisional Commander Maintenance was responsible for Maint Ops, equipment availability and engineering support within the division and I advised on sustainability and all equipment matters behind the divisional rear boundary.

E Man issues were also becoming clear. The Equipment Manager, as General de la Billière's advisor on equipment matters was a member of his staff working on his authority. He was located in Jubail where all the equipment problems were centred. This arrangement was effective by virtue of his being on the staff of the Commander FMA as REME advisor and Head of Service. There were many agencies involved in E Man matters: the operations centre at Joint HQ High Wycombe contained an E Man cell, MOD had its own Land Logistics Cell, HQ BAOR & HQ 1 British Corps were still involved in producing essential spares and prioritising the output of 23 Base Workshop, the base work-shop in Germany repairing engines. The staff at Headquarters Director General of Electrical and Mechanical Engineers (HQ DGEME) in Andover had global responsibility for all equipment management matters. Finally there were the defence contractors all of whom had their own concerns and priorities and some of whom were represented both in theatre and in Whitehall. All five levels of headquarters were demanding much data to brief their commanders. Most were interpreting them in their own way and coming up with different sustainability conclusions. On the arrival of Colonel Peter Gibson in Riyadh (300 kms distant from Jubail) as Theatre Commander Maintenance all E Man matters were briefed through him to JHQ in High Wycombe. He placed an embargo on direct communication outside the chain of command and a strict régime of reports and returns was eventually established.

There was an unlooked-for benefit to the uncertainty of status and authority for me, the equipment manager. I was not issued with an order on the functional chain by anyone, from arrival in theatre until the day before the land war started!

Equipment Modification

Modifications to equipment were a major E Man task throughout the whole operation. Firstly Challenger and Warrior had to be 'desertised' on arrival in theatre by means of the Quayside Modification Programme (QMP). Subsequently many key battle winning equipments were fitted with modifications designed to enhance the capability of these vehicles and their crew protection.

In the event, the QMP for Challenger consisted of installing 14 separate modifications in the 24 hour period that Brigadier Cordingley allowed for each armoured squadron before its deployment to the training area. The bulk of the work was to improve the air filtration and cooling systems. It was carried out by the tank crews, the regimental LADs and a dedicated production team from 7 Armoured Workshop together with a composite mix of key civilian defence contractor representatives.

A total of 221 Challengers went through the QMP during which power packs were removed, all automotive and turret systems were thoroughly inspected and repaired or replaced if found suspect. This production line approach was a triumph of co-operation which allowed crews and REME tradesmen and technicians to learn a good deal from the specialist civilians. LADs and FRTs gained much valuable knowledge and experience by removing and refitting the power packs under controlled conditions.

All 324 Warriors were put through a similar but smaller scale programme in which a thorough inspection and health monitoring was carried out. The first 80 were fitted with a modification to insulate the driving compartment from the heat of the power pack. This required pack removal and replacement. All Warriors were fitted with modified air filter seals by a REME team supervised by GKN (the manufacturer of Warrior) specialists. All Warrior turret rings were packed with grease.

Many other equipment modifications were fitted after the QMP right up until the start of the land war. The major task was the uparmouring of Challenger, Warriors and engineer armoured vehicles. The fit was successfully piloted by an E Man team, first in workshop conditions – specifically on some form of hard standing with overhead cover – and then in the open desert. Following this, the Divisional Commander agreed to the E Man proposal that a quick and simple trial should be carried out to compare standard Challenger and Warriors with their uparmoured counterparts for manoeuvrability, fuel consumption, mobility and recoverability. The Divisional G3 staff controlled this trial and reported no appreciable disadvantage on any comparison. Thereafter, a fleet-wide fit was ordered. As time became short the Divisional Commander decided on Warriors as top priority for fitting, and then Challenger. The fit was done one squadron or company at a time in the desert by crew, LAD and a specialist supervisor warrant officer from Vehicles and Weapons Branch REME (VWB) in the United Kingdom. Over three tons of specialist armour (Chobham and Explosive Reactive) were fitted to each Challenger.

Other enhancement modifications included modified (Jericho) racking – only three squadrons of Challenger were fitted before the operational decision was taken to halt the programme – Armoured Charge Bins were trialled and pilot fitted by an E Man team led by a RARDE (Royal Armanents Development and Research establishment) scientist with 2 VWB specialists. This fit was completed in one tank squadron with the latest Challenger. Some reserve Challenger of this build standard were also modified. Shortage of time precluded a full fleet fit.

Dozer blades were not available for all Challengers fitted to take them. A quick modification and fitting programme was carried out and went some way towards allowing an even balance of dozer tanks across the armoured regiments.

Smoke generators were fitted to 20 Challengers. Two extra fuel drums were fitted to the top decks of all Challenger. Engineer Chieftains and Centurions were uparmoured by regimental workshops personnel. Armoured bridge-laying tanks were also uparmoured by their crews and specialist mine detection and destruction modifications were fitted to some of all engineer equipment types.

Air conditioning was fitted to several key communication equipments. These were installed and maintained by a civilian contractor from Howdens. A modification was funded and developed for the installation of air conditioning in both Challenger and Warrior. Had the war gone on into the late Spring of 1991, it would have been necessary to install this modification. The BAOR Electronic Warfare capability was moved to the Gulf and fitted into FV 432s (armoured command vehicle). Challenger, Warrior and other battle winning equipments were fitted with secure radio. All command vehicles were fitted with Global Positioning System equipment (GPS).

Chemical Agent Monitoring (CAM) equipments (135) were fitted with a GRANBY modification. Artillery positioning computers (PADS) were converted to be compatible with the local Grid system.

It was of some concern that there were over 100 Urgent Operational Requirements (UOR) authorised for deployment to support GRANBY. These extras were sent out to the theatre, seldom as stand alone equipments but predominantly as modifications to existing equipment. They created considerable pressures on an already overloaded supply system. For instance, the material for the uparmouring programme weighed 1500 tons and consumed 80 C130 flights from the United Kingdom to Saudi Arabia. Many of these good ideas were not staffed fully and some were not required by the Divisional Commander. Some could not be fitted on time. A few were left to rust or rot on the airhead or quayside.

Technical Spares

The rationale used in deciding the breadth and depth of spares scalings was to provide as near as possible 180 days[4] worth of historical BAOR usage against the declared equipment holdings. In BAOR at that time there were many known spares shortages across the whole equipment range. Historical BAOR usage for Challenger and Warrior bore little relation to actual usage in the Gulf. The supply team deployed to the FMA did not include any of the HQ BAOR supply managers who at that time worked very closely with E Man and understood intimately the equipment spares problems. Combat supplies specialists were the highest priority, quite rightly, but perhaps in this case at the expense of specialists for 'B' vehicles and technical spares.

Managing the spares system was made extremely difficult by the sheer volume of demands generated by engineering support problems. The numbers of power pack components, other used spares stripped from BAOR equipment, many extra air filters, modifications kits, tools, and repair kits required to be sent out to the Gulf were many times greater than had been envisaged at the planning stage.

More seriously, the agreed equipment holdings were greatly exceeded by divisional units. There were many more equipments on the dependency than were planned. For instance, the agreed quantity of FV 432 was under 400 but ultimately over 700 required spares support. Some equipments requiring support were not in the spares support plan. These included American tracked artillery ammunition carriers (M548), secure radio, satellite communications, and special NBC and recce vehicles from the German Army. Several of the equipments deployed were new to service and had spares support arrangements which were, at best, ad hoc. In this category, were the Challenger Armoured Repair Recovery Vehicle, specialist Warrior variants for Royal Artillery units, Multiple Launcher Rocket System (MLRS), DROPS and new All Wheel Drive (AWD) logistic vehicles.

The Stockage Support System was seriously overstretched. Large quantities of spares were arriving continuously at 62 Ordnance Company in the FMA and a backlog built up as the processing system became overwhelmed. Priority 1 demands were the norm. A special Operationally Vital Items (OVI) status was created to ensure appropriate priority for air freight out to theatre but OVIs became so numerous that items often lay undiscovered for weeks. Many items were poorly labelled. Others were not successfully loaded on aircraft because of other equally high priority freight. Despatch from the United Kingdom was no guarantee of arrival, identification and delivery in theatre, even with a team of supply specialists on departure and arrival airfields. (For further details see Chapter 6.)

Sea freight for less urgent spares was also a problem for 62 Company which was still trying to unload and process the hundreds of containers already in their location full of assorted spares.

The most labour intensive part of the E Man workload was searching the Central Distribution Point (CDP) for the critical spares of the moment – and too often without success. In the weeks prior to the land war, the Maint/E Man cell in the FMA, which by this stage had grown to 13 officers and 32 soldiers, had up to half of its personnel scouring airfields, the port, and 62 Company dumps and containers, day and night, looking for critical items.

Spares for fuel tankers, generators and radios in particular had their demand priorities downgraded in favour of other vital spares. During the setting up of the Armoured Delivery Group (ADG), demands for such items as Thermal Imagers and NBC filters for Challenger; and RARDEN (30 mm cannon) gun spares for Warrior; and general items for both had to be placed at Priority 2. Not one such priority demand for the ADG was met in this critical three weeks preceding the land war. At one stage, spares for mobile Ptarmigan system radios were being 'controlled' by staff branches in Andover and London.

Turret System spares were extremely hard to 'find' at all times. In January 1991, it was discovered that a large batch of vital Challenger turret systems Line Replaceable Units (LRUs) had been 'found' in Dulmen, Germany after repeated assurances that it had been despatched to the FMA three months previously. Their arrival in theatre greatly reduced concern about the sustainability of the Challenger turret systems. However it was against E Man advice that the 'control' of these items was delegated to the divisional staff the day before the land war started. It was not possible to assess whether the divisional logistic system could have co-ordinated the backloading of repairable items and controlled their subsequent re-issue in a war of any duration.

As has been traditional in the British Army, there was evidence that units built up 'unofficial' buffer stocks of items they considered to be critical. As it turned out, such 'hoarding' escaped retribution. However, for future conflicts, it is essential that a system of spares supply is devised which inspires confidence in the end user in sufficient measure to persuade him against taking this 'just in case' action.

Equipment Availability

Reporting of availability for battle winning equipments was a command responsibility carried out by operational (G3) staffs. Equipment was deemed available if the unit commander could take it across the Start Line. This pragmatic definition was accepted by the Divisional Commander and it worked effectively as a coarse measure of tactical readiness. The figures were volatile and at no stage were they considered in theatre as being precise. Comd Maint directed his repair resources on a day to day basis to improve availability figures by repair and replacement of defective assemblies. Commanding Officers were directed to design equipment husbandry and maintenance days into unit training programmes in an effort to improve and then maintain availability levels.

The availability of key equipments was reported back daily to BFME, JHQ and MOD. Challenger availability was regularly reported to the Secretary of State for Defence and, we were told, to the PM herself. It only dropped below 80 per cent on six occasions, each of which was explained by major training exercise activity and was swiftly improved.

Availability levels achieved on Operation GRANBY were greatly in excess of those reported routinely in BAOR a few months previously. During the build up an experimental Battle Equipment Reliability Return (BERR) system was operated within 7 Armoured Brigade for a period of three months in Autumn 1990. The BERR results were capable of providing objective availability statistics, although BERR figures for availability were consistently lower by 20–30 per cent than the comparative figures reported by G3!

During the land war, the armour covered over 300 km. The Challenger fleet fired over 1,100 rounds of main armament ammunition in day and night engagements. Challenger squadrons suffered approximately one automotive and five turret systems failures during each 24 hour period of the war. Start Line availability was 98 per cent and on cessation of hostilities was declared as being 95 per cent.

Sustainability

Provision of sustainability advice to the theatre and formation commanders was a crucial part of the E Man staff function. The operational plan is critically dependant on the ability of the fighting formation to sustain its battle winning equipment.

The theatre commander needs to know such things as 'how long can we sustain our armour in 75 km battlefield days at given intensity and attrition rates – can we keep up with M1A1 Abrams and Bradley?' (the American tank and mechanised infantry fighting vehicle).

I was summoned early in November 1990 to brief General de la

Billière in Riyadh on these topics. My 10 minute presentation was followed by 1½ hours answering questions from five senior officers who collectively sported 14 stars!

The formation commander requires advice on how rapidly he is using his E & MAs, and how quickly they are being repaired/replenished in order that he can balance his training usage against his operational reserve. This subject was briefed weekly to the brigade and subsequently the divisional commander throughout the operation.

Failure data on Challenger and Warrior were analysed by E Man, who then calculated from usage in theatre the current figures for Mean Distance Between Failures (MDBF). (For electronic units in turret systems this was expressed in time to failure (MTBF). During the early training phase, the MDBF results were close to the initial predictions made in Germany. Progressively, however, the trend line showed clear underperformance and quite quickly the brigade commander decided he had to eat into operational reserve stocks of E & MAs in order to continue his essential training. By December 1990 the figures had become critical as shown in Figures 7.1–7.6

Against a (BAOR) prediction of 1235 Kms between Challenger engine failures the actual results achieved reached a low point of 723 Kms on a cumulative fleet distance in theatre by 7 Brigade of about 60,000 Kms. This meant that for the given fleet size, every 5 Kms one Challenger would require a power pack change 20 Challenger would not make the Start Line after a 100 Kms approach.

The figures for Warrior were even more alarming, giving an MDBF for CV8 engines at 1,205 Km against a (BAOR) predicted figure of 2,902 Km (see Tables). Warriors would drop out of an unopposed approach at a rate of one every eight kilometres. It was just then, in December 1990, that the Warrior air filtration problem was clearly identified by the GKN team leader and I, who were not about to have a Merry Christmas. During the health monitoring checks on the newly arrived Warriors of the 1st Battalion The Royal Scots (1RS) the GKN specialist demonstrated the routine refitting procedure for the engine air filter. He then repeated exactly the same sequence of actions but had, in fact, knowingly left a 1-inch gap between filter and housing which allowed neat dust to be ingested into the engine. Needless to say, procedures were subsequently tightened up! The Warrior air filtration problem was solved – except for these vehicles in which the rot had started and residual failure was still awaited.

At this critical time, following the deployment of 4 Armoured Brigade, Major General Smith had progressively to reduce his operational reserve from 30 to 20 and then to 12 Battlefield Days to allow training to continue whilst awaiting the expected improvement in MDBF figures.

All training was now carried out at a firing area about 50 kms north of

DATE	P/P		ENG		G/BOX		APU		DIST	AV DIST	
	QTY	MDBF	QTY	MDBF	QTY	MDBF	QTY	MDBF		PER	VEH
CR		617		1235		1235		1802	KM	KM	
14 Nov	47	734	37	932	10	3450	20	1725	34510	295	
21 Nov	60	745	51	877	13	3440	20	2236	44717	383	
28 Nov	72	683	61	806	18	2733	26	1892	49195	421	
5 Dec	88	607	74	723	19	2816	32	1672	53503	457	
12 Dec	95	619	77	763	20	2939	43	1367	58778	502	
19 Dec	104	587	80	763	23	2653	50	1221	61027	522	
26 Dec	111	598	82	810	27	2460	53	1253	66433	567	
2 Jan	116	583	83	815	29	2332	62	1091	67649	578	
										4BDE	7BDE
9 Jan	128	614	92	855	33	2384	67	1174	78697	58	65
16 Jan	142	603	101	847	35	2445	77	1111	85595	41	38
30 Jan	169	682	122	946	37	3119	84	1374	115417	379	63
16 Feb	206	774	138	1156	44	3627	107	1491	159599	253	249
13–30 Jan	53	901	39	1224	7	6824	22	2171	47768	379	63
31 Jan–16 Feb	90	1021	55	1672	15	6130	45	2043	91950	253	249

					PACK MDBFs		
				DATE	1DIV	4 BDE	7 BDE
				9 Jan	921	4231	586
			Cumulative	16 Jan	690	2220	567
				30 Jan	901	1530	531
				13 Feb	1021	1572	773

CHALLENGER: Power Pack (P/P), Engine (ENG), Gearbox (G/BOX) and
Auxiliary Power Unit(APU) failures, distances run (DIST) and
Mean Distances Between Failures (MDBF)

Figure 7.1 CHALLENGER: Major Assembly Failures and Mean Distances Between Failures

				ACHIEVED			BASED ON FIGS				
BDE	FLEET	PREDICTED	19 Dec	26 Dec	2 Jan	9 Jan	16 Jan	30 Jan	3–30 Jan	3 Jan
		(503 KM/PACK)	(619 KM)	(597 KM)	(583 KM)	(583 KM)	(603 KM)	(682 KM)		34381
7 BDE	117	5	5	5.1	5	5.25	5.15	5.82	4.5	6.6
4 BDE	59	9.9			9.9	10.9	10.22	11.56	25.9	26.6
7 BDE	176	3.3	3.3	3.4	3.3	3.48	3.42	3.8	5.1	5.8
4 BDE										
7 BDE										
4 BDE	221	2.7	2.7	2.7	2.7	2.77	2.72	3.09	4.1	4.6
WMR										

Figure 7.2 CHALLENGER: Fleet Kilometres per Power Pack Change

STOCK	WMR		ASSY'S DUE GULF			POOL ARMD WKSP	62 ORD COY	BALANCE
	REQ	LOG BASE E	USED JAN	BOH OR NEW FEB	MAR			
POWER PACK	80	49	0	–	–	26	18	+13
ENGINE [59% × 124] – 80		50		25	33	10	18	+103 (+33 in Mar)
GEARBOX		20		25	33	14	66	+125 (+33 in Mar)

176 Challenger (2 regts × 57. 1 regt × 58)
1 BFD at 60 Kms = 10.34 pack changes
12 BFD = 12 days WMR (124 pack changes)

At the current usage of engines in p/p repair the good engines salvaged from failed packs would enable the generation of the full 124 power pack changes required for 12 days operations.

IGNORING GEARBOXES (Not critical)

SURPLUS PACKS   = 13 P/P with replacement g/boxes = 22 P/P
SURPLUS ENGINES   = 103 = 174 P/P
GROSS SURPLUS   = 196 P/P
                           = 19 days WMR (giving 1137 Km/Veh or 905 Km/Veh incl WMR)

Figure 7.3 CHALLENGER: War Maintenance Reserve Requirements

the initial Brigade training area. The terrain was much more user-friendly. The new brigade quickly learned the lessons of desert equipment husbandry. Training for war was arranged on the basis that 4 Brigade were allotted the lion's share of available E & MAs. Training was no longer based on track mileage but on Power Pack Usage. The GOC, from the weekly E Man sustainability brief, allocated his brigades a set number of Power Packs. When they were used up, no more training could take place. By late January 1991, it could be seen that Warrior engine MDBFs were rapidly responding to the air filter fix.

The tables show considerable difference in MDBFs between the brigades. This strongly influenced the GOC's decision on which brigade

| DATE | P/P | | ENG | | G/BOX | | DIST | AV DIST |
	QTY	MDBF	QTY	MDBF	QTY	MDBF		PER VEH
WR		1451		2902		2902	KM	KM
14 Nov	19	1523	9	3215	3	9646	28939	315
21 Nov	27	1319	15	2373	3	11867	35602	387
28 Nov	34	1212	18	2289	3	13733	41198	448
05 Dec	41	1104	23	1969	3	15099	45295	492
12 Dec	48	1084	30	1735	3	17347	52042	566
19 Dec	60	994	41	1454	3	19877	59630	648
26 Dec	76	862	52	1260	4	16377	65508	712
02 Jan	81	818	55	1205	7	9470	66291	721
								4 Bde / 7 Bde
09 Jan	96	852	66	1240	10	8185	81859	68 / 64
16 Jan	108	958	73	1418	12	8627	103525	104 / 60
30 Jan	123	1281	77	2046	14	11254	157564	294 / 75
16 Feb	139	1644	90	2538	14	16318	228456	277 / 288
03 – 30 Jan	42	2120	23	3872	6	14842	89054	294 / 75
03 Jan – 16 Feb	50	2795	35	4633	7	23116	162165	277 / 288

| CUMULATIVE | PACK, MDBF | | |
	1 Div	4 Bde	7 Bde
09 Jan	1038	2914	568
16 Jan	2001	4493	342
30 Jan	2120	6897	628
16 Feb	2795	5379	1329

Figure 7.4 WARRIOR: Power Pack, Engine and Gearbox Failures. Distances and MDBFs

BED	FLEET SIZE	PREDICTED (1451 Km/Pack)	26 Dec (862 Km)	02 Jan (919 Km)	09 Jan (852 Km)	16 Jan (958 Km)	30 Jan (1281 Km)	03 – 30 Jan	03 Jan – 16 Feb
			ACHIEVED					BASED ON FIGS	
7 Bde	101	8.1	8.5	8.1	8.4	9.5	12.7	6.6	13.2
4 Bde	158	5.2		5.2	5.4	6.06	8.1	43.7	34
7 Bde + 4 Bde	259	3.2	3.3	3.2	3.3	3.65	4.9	8.2	10.8
7 Bde + 4Bde + WMR	316	2.66	2.7	2.66	2.69	3.03	4.05	6.7	8.9

Figure 7.5 WARRIOR: Fleet Kilometres per Power Pack Change

1 BFD AT 60KM = 5.56 PACK CHANGES							
12 BFD = WMR 12 DAYS = 67 PACK CHANGES							
	WMR		ASSYS DUE GULF				
STOCK	REQ	LOG BASE E	USED JAN	BOH OR NEW FEB	MAR	FIT POOL ARMD WKSP	62 ORD COY	BALANCE
POWER PACK	70	42		–	11	30	19	plus 21 (plus 11 in Mar)
ENGINE (60% ¥ 67) – 70	–	52	17	38		15	4	plus 84 (plus 38 in Mar)
GEARBOX	–	31	10	15		16	37	plus 94 (plus 15 in Mar)

On current standars of performance stock of power packs exceeds number of pack changes required, therefore, all engines and gearboxes are surplus to the 12 day requirement. At this stage of operations all stocks are WMR, therefore, since a 12 day WMR is not reqiured a WMR is not quoted for engines and gearboxes.

SURPLUS PACKS	=	21 POWER PACKS WITH REPLACEMENT G/BOXES = 35 P/P
SURPLUS ENGINES	=	84 ENGINES = 140 P/P
GROSS SURPLUS	=	176 P/P
	=	1899 KM/VEH or
	=	1557 KM/VEH INCL WMR
	=	31.7 DAYS WMR

Figure 7.6 WARRIOR: War Maintenance Reserve Requirements

was to lead through the breach and on the subsequent phases of the operation.

The Role of Defence Contractors

The Gulf War created a giant market place for defence equipment. Nations of the Coalition were keen that their equipment should be seen in a good light compared with that of their competitors. The outcome of the multi-national competition to provide the new British tank could well be decided on its relative performance on operations. GKN was engaged in a marketing campaign to sell a desertised version of Warrior in the Gulf Area as the invasion of Kuwait began.

The soldiers had a great deal at stake but their country's defence industry saw both the grand threat and the unique opportunity. Great Britain plc was on display. Soldiers and defence contractors had a happy unity of purpose.

All British contractors were placed under my control and I directed their work and authorised their movements as defined in a standard contract based on an agreement between the Chairman of Vickers Defence Systems (VDS) and the Ministry of Defence. They had to be documented; given such uniforms, accommodation and administrative support as they requested; protected if necessary and guaranteed a safe passage out of theatre if and when they wished to depart. At the height of the pre-war phase there were over 40 individuals working with soldiers on British military equipment in theatre. The companies represented were:

VDS, GKN, Perkins, David Brown Gear Transmissions, Barr & Stroud, Marconi, Howdens (Air-Conditioner), Leyland DAF, Landrover and Alan Mann Helicopters.

VDS headed up the composite team of system experts for Challenger known by the soldiers as the 'Vickers Volunteers'! The engine expertise from Perkins was shared by the GKN Warrior team.

The contractors were deployed firstly to contribute to Challenger and Warrior desertisation under the Quayside Modification Programme (QMP). They advised on the detailed implications of fitting or not fitting a particular modification and helped to design the QMP package. This sort of advice would normally be given through Project Management staff and HQ DGEME.[5] It would thus be much more measured and take a long time to produce. Apart from the team leader and one design engineer from VDS, the contractors were very much hands-on specialists from the shop floor, where they had been involved in prototypes, trials and production. They knew their part of the equipment intimately and explained the niceties and the finer points of detail to crews, REME tradesmen and technicians and the FRTs. The relationship between contractors and soldiers which started at the QMP stage was very positive.

As Challenger and Warrior deployed for training the efforts of the defence contractors divided between continued support to the QMP and support to training. A novel scheme was devised and welcomed by Brigadier Cordingley and his unit commanders under which an individual contractor was seconded to a particular unit to work and live in the desert with 'his Regiment' as it underwent training. Crews and maintainers worked closely with and learned a great deal from 'their' contractor on user operation, maintenance, fault diagnosis and correction.

Contractors were also extremely useful in the trouble shooting role, and their intelligence network on significant faults and defects rapidly outshone the existing reporting system. Happily, they shared this information freely and discussed the issues and proposed remedies in detail with the equipment manager. All their communications back to the UK were agreed by and copied to E Man who reciprocated, copying relevant reports and returns to the contractor concerned.

Good advice was given on many general aspects of maintenance and repair procedures. This resulted in improved repair processes which, in turn, improved reliability and sustainability figures. Soldier/contractor co-operation extended to the Brigade Commander allowing VDS to set up a marketing opportunity by which the Saudi Arabian Defence Minister participated personally (complete with red carpets and boarding ladder) in a fire and manoeuvre exercise on Challenger during the advanced brigade training exercise.

The contractors often set up diversion orders from UK factory production lines to obtain vital spare parts. They agreed to facilitate the advancement of fielding the Challenger Armoured Repair and Recovery Vehicle (CRARRV) and help with provision of training and spares support for it.

It was unfortunate that the VDS team were required to take the option to withdraw from theatre as the air war started. The reason for this was difficulty over the company obtaining life insurance cover for their employees, many of whom were reluctant to depart. A second VDS team was deployed within a few weeks when the life cover problems were solved. Most other contractors remained and continued their excellent work.

The VDS team, with an E Man representative, went forward to Kuwait very soon after the land war ended and gathered invaluable data from every single crew on how Challenger performed on the operation.

Contractors not involved with Challenger or Warrior came out on the whole at E Man request to resolve specific problems with their equipments. For instance, helicopter contractors came out to carry out an agreed modification programme.

The contribution of defence contractors was extremely beneficial to equipment availability, sustainability and performance. Their specialist knowledge and advice enabled crews and REME to operate and maintain their equipment to a significantly better standard than their previous training would have allowed. This co-operation between defence contractor and soldier must be maintained and be capable of development for future such conflicts.

Acknowledgements: *VDS teams*   *GKN teams*
                       John Slade   Paul Harris
                       Brian Trueman   Dave Tomes
                       Bob Armstrong

In Depth Repairs (IDR)

By November 1990 it was clear .hat engines for Challenger (CV12) and Warrior (CV8) were being used up much more quickly than they could be repaired or replaced. Even taking into account all additional stocks obtainable from Europe including 'part-worn' engines cannibalised from equipment in Germany, the capability to train and then go to war and sustain an operation was now becoming limited.

A pilot study was carried out in theatre in which a specialist team stripped down CV8 and CV12 to identify the repair requirements. Judging by evidence of erosion on the air intake systems and in particular the turbo fan and cylinder liners there was a fundamental sand/grit/dust ingestion problem. Even after identifying and rectifying the dust problems on CV12 (scavenge system flap valves, air filter completeness and rigidity) and CV8 (incorrect fitting and sealing of primary and secondary air filters) there was clearly residual wear on all engines which had been exposed to Soltau (the British training area in Germany) dust and Saudi sand and had not yet failed.

It was now imperative to guarantee to the operational commander sufficient good engines, particularly CV8, to meet his requirements. The supply system was already seriously overloaded and adding to it by requiring repaired CV8s to be flown in quantity from 23 Base Workshop in Germany or from Perkins factory in Shrewsbury, was not a favoured option. In-theatre calculations for turn-round times from point of failure to returned fit and assembled into a power-pack suggested a time scale of six to nine weeks. The war hopefully would be over before the repaired engines were returned.

The decision was taken in theatre to select those failed engines showing classic signs of ingestion wear and to carry out in-depth repairs (IDR) to them in Jubail. This would produce many engines more quickly than the regeneration loop time frame.

On 6 January 1991 an IDR facility was set up within the FMA workshop (6 MRG) on the outskirts of Jubail within a 'RUBB' shelter (polythene covered, steel framed hangar). Basic equipment, special tools and overhaul kits had been sourced and acquired. Perkins specialists supervised instruction on engine overhaul and workshop production control procedures. Within a few weeks REME vehicle mechanics were carrying out engine fault investigation, diagnosis and overhaul. No attempt was made to repair engines showing signs of crankshaft distress. All efforts were concentrated on those engines which could be repaired by replacing pistons (having topped, machined, set and checked them), liners, turbo, bearing shells, setting tappets and 'decoking' cylinder heads.

In the eight weeks from set up to end of the land war 47 failed CV8 engines were examined by the IDR team of which 31 were repaired/overhauled on site and returned to stock. They had their rocker covers painted red for identification. The Red Tops fitted to power packs have to date performed just as well as their factory overhauled counterparts. The opportunity was also taken to pilot overhaul/repair three CV12 engines for Challenger and the Commander Tank Transporter with similar success.

The IDR concept in an Out of Area operation proved extremely successful and can easily be repeated. Standard REME skills and procedures would again have to be developed to ensure a consistently high quality product but, with expert training this can be achieved with minimal delay.

Acknowledgement: Without the expertise, commitment and dedication of the civilian members of the IDR team, in what were trying and potentially dangerous circumstances the remarkable IDR achievements would not have occurred.

Bryn Morton   – Perkins Team Leader
Dave Harris   – Perkins Service Engineer
Dave Chawley   – Perkins Service Engineer
Kevin Francis – GKN Power Pack Engineer
Mark Fearn   – GKN Project Engineer.

Lessons Learnt and Future Application

The time between initial deployment and the land war was well used to correct equipment capability shortcomings and to improve operator and maintenance skills. It is most unlikely that so much time for preparation will be available in any future operation. Marked improvements in equipment performance, reliability and the availability of a realistic scaling of spares, together with a general lifting of training standards, are essential if units are to be able to fulfil their missions.

A partnership should be nurtured in peace and developed in war to allow Army standards to be raised to the levels achieved in the Gulf War and to enable IDR to be carried out as standard practice when appropriate.

The spares system was overwhelmed. There is an absolute requirement to ensure that Army equipment is reliable and that MDBF figures do not impose an undue burden on the spares system. Full use must be made of Information Technology to enable the collection of accurate failure data and to calculate objectively an appropriate depth and breadth of spares holdings.

Equipment Management is now rightly recognised as an important strategic staff function. The status and authority of the equipment manager in the operational theatre should be redefined to reflect this.

Chapter Eight

The Small Cogs

Lieutenant Colonel M C Le Masurier RLC
(Staff Officer Grade 1, Labour Resource, HQ FMA)

The logistic support of any operation is inevitably dominated by the major functions of supply, movement and equipment and medical support and in this respect Operation GRANBY was predictable. However, the size of the British commitment, the speed with which it was necessary to mount the operation and its location in a theatre which contained no British military infrastructure was unusual. Whilst much thought and training had been given to brigade and divisional level operations and their immediate logistic sustainment on exercise in Germany, proximity to the UK base and an in-place infrastructure had tended to blur some of the equally important, but rather less exciting, aspects of support. These were to be emphasised with a vengeance in the peculiar circumstances of the Gulf.

G1 Operations is a particularly important branch, dealing as it does with personnel aspects of support to the soldier. It is G1 Operations that is responsible for such morale sustaining matters as pay – not just to the individual in theatre, but to his family in Germany or UK too – mail and welfare. G1 Operations also deals with field records, reinforcement, prisoners of war and evacuation of the dead, all matters little practised on exercise in Germany but which were to become of considerable importance in the real-life circumstances of Operation GRANBY. It was discovered, for instance, that mail is not just a morale booster, but can present major logistical difficulties too by its sheer bulk and quantity. Prisoners of war need not only to be collected and disarmed, but fed, housed and documented, and their care and collection alone called for the deployment of the equivalent of an infantry brigade, which of course, itself required support! Modern communications are such that it is essential to know exactly how many soldiers are present, where they are and be able to keep track and swiftly and securely inform the UK base should they become casualties.

It is peculiar to the British Army that, at the time of Operation GRANBY, many of these functions were carried out either by small corps, or by small specialised branches of larger ones. This characteristic had led to the development of a high degree of expertise by such organisations often in relatively narrow fields. An example of this was the Army Catering Corps (ACC), a corps dedicated to the preparation and presentation of food, whose chefs were able happily to switch from preparation for a banquet to provision of hot, properly balanced meals in virtually any situation. Such was their renown on Operation GRANBY that British kitchens served as a magnet for American servicemen, many of whom presented themselves at mealtimes. The Royal Pioneer Corps (RPC) too was a small corps which prided itself in being able to take on any job and do it well. Pioneer soldiers trained as infantrymen and in peacetime often deployed to remote locations under the command of young officers or NCOs. This early independence bred a healthily robust attitude; the individual Pioneer officer and soldier would quite happily take on even the most unfamiliar task, and the 400 present in the Gulf provided commanders with a flexible and much sought after resource.

The purpose of this chapter then is to relate the experiences of these small cogs in the logistic machine. Starting with G1 Operations the following sections illustrate how the operation was seen from the specialised aspects of the Postal and Courier Service, Military Police, Pioneers, ACC, Financial Services and Field Records. They illustrate the complexity of functions often taken for granted and even more, the determination of their practitioners to provide the highest degree of service in what are best described as unusual circumstances.

There have been considerable changes in the British Army since the end of the Gulf War. The RMP and Royal Army Pay Corps (RAPC) (who supplied the financial services) are now part of the Adjutant General's Corps (AGC). The Postal and Courier branch of the Royal Engineers, RPC and ACC are no more and have joined the RCT and RAOC to form the Royal Logistic Corps (RLC). For these particular small cogs then, GRANBY was a final fling, and whilst their functions remain in the new corps, they are rightly proud to have gone out on such a high note.

* * *

Part One

Headquarters Force Maintenance Area
G1 Operations

Lieutenant Colonel S C Howe MBE RAMC
(Staff Officer Grade 2, G1 HQ FMA and HQ RAMC Armoured Division)

Following the decision to deploy to Saudi Arabia, thought was given to just what G1 representation was required in HQ FMA. It was initially decided that an SO2 and SO3 would deploy. This was later enhanced by a second captain SO3 and a lieutenant. Major Steve Howe RAMC was seconded from his post of SO2 G1 HQ 1 Armoured Division to become one of the first half dozen HQ FMA officers to start planning with Colonel Martin White in Rheindahlen. It soon became clear that planning for operational G1 matters such as care of prisoners of war and repatriation of the dead could only be based on assumptions and would have to be modified after arrival in theatre. However, the staff at HQ BAOR were quick to identify the requirement for welfare support for both the troops deploying and their families who were to be left in Germany. Shortly before their departure to Saudi Arabia Colonel White and Major Howe were briefed by Assistant Chief of Staff (ACOS) G1, Brigadier David Burden, on the impressive welfare package that was being assembled. This included:

The establishment of a Command Information Team. Its brief was to ensure that families were given up-to-date information on what was happening in theatre by a combination of daily telephone messages to be broadcast on BFBS radio, and GRANBY text pages on teletext. In addition, written narrative and pictures were to be published in Sixth Sense, the BAOR weekly forces newspaper.

Operation GRANBY was to be given precedence for the allocation of welfare funds. The staff were told that, within reason, they had authority to purchase any items that would contribute to the welfare and morale of soldiers once in Saudi Arabia. In addition, each unit was to be issued with a number of welfare packs containing sports equipment and board games.

The Services Sound and Vision Corporation (SSVC) had acquired a large number of short wave radios, capable of receiving BBC World Service broadcasts in the Gulf area and these were to be sold exclusively to troops deploying on Operation GRANBY. There was a promise that a BFBS radio station would be established in Saudi Arabia as soon as was practicable, however, account would have to be taken of local sensibilities. Similar constraints were also affecting planning for CSE shows, if operations allowed, and an ambitious plan for two Land Rovers to be equipped to act as mobile desert cinemas.

The last week of preparation before the official form up of HQ FMA was spent in finalising staff lists. The Headquarters was subject to 'rate capping' and difficult decisions had to be made about just what its shape should be. To this end the Military Secretary's (MS) branch at HQ BAOR, headed by Colonel Martin Gibson, provided an invaluable service, finding individuals at short notice to fill slots. This intimate level of support was to continue throughout the operation and it is of note that while other reporting chains were to change, the MS reporting chain for the brigade group and, latterly, the division remained unaltered.

The G1 staff deployed to Saudi Arabia with the brigade advance party on 11 October. On 12 October the cell opened for business, sharing a room with the G4 (Ops) staff. Whilst this was far from ideal in preserving matters of confidentiality, it had the advantage of becoming an all-informed cell and assisted in rapidly developing a strong G1 and G4 team.

Initial tasks included liaising with the personnel staff of HQ 1st (US) Marine Division. The US and British staff systems had similar divisions of responsibility and an easy rapport was quickly established. The British were keen to conform with directives on movement within the port area and out of bounds areas that had been promulgated through the US chain of command. This early attempt at conformity won friends and reaped benefits far beyond an inconvenience felt by the force.

Experience in Germany had taught us to expect casualties once the brigade began training in earnest. It is normal practice to employ a local undertaker to handle the dead. No such facilities existed in Jubail and it was clear from the outset that we would be expected to handle and repatriate any dead that resulted from training ourselves. The problem would be further compounded in war, as the Saudis would only allow emergency burial on their soil and all remains would have to be removed from the country as soon as was practicable.

The Americans had deployed a small graves team under the command of a lieutenant colonel to handle their dead. They had set protocols for identifying and processing remains, borne from hard experience in Vietnam. Their ability to take dental x-rays and finger prints to aid identification was impressive. The commanding officer of the unit agreed that they would handle and store any British dead until we had established our own facility.

Sadly, we were to take them up on this offer within a few weeks. A British Army War Graves Team deployed into country in mid-December and established a mortuary facility. This was to prove invaluable when the time came to repatriate dead at the conclusion of the land war.

The next most pressing G1 operational issue was the handling of prisoners of war. The intelligence assessment at that stage was that we could expect a capture rate of 2,500 per day and that planning should be based on holding 12,500 for one week. British doctrine for handling prisoners of war is laid down in JSP[1] 391, 1990.

Based on the guidelines in that publication it became clear we would need a force of at least three battalions to care for healthy prisoners and the burden on the medical services of having to deal with injured ones would require the allocation of additional medical resources. A paper was prepared at HQ FMA and forwarded through the chain of command, recommending that a prisoner of war guard force be established; given that the force was still subject to a manpower ceiling, we held out little hope of receiving additional support. However, the manpower bill was met in full and the guard force deployed into theatre in January 1991.

On 25 October HQ FMA was visited by a delegation of expatriates headed by Mr Arthur Gray and Mrs Anne Berry, the mother of one of the soldiers deployed with 7th Armoured Brigade. The group were all based in Dhahran and were keen to do whatever they could to show their support for the 'Desert Rats'. A scheme was developed whereby soldiers were bussed to Dhahran to spend an afternoon in the company of these kind people. The men were given some home cooking and, most importantly, the opportunity to phone home and generally unwind in congenial company. In all there were places for 210 soldiers per week and competition to attend was fierce.

The absence of international telephones was keenly felt by the force. The problem was that telephone lines did not exist in the area where British troops were billeted. Negotiations with a representative from Mercury began early and within eight weeks 50 card phones were installed in Camp 4, our main transit facility. The company had pulled out all the stops to lay lines and install phones and earned the gratitude of all ranks in the force.

Given the local conditions and restrictions, the search for recreational facilities took on a high priority. These were necessary not only for the benefit of morale but also as an aid to the maintenance of fitness, which would deteriorate in those men living in desert conditions for four weeks at a time. A number of expatriates allowed the free use of the swimming pools in the camps they ran. Within two weeks of arrival, we had established a rota system that meant close to two thousand men per week would have the opportunity to use a swimming pool in at least one of the compounds, albeit for only an hour or so. The greatest boon was to be the discovery of the A1 Huwaylat Centre, a western style sports centre located in Jubail. The centre offered a swimming pool, tennis courts, squash courts and a very impressive gymnasium. An additional bonus was a 550 seat theatre, which was to become a venue for future Combined Services Entertainment (CSE) shows. Once initial negotiations had begun with the British managers, civil servants from HQ BFME in Riyadh approved the hiring of the facility and negotiated a contract. These formalities completed, over 1,250 soldiers per week attended the facility, under the watchful eyes of British Physical Training Instructors (PTIs) who were determined to ensure the benefits to the maintenance of fitness were maximised to the full!

The administrative staff at HQ BFME and under the enthusiastic and able direction of Colonel Bill Strong were also working hard to ensure that soldiers received the best possible welfare package. British newspapers were received daily, normally within forty – eight hours of their production. These were distributed on a per capita basis through the postal and courier detachments and were an important source of information. A British Forces Broadcast Services (BFBS) disc jockey (Alton Andrews) arrived in Jubail in early November and managed to persuade the Americans to give him prime air time on their local AFN station. This service was popular with both the British and US troops and contributed to the sense of alliance. BFBS eventually began broadcasting from their own station at Camp 4 on 14 December 1990.

Over 100 television and video recorder sets were issued to 7 Armoured Brigade Group. A short time later a video film library was established in Riyadh and these films were supplemented with those sent to units from rear parties and families. We all welcomed the opportunity to watch films and, given the nature of shift work, it was not unusual for the videos and televisions to be working 20 hours a day. The small screen was later supplemented with the two mobile desert cinemas where the small civilian crew lived a peripatetic life travelling from unit to unit giving film shows. They were later to follow 1 (UK) Armoured Division into Kuwait and started operating again within two days of the end of the war.

As a result of understandable local sensitivities, a directive had been issued that religious services were to be kept low key and that army padres were to be referred to as welfare workers. However, in spite of this directive, a Remembrance Service was conducted in a port hangar on Sunday 11 November with full military ceremony. The service was attended by over 1,500 soldiers and guests from the local expatriate community. It was a poignant moment and few who attended could have failed to be moved.

On 12 November, a reconnaissance was carried out for a potential CSE show. The Al Huwaylat Centre was an obvious site for those based in the port area, but a desert location would also be needed if the majority of those based outside the port were to have the opportunity to see the show. Engineering work began on enhancing a natural amphitheatre in a quarry close to 7 Armoured Brigade's brigade administrative area

(BAA) and when Bob Carolgees and his troupe visited in late November over 6000 troops enjoyed the show.

A number of celebrities visited in the run up to Christmas including Sir Harry Secombe and Paul Daniels. The visits inevitably placed a strain on a very busy G1 cell, as did the distribution of British Legion welfare packs and the hundreds of parcels simply addressed to a soldier or a female soldier. The kindness of the British public was literally over-whelming at times. However, the benefit to morale both to the troops deployed and their relatives of knowing that they had the support of the vast majority of the British public and media was incalculable.

At the same time as dealing with the huge welfare effort, the G1 staff were also having to deal with more traditional matters. Over 266 battle casualty replacements (BCR) had been deployed into theatre. With hind-sight it can be said that these reinforcements were sent to Saudi Arabia too early. Initially their morale was understandably not too high. The mere fact of being a reinforcement meant that they did not know which unit they would be posted to, or what the immediate future held. An early decision was made to reduce the administrative burden on the FMA and move the reinforcements to foster units selected on the basis of their Corps or trade. The subsequent establishment of a reinforce-ment holding unit to cater for the divisional BCRs was to be a far more satisfactory solution.

During the period between October 1990 and January 1991, the FMA were processing between three and five compassionate leave cases each day. The majority of these were classified as type B, which under the strict letter of the law were not entitled to return to the United Kingdom. However, it proved possible to fly the great majority home on the next available plane and most returned into theatre within 14 days. The disci-plinary record of the force during this time was impressive. Hard work, the absence of alcohol and high motivation ensured that there were very few disciplinary problems.

The G1 matters dealt with at HQ FMA were vital to the success of the operation. Following the deployment of 1 (UK) Armoured Division and HQ FMA, HQ FMA remained the focus for a myriad of operational and non operational issues. They had the benefit of stable communi-cations and had developed sound operating procedures which were understood by all staff involved in G1 matters from unit, brigade divi-sion right through to JHQ and MOD.

Part Two

Postal and Courier Services

Lieutenant Colonel H A Hughes RLC
(Officer Commanding 3 Postal Squadron)

*'Another medium of communication I considered vital was the post –
the "bluey", a single sheet airmail letter form is a war winning factor,
nothing less'.*

General Sir Peter de la Billière.

Training, exercises and even study days, seldom produce realistic
scenarios for war. The difficulties which cascaded throughout the entire
period of Operation GRANBY were unique and completely different
from anything those of us in the Royal Engineers Postal and Courier
Services (PCS) had experienced before.

For years PCS had trained successfully in BAOR, their main exercise
commitment being the secure carriage and delivery of rapid response
courier service (RRCS) items. This was in line with set priorities, viz,
a descending scale from RRCS, official mails, private mails, forces post
office counters to parcels. The theory was (it always seemed) sound!
Manpower being limited, PCS would execute its given tasks in order
of priority, the courier service would be the last to go, and well ... if
counters had to be closed or the parcel service suspended so be it, the
exercise would soon be over.

As a consequence of repeated assurances that this would be the way
any war would be supported, PCS very rarely carried 'real mail' on exercises, and the result of this was that there was almost no conception
among the staff of the colossal amounts of business in all five priorities
that would come our way!

The reality of a massive force deployed to the Middle East hit the
Postal and Courier Services hard. The initial PCS team of 19 men and
women from 1 PC Regiment in BAOR trained and equipped itself in
a frantic hurry to join 7 Armoured Brigade Group when it deployed
in October 1990.

Having established a Forces Post Office (FPO) and Distribution Office
in the laundry at Camp 4, and an FPO in the vast port area in Jubail,
this advance element deployed a small detachment in direct support of
7 Armoured Brigade in the desert about one hour's drive north of the
port itself. A further six FPOs were established to serve the main body

of 12,000 troops as they arrived in theatre. As mail increased, PCS soon found that they had insufficient manpower.

When 1 (UK) Armoured Division arrived in theatre, it was clear that PCS reinforcements were required. These were provided by two small PCS squadrons of about 30 soldiers each; one under command of Major Rod Small in support of 1 Armoured Division, and one in the FMA under command of Major Howard Hughes. Small PCS detachments at Bahrain, Dhahran, Oman, Riyadh, and Tabuk had already been established.

The laundry, which had given faithful service, was soon abandoned in favour of a hastily converted laboratory building situated about half way between the port area and the airport. Its location next to the largest petro-chemical plant in the world was not ideal and thoughts of a pre-emptive Scud attack concentrated the minds of us all! However, in the latter half of December most minds were grappling with plans for the operation that would soon come.

It was clear that, even with the two PCS squadrons collocated in Jubail (the 1st Armoured Division PCS Squadron had not yet deployed to the desert), we were only just keeping our heads above water. Mail was increasing at an alarming rate as force levels grew. The standard of service was still between two to three days from Great Britain which did much to keep the troops' morale high. It was nice to learn that our 14-hour days were appreciated. Little did we know that when the Division arrived we would become completely swamped!

We knew that it was only a matter of time before the divisional PC squadron would deploy and rob us of half our workforce. By this time we were running 11 FPO counters, one of which operated 24 hours a day, and the levels of counters business were staggering. To cope with this, we established an Accounts Branch run by two senior NCOs and a junior NCO. This branch ordered and issued all postal stock and balanced the accounts daily. An enduring memory is of huddles of posties pondering over account books at two in the morning desperately trying to get the figures right. The branch junior NCO spent almost all her time counting massive piles of Saudi riyals which not only had a strange aroma but which had also deteriorated to the point where many notes resembled pieces of fine lace.

Our first lesson was that contrary to training beliefs, we simply could not close counters and concentrate on mail and courier matters. New camps were being opened in the Jubail area (such as Blackadder and Baldrick Lines) and these demanded and deserved a counter service. Most business was not simply the sale of stamps but revolved around long queues of soldiers paying water money (a local allowance) into their National Savings Bank accounts. The accounts branch served both PCS squadrons, and at its peak was handling over £350,000 per week, a monumental responsibility for a couple of sergeants.

The main sorting office in Jubail was christened the Force Distribution Office and new branches were established. A registered letter enclosure (RLE) with a forces courier office (FCO) collocated was built. Also, because of the growing numbers of misaddressed mail, we established a locations branch. Working from field records print-outs, this office was redirecting some 2,500 items of mail per day. Letters addressed to 'Cpl Jones The Gulf' were not uncommon! A postal inquiry branch was set up to deal with losses and damage. These branches, although vital, greatly reduced the manpower for mail sorting and courier work.

In early January the divisional PC squadron was deployed forward and was served by the road link (MSR DODGE) from Jubail. On 20 January elements of the FMA (PCS) moved to form the FFMA PCS detachment. To ensure a workable mail plan we also deployed a PCS section to the Al Quaysumah airhead, 70 kms forward of the FFMA. This was a prime example of the amoeba effect; assets which were adequate in one location were beginning to become stretched as lines of communication opened and expanded. The divisional PC Squadron was likewise fragmented with detachments at both divisional headquarters, both brigade administrative areas and the divisional administrative area.

A greater worry began to manifest itself when the Division moved north west across the Wadi Al Batin and well ahead of the logistic tail. Now our transport assets were quite insufficient to cope with the volumes of mail to be carried over such long distances.

In addition to normal mail and parcels being handled we began to be inundated with welfare parcels – donated by well-meaning companies, clubs and individuals in the United Kingdom. The generosity of the British public was quite overwhelming – as was the problem for us! We urgently needed more manpower, transport to move them and more space in which to sort them! Space was solved in the short term when Sappers fixed arc lights to the palm trees to our immediate front. This area became our parcel sorting office, and was in use day and night. Fortunately the rain stayed away until we moved into an adjacent factory complex. In fact we moved in illegally when the rain did start, much to the annoyance of the staff – but thoughts of damp mail encouraged the final approval! The sight of thousands of mail bags spread over an area the size of several football pitches did arouse some comment. We were accused of holding a massive backlog, and delaying mail, a misconception quickly displaced when I informed such Cassandras that this was no backlog, merely the daily delivery! Our rather public sortation did serve to concentrate a few minds and we were fast becoming a favourite venue with visiting senior officers.

The transport problem was more troublesome. What was needed was much larger transport than our five Mercedes Benz trucks which plied the Jubail and Dhahran airhead routes; 40-foot containers and plenty of them. The ordnance companies proved extremely obliging and frequently lent us freezer wagons for the task, but this was rather ad hoc. Quite clearly a system of transportation urgently needed to be established. The staff tended to think that Hercules air lifts were the answer and while I agreed that a 'Herc' a day for letter mails would be ideal, I was less than optimistic that sufficient would be available for parcel mail. On one memorable day we managed to obtain clearance for six 'Herc' lifts! Having worked all night palletising parcels we then found that there were no flatbed trucks to lift them! Much screaming around eventually threw up three which were loaded up and sent to Jubail airhead where the 'movers' complained as they had no room to hold the pallets. Eventually we managed to get them unloaded and the vehicles returned to pick up the rest! By the end of the day we had despatched all six aircraft loads but, although it sounds like an enormous amount of mail, in overall terms we had hardly scratched the surface.

Meanwhile, within the division, extensive exercises in preparation for the forthcoming battle were disrupting the mail system. This was partially solved by the use of support helicopters on CASEVAC missions to carry mail forward.

Mail was arriving in from a variety of locations, sometimes from Riyadh and Dhahran, sometimes mixed in with freight to 62 Ordnance Company and, in one case, ten 40-foot containers driven all the way across the desert from the Red Sea. In all cases, these wagons had to be unloaded, the bags opened and the contents sorted to units and the whole consignment re-despatched forward. Containers, some of them RAF, arriving from Dhahran, were commandeered and sent forward with their Arab drivers (and PCS escorts). This direct approach was unpopular with the RAF who had very decently helped, and also with the Arab drivers who were understandably less than keen to go too far forward. Methods of persuasion varied, but even the issuing of NBC kit didn't cheer them much! Once containers were despatched along MSR DODGE we had no further contact until they arrived in Al Quaysumah – oh for a system of asset tracking! In some cases our mail containers failed to arrive at all for days and we therefore not only lost the asset but were gripped with anxiety over the fate of our mail and soldiers. One wagon overturned on the MSR, fortunately without injury to anyone.

Fatigue was widespread and was a constant source of worry. HQ FMA was sympathetic and quickly authorised the use of battle casualty replacements (BCRs) and some local labour in the form of orange boiler-suited Filipino workers. While these did help us with the basic humping and dumping, their usefulness was limited in that the BCRs changed almost daily and the Filipinos couldn't speak (let alone read) much English. But they were all extremely cooperative and we thoroughly enjoyed their company. Our lobbying for extra PCS personnel had achieved no success due to MOD's policy of 'rate capping'.

Our parcel sorting problem was solved when on 21 February, Lieutenant Colonel Barry Cash, as acting Commandant, instigated parcel sorting at our main depot at Mill Hill before despatching to us, and this greatly eased our problems. We had been asking for this for some time but Mill Hill itself was also under extreme pressure; had the war been prolonged and Mill Hill not began pre-sorting, we would certainly not have coped! Coincidentally, it was also on 21 February that the Division asked us to freeze parcel mails as they were about to go through the breach into Iraq and obviously did not want the extra clutter of parcels! This freezing meant that parcels had to be stock-piled at all links in the mail chain which caused some fairly frantic decision-making back in Mill Hill where Parcel Force containers continued to arrive daily but could not be unloaded. Indeed, so enormous was the problem that Parcel Force itself became critically short of its own containers!

The difficulties experienced in the Jubail – Al Quaysumah – Dhahran – Bahrain network were, of course, mirrored at Al Quaysumah itself where our forward detachment received the divisions's and HQ FFMA mails. This detachment was located at Al Quaysumah airhead under command of Captain Brian Felks. The dozens of 40-foot containers arriving there could not proceed further and had to be crossloaded to transport from 10 Regiment Royal Corps of Transport and the mails sent on to the divisional distribution area for collection by units. Transportation of mails was a constant headache. It should not be forgotten that mails had to be processed outwards as well as inwards and at the peak we were handling nearly one and a quarter million forces free aerogrammes ('blueys') outwards per month!

The courier service was based in Riyadh and consisted of a small number of PCS senior NCOs who operated on a Hercules network throughout the Middle East. The service was well used, but more often than not despatches were so urgent that special RRCS tasking had to be implemented. Maps, operations orders and the like necessitated us scrambling various aircraft from helicopters to the VIP HS 125 from Riyadh to get them to their destinations on time! The RRCS had travelled over 200,000 miles to deliver 7,000 highly classified items by the end of the war.

The division moved into Iraq in wet, misty conditions with the PCS element enhanced with two AFV 432s (British Armoured Personnel Carriers) to provide protection for the RRCS Teams which had their Armstrong motorcycles mounted on top of the vehicles. The advance was conducted at incredible speed but the mail plan worked well with 4 Armoured Brigade and the divisional troops receiving mail during short breaks. But 7 Armoured Brigade moved so quickly that their mail did not catch them up until they were consolidated in Kuwait.

On 2 March, an element of the FMA PC Squadron, on its own initiative, moved up the coast into Kuwait and, after leaving a section at the international airport, moved north into the desert to close the loop and meet up with the division in order to establish the future mail plan.

In all, over 626,000 kgs of letter mail and 1.5 million kgs of parcels had been handled, including over 9 million blueys. Forces Post Office counters had turned over in excess of £6 million. Like so many conflicts before, the enduring feature of the entire mail operation was the sheer ingenuity of the postie soldier who, sometimes against all the odds, refused to be stayed in the execution of his appointed rounds, as Heroditus put it so many hundreds of years before.

*   *   *

Part Three

Military Police Operations

Major D J A Bergin RMP
(Force Provost Marshal, HQ FMA)

The decision to send a force to the Gulf had major implications for the Royal Military Police (RMP), as any field deployment would impact severely on an organisation which had dual peace and war roles. The IRA threat to the Army in Germany was at its height and the military police were at the forefront of the fight against terrorism. The choice of a military police unit to support the 7 Armoured Brigade group was not easy; the task would include all the normal police functions so there would be a requirement for policing the force, for investigations, crime prevention and advice to the commander, as well as field operational responsibilities, such as traffic control, route signing and close protection.

Although 174 Provost Company in Tidworth had a world-wide role, it was decided to use Germany-based military police who were more familiar with armoured formations. Rather than remove an entire unit from its peacetime area of responsibility, a composite unit, 203 Provost Company was formed from military police units throughout BAOR. Such a decision is always difficult and perhaps, with the benefit of hindsight, it might have been better to take a complete company, notwithstanding the impact on the peacetime policing of the British forces in Germany. Major Desmond Bergin was appointed Force Provost Marshal (FPM) and Major Nick Ridout was selected to command the company. 203 Provost Company assembled at Werl and embarked on rigorous and rapid training to prepare for deployment.

Sadly, there was no room on the reconnaissance for any MP representation, so all planning for operations was done from the reports of those who had been able to go, together with other sources such as Second World War recollections, the RMP Corps history and current army doctrinal publications on desert warfare. As with all the other elements of the brigade preparing for this operation, there were frustrating moments for the military policemen and women, pooling vehicles, radios and equipment from all over BAOR, as well as trying to mould themselves into a cohesive force ready to deploy on the British Army's biggest operation since 1945.

The RMP deployment to Jubail was led by the FPM, who moved on the Pre-advance Party, followed shortly by a headquarters element and a platoon of 203 Provost Company. The whole Jubail area was the responsibility of the USMC MP; liaison was quickly established and joint policing operations were set up from a shared military police station in Jubail port. The sensitivity of the Americans to the absolute obedience to the very low speed limit in the port meant that traffic policing quickly became a vital task. The imminent arrival of the main body of the brigade dictated that preparations for their reception could not be delayed; the military police were concerned with providing traffic control and direction in the densely packed port area and signing a route from the port to the brigade base location at Camp 4. Once the armour had arrived, the RMP task of moving the brigade to its desert training area began. Under the command of Captain John Petrie, a brigade Provost unit of two platoons and a small headquarters deployed to the brigade maintenance area (BMA)[2] while the remainder of the company provided support to the FMA and the growing line of communication from Jubail port to the BMA.

One of the first problems encountered was the relative unsuitability of the signing system which had been brought from Germany; the standard signs of bitumen covered card mounted on three foot pickets soon proved of limited value and various other methods were tried in order to provide effective route signing both on the main deployment routes and later across the desert. A particularly useful system employed in the desert involved the use of cyalume chemical sticks mounted on six foot angle-iron pickets; these commercially manufactured luminous markers proved very effective and their eight to twelve hour life was more than adequate for most applications.

A section of the Special Investigation Branch (SIB) deployed to Saudi Arabia with 203 Provost Company and set up in the port alongside the USMC MP CID branch. Initially the SIB section was not fully committed but, sadly, after the first few weeks fatal traffic accidents began to take their toll on the force and all of these were investigated by the SIB. Criminal investigations at first centred on illegal alcohol stills and some of those found proved that the inventiveness of the British soldier had not been dulled by the heat; one particularly memorable find by the SIB involved a make-shift still producing alcohol from onions. The smell alone was enough to prevent anyone from trying to drink it!

Liaison with the local authorities was usually very harmonious although at times it could be quite frustrating. The basic problem was that a memorandum of understanding (MOU) between the United Kingdom and the Kingdom of Saudi Arabia took some time to negotiate and took even longer to reach the FMA. The local police, not unnaturally, had only limited experience in dealing with foreigners and the arrival of Westerners in their thousands caused some initial difficulties; a liaison office established by the US Marines went a long way to easing both British and American problems and provided a point of contact for quickly resolving even routine matters. Although no British liaison officer was attached to the Saudi Arabian police, almost daily direct contact, combined with the efforts of the Arabic-speaking American liaison officers, ensured that most issues could be resolved quickly. Even when the MOU was signed, however, there were still difficulties and frustrations; the agreement negotiated by the Foreign Office conferred on British soldiers a legal position similar to diplomatic status and this did not immediately find favour at the local level; more than a little further negotiation was required between the RMP and the Jubail civil police in order to ensure the proper implementation of the MOU.

Close protection (CP) operations by RMP were conducted in two main areas; in Riyadh, a team of RMP NCOs provided round the clock protection for General Sir Peter de la Billière; in Jubail and the Eastern Province, CP was provided for the commander of 7 Armoured Brigade and for visitors who warranted such protection. 203 Provost Company was not particularly suited to coordination of CP operations as it was focused mainly on conventional policing and support to 7 Armoured Brigade, so the task fell to the FPM's operations NCO, Sergeant Peter Cassidy, with bodyguards drawn from 203 Provost Company. This arrangement proved satisfactory although more than a little tweaking was necessary both to convince the Brigade Commander of the need for his CP and to acquire the hardware to ensure that a discreet yet effective service could be provided.

The decision to increase the British contribution to the operation had a significant impact on the RMP. In order to support a division with an extensive line of communication, reinforcement was required and the deployment of 174 Provost Company from Tidworth under the command of Major Dick Bishop was authorised. A new plan was drawn up by the FPM which moved the whole of 203 Provost Company to support 1 (UK) Armoured Division while 174 Provost Company supported the FMA and the main supply route (MSR) forwarded to the division. At the same time, a more senior Provost Marshal, Lieutenant Colonel Stewart McLean, was deployed to take over from Major Bergin, who then moved to the US Army Central Command[3] to help with the planning of the movement of the British division and its logistic support to its forward deployment area.

By early January, all RMP assets were in theatre and the two companies had taken on their new roles. 174 Provost Company had deployed a series of traffic posts (TPs) along MSR Dodge to support the FMA's massive outloading task in order to establish the FFMA while at the same time providing all military police support to the port area and Jubail. 203 Provost Company had joined 1 (UK) Armoured Division and was heavily involved in work-up training for the expected ground war.

The start of the air war in mid-January introduced a new sense of urgency to the work of the companies although the Iraqi response to the allied attack posed no effective threat to military police operations; the dispersed section-strength TPs continued to function with little disruption. The SCUD attacks were mainly targeted against the air base at Dhahran and at Riyadh and only isolated attacks fell on desert targets; nonetheless RMP units, like all others, were constantly operating under the threat of chemical weapons attack and were able to provide, through the TPs, a chemical monitoring and warning system for the deployment and supply routes.

The 1 (UK) Armoured Division build-up included several large-scale rehearsals leading the force to the final assembly area and 203 Provost Company was intimately involved in this important phase; at first there were problems of command and control but the rehearsals ensured that when the time arrived to launch the ground attack, the company was ready for war. 174 Provost Company had the daunting task of continuing to provide a police and security element in Jubail while also manning a line of TPs from the FMA at Jubail to the FFMA near Hafr Al Batin and on to the Divisional rear boundary.

In order to find their way across the often featureless desert, military police sections had by now been issued with GPS which gave superbly accurate positional fixes and enabled incredible precision in the siting of TPs and administrative areas as well as the layout of routes. Although most users of these routes only saw them after much traffic had passed over them, the military police recce parties actually laid the routes out on unmarked desert. Signing continued to be a problem and many different solutions were pursued in an effort to provide a system of value to the formations moving forward; as discussed earlier, the bitumen signs brought from Germany were difficult to see and the issued Bardic electric lamps needed to be recovered and to have their batteries changed. The best answers were to have bigger signs when there was a need to convey information and to use the American chemical sticks, or cyalumes, to define routes. For the crossing of the Iraqi front line, special six foot signs were made by the Royal Engineers.

Functional command and control of military police units was always difficult and Colonel McLean spent many days on the road trying to keep in touch with his assets spread from Major Bergin in Dhahran to 203 Provost Company several hundred kilometres further north; the company commanders had similar problems and they spent long hours in their Landrovers moving between their platoons and sections, ensuring not only that their men were in 'good order' but also that battle plans were understood by all.

By the eve of the battle, the RMP disposition in the forward area saw a platoon with each of 4 and 7 Armoured Brigades to help move the Brigade Administrative Areas (BAAs) with the remaining four platoons grouped together with the elements of 32 Armoured Engineer Regiment to form the Route Development Battle Group (RDBG) under the command of Lieutenant Colonel Alwin Hutchinson (see Chapter 10).

In the hours before the ground attack was launched, military police signed and manned the four staging areas leading to the breach in the Iraqi defences which would be made by the leading elements of 7 US Corps. The RDBG then led the British armour of 4 and 7 Brigades through the breach before the breakout by the Division. As the brigades moved forward, their BAAs were led through obstacles and minefields by the military police; besides the obvious threat from land mines, they also had to cope with mines and bomblets which had scattered from air-launched munitions and it was during one of these daring operations that Staff Sergeant K M Davies and his platoon used shovels in order to clear the route of bomblets for 7 Armoured Brigade; for his outstanding leadership and his personal bravery in this most hazardous situation, Staff Sergeant Davies was awarded the Distinguished Conduct Medal.

The British advance was as rapid as that of the Allied forces and the task of keeping the supply routes open and the convoys moving, even as the weather deteriorated, meant that there was no rest for the RMP sections of 174 and 203 Provost Companies who, by the end of hostilities, were strung out in a very thin line from Jubail in the Eastern Province of Saudi Arabia, to Hafr Al Batin in the north of the country, through the breach into Iraq and then on into Kuwait to a final position just to the north of Kuwait City. The troops still needed to be fed and watered, so the need to keep the supply routes open continued even after the signing of the surrender. The cessation of hostilities also heralded new tasks for the military police as patrols were mounted around Kuwait City to enforce out-of-bounds regulations and to prevent looting. Soon after that, the plan to move the division back to Jubail was drawn up and the military police deployment moved full circle in order to provide route signing and traffic control.

Although other allied nations used their military police to control enemy prisoners of war, this is not normally a task given to the Royal Military Police, however it is an RMP function to advise the staff and to escort special category prisoners. The Prisoner of War Guard Force (PWGF) formed collection, escort and guard units; a prisoner of war compound was established at Al Quaysumah and enemy prisoners processed through this facility before being handed over to the Americans and thence to the Saudi Arabian forces for holding prior to eventual re-patriation after the war. RMP involvement was limited to Major Bergin, the former FPM, and Corporal Moon, who formed a British prisoner of war liaison cell at the headquarters of 800th US MP (EPW) Brigade in Dhahran and two female Provost NCOs, Corporals Chessington and Carrington who worked with the guard force at Al Quaysumah.

In the aftermath of the Gulf War the Royal Military Police examined operational procedures and unit organisations in order to make best use of the lessons learned; there was a requirement identified for improved command and control of any future Military Police force deployed on operations so that formed units might deploy rather than composite ones; the shortcomings of some communications equipment and the excellence of others such as Ptarmigan (the Army trunk communications system) was recognised; vehicles performed well but there was never enough space particularly in administrative vehicles. Above all it was confirmed that, as at El Alamein and in Normandy, effective military police in the right numbers are an essential part of offensive military operations.

*   *   *

Part Four

Pioneer Operations

Lieutenant Colonel M C Le Masurier RLC

Early in the planning stages, it was appreciated that there was likely to be a requirement for considerable numbers of civilian workers to assist the logistic effort in the theatre of operations. The recruitment, administration and payment of local civilians in a theatre of operations is the responsibility of the Royal Pioneer Corps (RPC), who carry out a similar function for the Army in Germany through a number of Pioneer Labour Support Units (PLSUs) and it was therefore decided to form a mobile PLSU for the Middle East.

Further forward, where it is too dangerous to employ civilians, Pioneer soldiers of the RPC carry out a similar role. However, Pioneer soldiers are much more than just labourers in uniform; trained as infantrymen and with a multitude of skills they are frequently deployed overseas at section and platoon level either in support of other logistic units or in an independent role. Such tasks are normally carried out by men from 23 Group RPC, based at Bicester, and 518 Company, a field force company, was earmarked for the operation in order to allow the logistic commander extra flexibility.

The initial Pioneer contribution thus consisted of 908 PLSU, commanded by Major Martin Wyke, specifically formed for the operation, and 518 Company, commanded by Major Colin Code, consisting of a company headquarters and six platoons. To coordinate Pioneer matters a small Labour Resource branch was established at HQ FMA. In addition, a further Pioneer platoon under command HQ 7 Armoured Brigade provided security for the brigade headquarters. Later in the operation, as force levels were expanded, a second Pioneer company, 187, commanded by Major Colin Langford, was added to the Pioneer order of battle.

First to arrive at Jubail was a platoon of 518 Company with the activation party in early October. They helped 39 Engineer Regiment erect tents for 2,000 men in the commercial port in Baldrick Lines, and a number of carpenters were discovered to help with the construction of showers and field ablutions. Within a fortnight, the whole company had arrived. In the early stages, Pioneers were used to provide escorts and guards; they loaded rations and trained as chemical decontamination teams to deal with both personnel casualties and vehicles: a necessary precaution in view of the perceived Iraqi chemical capability. Another task the Pioneers took on at an early stage was the protection of the huge Ammunition Supply Point (ASP)2 to the north of Jubail. This released a company of USMC but tied down a Pioneer platoon until the end of the operation.

After the Brigade deployed into the desert to train, second line support was via the Brigade Administrative Area (BAA) where HQ 518 Company and four of its platoons were established. Throughout the training phase, the company was tasked daily by HQ BAA with tasks which included construction and protection of the brigade water point, a bulk fuel installation (BFI)[4], transfer of engines and major assemblies from forward units to repair teams, breaking bulk, provision of chemical decontamination teams to the dressing stations and the ubiquitous security tasks. This proved the value of Pioneers on hand at second line and experience was also gained in living and working in desert conditions.

As part of the reinforcement to divisional strength, a second company from 23 Group, 187 Company RPC, arrived in Saudi Arabia in January 1991. This company was five platoons strong, although one was immediately detached and put under command of 518 Company. It now became possible to put 518 Company under command of 1 (UK) Armoured Division at second line, drawing on the lessons learnt from the training phase, and the company remained with the division until operations ceased in March. The company headquarters was located in HQ DAA, which it administered and protected, and platoons were tasked by G1/G4. For the most part they were detached to dressing stations and Ordnance companies.

187 Company moved north to the FFMA where its headquarters was tasked with administration and protection. Platoons were deployed to protect bulk fuel installations and ammunition supply points just south of the Kuwaiti border and the company remained at third line under command of HQ FMA throughout the operation. As a late arrival to the theatre, 187 Company was retained to assist in the recovery operation, returning to the United Kingdom in July. One of its more unusual tasks was to recover the pipeline over the desert (PLOD).

The task of 908 PLSU was to recruit, administer and pay civil labour in support of the operation and its working procedures were based on current practice in Germany, information gleaned from commercial companies operating in Saudi Arabia and experience gained in Bahrain and Sharjah in the late 60's and early 70's. However, whereas in Germany civilian employees are recruited either through local labour exchanges or direct recruitment, no such system existed in Saudi Arabia. Instead individual contractors are licensed by the Saudi authorities to recruit workers for specific purposes. Contractors are also responsible for providing accommodation and food for their employees, most of whom originate in the Indian sub-continent, the Philippines and South Korea.

The system developed was for the PLSU to recruit the labour authorised by the staff from contractors, who in turn recruited from the countries of origin. Rates of pay were agreed with the Civil Secretariat in Riyadh and payment made monthly to contractors. As a result of this somewhat convoluted process recruitment was slow, but by March some 600 of these employees, known locally as Third Country Nationals (TCN), were working in the Jubail area. The great majority were labourers, but translators, clerks and tradesmen were also recruited, releasing soldiers to carry out military tasks.

As a result of the Falklands War the RPC had been given the task of recovering the bodies of British military war dead, and four Graves Registration Teams (GRT) were deployed to the theatre in early 1991. Past practice has been for the dead to be buried in centralised cemeteries in the theatre of operations, but pressure of public opinion after the Falklands War had resulted in an option of recovery to and burial in the United Kingdom being offered. Moreover the particular status of Saudi Arabia within Islam precluded local burial for non-Muslims and a system for recovery to the home base was established. In the event it was decided late in the day that a revised system involving increased manpower was necessary in order to evacuate the dead to Jubail in a similar way to the casualty chain, and volunteers were recruited from a number of non-RPC sources. The GRTs were responsible for the recovery and evacuation of the dead before and during the war and, after it, of those bodies returned from Iraq. They were also concerned with the local burial of Iraqi war dead.

Operation GRANBY resulted in the deployment to the Middle East of one third of the total manpower of the RPC, no mean task when further operational duties in Belize and Northern Ireland had to be maintained at the same time. The peacetime deployment of RPC officers in the Labour Resource service in Germany, which manages BAOR's civilian workforce, proved an excellent training ground for 908 PLSU. Officers used to a sophisticated and immensely complicated German industrial relations environment were able to come to grips quickly with a less complex but more idiosyncratic system, and the employment of civilians released soldiers for purely military tasks. The fact that GRTs had been trained prior to the war was important in that their sad task could be carried out quietly, effectively and with the minimum of fuss. The last minute expansion of the function also proved that a sound basis had been provided on which to do so, and much credit is owed to the officers and men involved.

The two Pioneer companies were given a great variety of tasks, many at platoon or section level. Once again the individual Pioneer soldier demonstrated his great versatility and ready acceptance of even the most unfamiliar task. Morale was invariably high, and the normal peacetime deployment of Pioneers at platoon and section level was again proved to have bred fine, confident junior leaders used to looking after their men away from their companies and working to a broad directive. Company headquarters too were of sufficient size to be able to take on such tasks as the administration of logistic groupings at HQ DAA and HQ FFMA. The detachment of a company to second line provided the division with a highly flexible and uncommitted resource. However, it did draw attention to the paucity of integral transport in Pioneer units which had to be rectified during the operation. Similarly, a lack of suitable radio, night vision and light support weapons was highlighted and addressed. Above all Operation GRANBY demonstrated yet again the versatility and 'can-do' ethos of this small corps.

*   *   *

Part Five

Catering

Lieutenant Colonel C H Noons RLC
(Staff Officer Grade 2, Catering, HQ FMA)

The deployment of a major British contingent to the heat and sand of the Middle East under operational conditions inevitably presented a considerable challenge to the catering system. An initial appreciation identified the most likely problem areas as manpower – ensuring units had enough chefs, rations, hygiene and cooking equipment. None of these problems was unique, but taken together it looked likely that Operation GRANBY would fully test the catering system to provide hot, attractive and sustaining food to the British soldier in the desert.

The first job prior to deployment was to bring GRANBY units up to their war establishment of chefs. This was very largely achieved from within BAOR and kept initial turbulence to a minimum. However, it caused a knock-on effect later when the size of the force was increased with reinforcing major units also coming from BAOR. Many which had donated chefs to bring the original force up to strength were now themselves bound for the Gulf and thus needed even greater reinforcement of chefs themselves. In Saudi Arabia itself, reinforcement resulted in transit camps such as Baldrick and Blackadder being set up. These had to rely largely upon chefs from units in transit. This was obviously unsatisfactory but manpower was now severely limited with 'rate capping' in full swing. No more army chefs were forthcoming, but the joint service approach proved more fruitful and RAF caterers were flown in, courtesy of the staff at HQ BFME. However, even this did not entirely solve the problem as units deployed forward leaving only small rear parties behind. Catering contracts were let locally in order to feed those remaining and, after some initial hiccups, standards were high. Battle casualty replacements next arrived on the scene and required careful control because of their small numbers and specialist skills. They did, however, allow catering teams to be formed to support ad hoc groupings and units, including a team formed for the reoccupation of the embassy in Kuwait.

Rationing
The peacetime rationing system involves a daily cash allowance per soldier which is then spent to buy food at service sources. However, the

wartime system is for actual issue of a fully constituted ration, rarely practised for long in peace and an inevitable source of argument when it is. Operation GRANBY was no exception and there was initially considerable disagreement between caterer and supplier. Honour was finally satisfied when the supply organisation was forced to admit that the fruit ration on one particular day, one lemon per soldier, was perhaps unsuitable. Such skirmishes rarely filtered down to the soldier and a better judgment was probably provided by the large numbers of US servicemen who contrived to find themselves in British camps at meal-times clamouring to be fed. Fresh rations were available in base areas from the start and the hire of huge refrigerated lorries even gave units in tented and field locations the ability to hold fresh stocks. Refrigerated lorries were usually driven by locally recruited drivers, including one legendary character who turned up complete with leg in plaster and waving crutches. By the end of the operation, he had progressed sufficiently to have discarded the crutches, although no comparable improvement was apparent in his driving ability. A good example of the versatility of the ration system was the provision of seasonal goodies at Christmas, including mince pies and turkey. These two items provided a heart-stopper for the chefs: thousands of mince pies arrived frozen and had to be cooked; and turkeys had to be defrosted and boned out in order to fit into field ovens. All of this, however, happened behind the scenes, the details known only to the catering fraternity.

Hygiene

Hygiene was of paramount importance in an environment of heat, dust and flies, and pertinent to both chef and customer. Normally much of the food left uneaten at one meal can be used in the preparation of another, but in the Saudi situation this was not possible and chefs had to be persuaded, against the dictates of their training, to discard anything left over. The refrigerated lorries too were extremely useful in this context and, indeed, one master chef was so determined to hang onto his that he personally drove it through the desert to Kuwait. Hygiene is also the province of environmental health advisers (see Chapter 5) and at first guidelines were rigidly applied: for instance chefs were advised to suspend business one morning when the temperature in the kitchen at Baldrick Lines reached 140° F. However, as no satisfactory answer could be provided on how to handle several thousand hungry soldiers when lunch failed to appear, this particular gem was ignored. Another major source of concern was the problem of hot water for washing up and its disposal. This was solved by continuing the US Marines' practice of issuing disposable plastic plates and cutlery at each meal. Finally, in forward areas, the practice was instituted of each soldier dipping his hands into a sanitising solution before being served. All of these precautions resulted in an excellent hygiene record and no cases of food induced illness were reported from any centralised food production unit throughout the operation.

Field Cookers

The most serious equipment problem concerned field cookers. The cooker on issue was designed to be fuelled with petrol and military chefs are well practised in field cookery. However, in practice, petrol is rarely used as it is considered to be too dangerous and LPG (Liquid Petroleum Gas) is preferred. This could not be practised on GRANBY as LPG was not available forward of Jubail and the petrol option had to be resorted to. Spares, too, were in short supply, cannibalisation was the order of the day and some non-stressed parts had to be found locally. There were a number of accidents, including explosions caused by failure in petrol vaporising tubes, and constant attention to maintenance was vital, resulting in many hours spent tightening or loosening even the smallest joint before and after each move. This time consuming process was essential in order to prevent equipment failures.

Conclusion

Operation GRANBY proved to be every bit as complex and testing for the caterers as anticipated. By and large training lessons proved sound, many long-forgotten ones were relearned together with newer strictures, such as the need to juggle specialist manpower in an artificially constrained manning environment. However, the motto of the Army Catering Corps is We Sustain, and sustain they did. Whatever crises developed behind the scenes were largely solved by the caterers themselves, and soldiers were invariably well fed throughout the operation.

*   *   *

Part Six

Finance

Lieutenant Colonel R W Thompson
(Staff Officer Grade 2, Finance, HQ FMA)

An early decision was taken to deploy myself (as SO2 Finance) and a warrant officer with the staff of HQ FMA. A Field Cash Office (FCO) was formed as the funding unit and was manned by a major and two senior NCOs. Saudi Arabian currency was not available on the London market and it was originally decided to obtain US dollars in order to pay the troops as they left Germany. The recce party, however, had confirmed that Saudi riyals was the appropriate currency except at American Service shops. As a result, the decision was made to pay troops in riyals as they arrived at Jubail.

The Arrival

First priority for the finance staff was to organise reception arrangements for the troops who would shortly be arriving. Field records had developed a system to ensure that everyone arriving in theatre was entered onto a database at a reception point between the airhead and final destination; it was at this point that other administration was also undertaken, including pay.

The finance staff opted to pay each person on arrival the sum of 200 riyals and $20. This was achieved by means of an acquittance roll[5] and included all British Army, RAF and Naval personnel including those attached from the Australian and Canadian armed forces. The pay desk was manned on a 24 hour basis by the finance staff from the advance party and was augmented in time by unit pay staff as they arrived with main bodies.[6] However, as the size of the operation grew from brigade group to division, the reception process was extended in much the same way for some three months and became a major commitment.

It soon became apparent that there had been an omission from the HQ FMA organisation in that there was no administrative organisation to look after pay and documentation for members of the headquarters itself. This would normally have been provided by the FMA signals squadron, but in this case the squadron had no integral pay support. It was necessary, therefore, for my warrant officer and I to 'double-hat' and fill that role too. The pay office was eventually supplemented by battle casualty replacements (BCRs) and was able to provide a basic administrative service, one of the most important aspects of which was the publication of Part 2 Orders.[7] As there were insufficient pay clerks amongst the BCRs, two female supply specialists were co-opted and trained in the intricacies of Part 2 Order publication. They made a significant contribution to the administration of the FMA.

Role of the Field Cash Office

The FCO soon moved to a permanent site at Camp 4 and became the focus for funding for the whole of the Jubail-based deployment. It even funded a second FCO which later supported the 1 (UK) Armoured Division. The tasks of the FCO were to issue cash to imprest (public) and non-public (regimental) fund holders and pay all bills. It was also responsible for taking in cash from units and other official organisations such as forces post offices, the Expeditionary Forces Institute and the operational canteen service. A currency exchange service was also provided and the FCO acted as pay office to those soldiers who had no unit pay support. In carrying out its role, the FCO issued £82.8m during the period October 1990 to February 1991, almost £63m of which was spent during December and January. The highest bills were for accommodation and amounted to £32m, with stores, £14m, and vehicle hire, £12m, running second and third.

One of the most important decisions concerning allowances which was made very early in the deployment was to issue a water allowance of 25 riyals per day (about £3.50) to those at Jubail and forward. This decision was taken by HQ BFME in Riyadh based upon a local regulation made some years before and without any reference to, or authority from, MOD. Water allowance was issued locally in cash. Once payment had started it was allowed to continue and did so until July 1991 when local overseas allowance (LOA)[8] was adjusted to take such factors into account. Until then, throughout the period of the operation, although Saudi Arabia was an LOA area, the LOA rate was zero for all ranks below lieutenant colonel.

The nature of the Gulf deployment resulted in soldiers not necessarily being able to visit their own pay offices. The pay system therefore required sufficient flexibility to allow them to receive cash, including water allowance, at any location. This raised a problem concerning safeguards as it was obviously undesirable for soldiers to be able to overdraw by going from one pay office to another collecting the same allowance several times. A safeguard was achieved by introducing a card, similar to the erstwhile army pay book, which every soldier and officer was required to carry. Cash drawn was recorded on the card wherever issued and unless a card was produced there was a limit to the amount that could be drawn. Use of the card was not at that stage a formal pay services procedure but as a result of our experience it was adopted for use in future operations.

The Problems of Medical Reservists

Some of the medical and dental officers deployed were reservists recalled for the emergency. Most were from civilian practices and, as a result, almost inevitably suffered financially. To compensate for this, a top-up allowance was introduced, and designed to enhance military salaries to the level of earnings lost as a result of the reservists' call up for military service. Doctors and dentists were required to provide evidence in support of claims and the process was slow and laborious. Many officers returned to their practices at the end of the operation with claims still not met. It was probably the only feature which could be considered to have been a failure as far as the pay services were concerned. It resulted in the paymasters of the field hospitals coming under a great deal of pressure and caused resentment amongst the officers concerned.

Telephone Cards

Another unfamiliar area that pay staffs became involved in was the control and issue of telephone cards. Mercury telephones were installed in a number of locations and phonecards were held by the FCO for issue to units for sale to soldiers. The FCO also sold cards directly over the counter. At Christmas the Royal British Legion donated sufficient phonecards to Operation GRANBY for a free issue to all serving in Saudi Arabia. This issue was controlled by my staff at HQ FMA using nominal rolls produced by the field records database.

Non Public-Funds

In addition to public fund accounting, every unit maintained some sort of regimental fund. Many operated shops selling sweets, drinks and even desert boots and there were a number of grants made to the operation which allowed items of comfort to be purchased. The HQ BAOR welfare fund, for example, gave £5,000 to set up the Operation GRANBY welfare fund which was controlled by the SO2 Finance. It was sometimes difficult to spend the money; much was made available from public funds or by donations from commercial organisations. A regular monthly rebate from the EFI (NAAFI) was shared among units with a proportion going into the GRANBY welfare fund. In March 1991, the £5,000 granted by BAOR was able to be returned as so much money had been accumulated in the theatre of operations.

Currency Exchange

There was always a brisk business in currency exchange at pay offices. Mostly it was exchange between Saudi riyals and US dollars to allow soldiers to shop at the American PXs.[9] Later, as troops prepared to return home, it became necessary to obtain sterling and deutschmarks so that they could dispose of their Saudi currency before leaving. Huge amounts of pounds and DMs were flown in by the RAF and taken on charge by the FCO. At one stage £4m was sent from Jubail to Kuwait by the only means of dispatch – the forces postal system. When, after three days it had not arrived, the officer commanding the FCO became visibly nervous for the first time since deployment. Needless to say, the box turned up intact.

Documentation
Pay documentation was kept simple and new Part 2 Order occurrences were designed in due course to take account of new entitlements. For example, soldiers living in married quarters in Germany were paying a facilities charge (community charge) which was abated by half while they were serving in the Gulf. A new standard entry was designed to report the occurrence. All Part 2 Orders were manual because PAMPAS, the unit administration computer system, had not been deployed. It was felt at the beginning that conditions would not be favourable to PAMPAS. Sand clogging the works was envisaged and maintenance was considered too difficult. In the event these fears were unfounded and many computers were used in the Gulf without problem. It was a serious mistake to revert to manual reporting and it slowed the passage of information considerably.

Conclusion
The role of Finance Branch and of paymasters and pay staff attached to units may not have been an overtly important contribution to the successful outcome of the war. Their role was to pay operational bills, to ensure that all troops received as much cash as they wanted while deployed, and to complete the documentation necessary for the correct administration of soldiers' pay. This included ensuring that recurring claims such as boarding school allowances were actioned on time. Soldiers are more effective when they are free from financial worry and concern over their families; the RAPC helped to eliminate some of these outside pressures. The post operation report revealed that little would change in the pay function area if a similar deployment were to be undertaken again. That in itself is a measure of the well tried systems in place.

*   *   *

Part Seven

Field Records

Major J Bailey RAPC
(Officer Commanding Field Records Office, Gulf)

In September 1990 I and seven soldiers were warned to set up a Field Records unit for the 7 Armoured Brigade Group. The last time such a unit had been mobilised had been during the Falklands War and those involved with running it had long since left the Army. Armed with the four page Falklands post-operation report and the Unit Guide to Administration of Personnel in War, the newly appointed officer commanding set to work to design a viable field records system for the Gulf.

Establishing the System
It soon became apparent that the sheer quantity of data involved would necessitate the use of some form of computer system and a prime requirement was that it would need to be sufficiently rugged to cope with the terrain and heat of the Gulf. At this stage a bid for equipment to be procured was initiated and a programmer tasked to write the software. At this early stage of the operation it was not known what statistical information would be required and, in the time available, properly structured programmes could not be written. The equipment was ordered on 20 September 1990; three days later a system was configured by GRID Computers engineers, and, on 26 September, it was delivered to 1 (UK) Armoured Division at Verden, ready to accept data. Whilst all this activity was taking place, units had been tasked to produce nominal rolls[10] and mobilisation prints of their personnel in order that data capture might take place. However, it was quickly obvious that, in the limited time available, it would not be possible to input all data manually; the RAPC computer centre at Worthy Down near Winchester was therefore asked to provide an extract of records from its mainframe of all units taking part in the operation. This extract was not a success and it was decided that the only way to establish an accurate theatre location index (TLI) would be to book each arrival into the theatre as personnel arrived from the airhead. In the meantime, vehicles, equipment and stationery were being procured, and the whole unit underwent a three day military training package. On 13 October 1990 field records flew to Jubail and the system was established in a hangar ready to receive 7 Armoured Brigade.

As the Brigade arrived in Saudi Arabia many hours were spent inputting data from officers and soldiers; the process taking around four minutes per person. Manual Part 2 Orders were used to pass information between units and field records in Saudi Arabia and the various documentation, manning and record offices in the United Kingdom, and many units were found to be very rusty on the necessary procedures. In November field records became a theatre asset and thus directly under command of HQ BFME at Riyadh. This made it necessary to take all land based Navy and RAF personnel in the Gulf onto the database, swelling numbers to 12,500. Once 1 (UK) Armoured Division was warned for Operation GRANBY, the sheer weight of numbers made it obvious that the system used to check in 7 Armoured Brigade on arrival would no longer be feasible and that some form of interface between PAMPAS (the units' computer) and Field Records was necessary. As a result a new programme was produced and each unit supplying soldiers was asked for a complete backup of its PAMPAS data to allow transfer to take place. This resulted in a PAMPAS table being built and as each soldier arrived in theatre, his regimental number was input by an operator who would then check details held with the individual. This reduced the time required for data input to an average of one minute per soldier. Once a chalk[12] had passed through the check-in point and the numbers tallied, a tape dump of new data was taken to Field Records (Main) and sucked into the database, allowing timely and accurate statistics to be passed to HQ BFME and JHQ at High Wycombe. By the end of the conflict, field records had 37,546 service personnel on its active database and 2,500 on its historical record. The manpower required to run this specialist unit had increased from the original one officer and seven to two officers and 54. There were also 66 Kuwaiti interpreters.

Once up and running, benefits of the system were quickly appreciated by the chain of command; and a further warrant officer was seconded to the Gulf to hot programme in order to produce prints and statistics which had not been envisaged when the system was established. It was also found necessary to deploy systems, with their associated manpower, to HQ BFME, and into the desert with the Divisional Administrative Area (DAA) of 1 (UK) Armoured Division, the prisoner of war cage and the two field hospitals. In order to allow these deployed detachments to communicate, the Ptarmigan tactical area communication system was adapted to allow data to be passed into the main system and into a series of laptop computers. The field hospitals, for instance, passed their admission and discharge books in signal format; field records updated their database, and then passed casualty notification signals directly to MOD via the MAPPER worldwide computer system.

Casualties

Although actual casualties during the war were light 2,500 casualty occurrences of one sort or another (mostly of a minor nature) were passed via Field Records to the United Kingdom. Ninety five per cent were reported directly from the hospitals and only a modest 5 per cent from units. This was largely a result of the first class communications between field hospitals and Field Records. Eventually individual units received laptop computers but too late in the day to be significant. Considerable political importance had been placed on the need for a system which could report casualties quickly and accurately to the MOD and it was recognised as essential that information was received and passed to relatives before being released to the media. To ensure that Field Records in Saudi Arabia and the casualty reporting chains in Germany and the United Kingdom could cope with large numbers of occurrences, a three day casualty reporting exercise was conducted prior to the commencement of hostilities. This resulted in some 12,000 casualty details being successfully passed, through Field Records to the casualty chains, at the same time producing accurate statistical information to commanders in theatre. This was the most extensive casualty reporting exercise to be conducted since the Second World War.

Prisoner of War

Initially, a low priority was afforded to establishing a prisoner of war database, but once the requirement had been identified some 26 laptops with the software loaded were deployed. These were used for data capture, and prisoners were asked a series of questions via interpreters at the divisional cage. Individual computers were downloaded onto a master every 12 hours, and thence via Ptarmigan to the field records computer at Jubail. Detail, such as photographs, capture cards and 'Anxious for News' letters together with back-up floppy discs was also passed daily by courier to Jubail for reconciliation and mail transfer to the Prisoner of War Information Bureau (PWIB) in London. To speed up the passage of information a disc fax link was established with MOD and data passed daily. This ensured that the PWIB had the same information as Field Records for the 5,200 prisoners of war who were eventually registered.

Conclusion

The operation demonstrated that computer systems were able to work in an environment such as the Gulf and that immediate statistical and casualty details were available from them. To ensure system resilience, duplicate equipment, which was updated twice daily, was located far enough away from the main system to survive hostile attack. The lessons learned in the Gulf have not been forgotten. As a direct result of the success of the Field Records unit deployed to the operation, the

Adjutant General commissioned a study which reported in April 1992 and was endorsed in May of that year. The study has now become a project and a second version of the Field Records Support System (FRSS) has been issued to various formations and training units. The FRSS is now available for deployment to any operational theatre.

Chapter Nine

Relations with the Host Nation and Support Arrangements

Lieutenant Colonel G A Hill RLC
(Staff Officer, Grade 1, Host Nation Support)

Major J Rigby, Coldm Gds
(Staff Officer, Grade 2, Host Nation Support)

Mr Andrew Moffat, *Defence Lands*

Any force deploying outside its home base is normally heavily dependent upon a wide range of Host Nation Support (HNS) such as transport, labour and goods of all sorts and the Gulf War was no exception. Interfaces need to be developed with government and commercial organisations and these are the primary responsibilities of the G5 Division of the General Staff. This branch tends to be the Cinderella of any headquarters as it lacks the glamour of the operational staff and does not decide and execute grand concepts. Instead, it responds to user needs or resolves problems which have already arisen. Its tools are diplomacy and negotiation backed up by an intimate understanding of what may be, to a greater or lesser extent, a different culture. Patience, flexibility and a capacity to understand another point of view are essential prerequisites for any G5 officer while an ability to apologise for perceived slights is an asset. The need for a G5 presence within HQ FMA was recognised from the outset, although resources were scarce.

There was always potential for political disaster and local misunderstandings during Operation GRANBY. The majority of the British forces committed had not been further east than Berlin and were used to a European Christian ethos. Although many briefings had taken place before deployment, the majority were not prepared for life in the Kingdom of Saudi Arabia. However, the Army was fortunate in having officers available who had previously been seconded to or served with Arab Forces in the Middle East. The quality of their spoken Arabic varied greatly, but their main advantage was that they understood and respected the Arab way of life and culture. The fact that problems were contained to relatively minor irritations demonstrated the innate ability of the British soldier to adapt, as well as reflecting the high standards of leadership and the sheer hard work of both the Saudi and British liaison staffs. The complete lack of alcohol also helped.

Early Days

By the time the FMA pre-advance party arrived in Jubail on 8 October 1990, much had already been accomplished. Lieutenant Colonel Barry Aitken, who had been left behind after the recce, had established a close working relationship with the USMC, HQ 1 Marine Expeditionary Force (MEF) in Jubail and with the officer nominated as Commercial Port Manager. He had started negotiations for the allocation of Camp 4 from the Royal Commission, various areas of hard standing and two cargo sheds in the Commercial Port. Of more immediate importance to the pre-advance party was his acquisition of the Port Clearance Office block which was to be HQ FMA until early December (see Figure 3.3).

Meanwhile, Lieutenant Tom Lishman and his Local Resources Section (LRS) RAOC had based themselves in the offices of a local shipping agent and were busy procuring goods and services on the local economy. Tom had also negotiated the lease of a large refrigerated store and adjacent land (Al Berri). This complex was to be expanded as our commitment increased, and would become crucial to the supply operation.

Major John Rigby took over G5 responsibilities on 17 October when Lieutenant Colonel Aitken returned to Germany. John spent the first week familiarising himself with the town of Jubail and establishing relations with his Allied opposite numbers, members of the Saudi Arabian military liaison organisation and officials of the Royal Commission. HQ MEF had several departments engaged on HNS, real estate, public affairs and contracts. All worked from the Commercial Port except the contracts department which had set up offices in the Royal Commission's industrial area to provide convenient access for local businessmen. A very large organisation indeed, compared to G5 HQ FMA which never numbered more than two officers and, for a brief spell, one Defence Lands Agent.

Lieutenant Colonel Ashaq Al Saqar was the Saudi Arabian Army Liaison Officer (SALO) for all Allied forces in the Jubail area. A big man in every sense, he worked tirelessly to ensure that our needs were met; that the local population was affected as little as possible by our activities and that the interests of the Royal Commission and other property owners were safeguarded. The Anglo-Saudi HNS agreement was still under negotiation, so although he gave valuable advice and assistance on the best or most reliable sources of supply, he was not, at that time, able to provide the burgeoning amount of support required. Consequently, authority to purchase goods and services, in anticipation of the HNS agreement, was given by the Civil Secretariat at HQ BFME in Riyadh. On their advice, G5 and Supply devised a system to monitor demands and to establish levels of authority consistent with degrees of expense. It also served to put Commander FMA's mind at rest! Completed demands were then passed to the relevant staff branch – Supply, Labour Resources, Engineer, Catering etc, or to LRS – for action. Contracts and bills were consolidated and sent to HQ BFME for later submission to the Saudi authorities. Contracts for real estate were managed in much the same way, but its acquisition was to be fraught with problems which would consume a large proportion of John Rigby's time during the next four months.

The Royal Commission for Jubail and Yanbu was set up in the seventies to provide port, industrial and manufacturing bases on the Gulf and the Red Sea. The Jubail project comprises large areas to the North of the town, divided into industrial, support, light engineering and residential sections. Units are leased to firms and businesses for specific purposes under strict contractual terms. Many of the units were vacant and many more, although occupied, would be offered to the Allies as our real estate requirements were established.

In many ways the modern town of Jubail was an anachronism which might well have become a white elephant. The Royal Commission had planned and begun a huge industrial area adjacent to the port but this was to be privately financed and the Commission had laid down stringent rules to ensure the proper completion of projects before commercial operations could begin. At the time that we deployed into the Jubail area much of the construction work was unfinished and the recession was beginning to bite. While the facilities were ideal for the logistic elements of a field force, the Royal Commission were determined to ensure that the Allies should not occupy any facilities until they were properly completed. While this was a source of irritation, it did demonstrate a very farsighted view by the local planners and perhaps even a confidence that Allied success would be swift.

The Americans had concentrated the vast majority of their assets in the Commercial Port and in the Royal Commission's industrial area. In drawing up our own deployment plan, there were many factors to consider. The USMC Port Manager and the Commercial Port authorities made it clear that we were expected to move out of the port as soon as possible; an understandable attitude in view of the huge numbers of American personnel to be accommodated and the vast quantities of vehicles and equipment to be dumped. It was, in any case, assumed that the Port would be an important strategic target and although HQ FMA and some units of the FMA would have to remain in, or near the Port, others could be dispersed. Other considerations included protection, security, communications and proximity to main routes. One further assumption was made: that at the conclusion of the operation, recovery would be made through Jubail. Other options were later to be considered, but it was agreed that the most logical option was to roll back the logistical tail to its point of origin. This would be significant because whereas during the build-up, troops and equipment were moving through Jubail in reasonably manageable packets, on recovery, all theatre assets could descend upon the town at the same time. Transit facilities would have to be provided, not only for battle-weary units, but also for their vehicles, weapons and stores.

Successes and Frustrations

Word soon got around Jubail that the British Army was in the property business. The Headquarters was inundated with 'phone calls and visitors, all of whom had exactly what we were looking for and at the right price! The first priority was for a field hospital and several sites had been recced before deciding on the Goodyear Tyre showroom in the Royal Commission area. It became apparent during negotiations that no special arrangement was possible and that market forces prevailed. Close liaison with the USMC G5 branch to rule out competition, and with the Civil Secretariat, negated this to some extent, but the sudden demand for property inevitably drove up prices.

Lieutenant Colonel Al Saqer was by this time working under a great deal of pressure and was spending most of his time looking after the interests of the US Forces, whose problems were obviously more numerous and on a greater scale than ours. Consequently, Commander FMA's request for a dedicated SALO was well received and on 1 November Captain Yusuf bin Musa'id bin Abdulaziz Al Saud (UKSALO) reported for duty.

His first suggestion was that we retain the services of a local agent, approved by the Saudi Ministry of Defence and Aviation (MODA), to advise on the selection of suitable properties, to ensure that contracts were drawn up in accordance with civil law and that realistic rates were charged. The appointment of Abdulaziz Hussein of the Arabian Supply & Architectural Contracting Company and the adoption of the official MODA leasing contract would, it was hoped, ensure that our contracts would be retrospectively accepted when the HNS agreement was signed. This was to be the case.

Several sites belonging to the Royal Commission had been identified as fulfilling requirements for a Bulk Refuelling Installation (BFI), a Helicopter Landing Site (HLS) for the hospital and a Medical Storage complex. Lessees were not allowed to sub-let without the permission of the Royal Commission and this was not, in some cases, forthcoming. A meeting was therefore arranged on 3 November between Commander FMA and the Director of the Royal Commission in order to establish contact; to submit our immediate requirements and to agree procedures for further requests. UKSALO was present at the meeting and it was largely due to his efforts that we were allowed to proceed with negotiations. Similar meetings were to take place throughout the operation and Major Rigby was in daily contact with the Royal Commission. Consequently, a good working relationship was maintained but there were problems; and these were caused largely by ignorance of local customs and by precipitate unilateral action by units in exceeding the terms of agreement.

These problems were invariably dealt with, on behalf of the Royal Commission and the townspeople, by Lieutenant Colonel Al Saqer. On 20 October, John Rigby was summoned to his office to be told that the Port Director had received complaints of indiscretion and nakedness in Baldrick Lines. The showers were by now up and running, and soldiers were drying themselves in the open. Such conduct was insulting to the local people and must cease. These summons were to occur frequently and involved a number of minor indiscretions by our soldiers; military vehicles exceeding the speed limits; female soldiers driving and being in public places with legs or arms bare, and so on.

When units began training in the desert, reports flooded in of camels being killed by tank and artillery fire. This involved the G5 staff picking their way gingerly through acres of craters and unidentifiable ordnance to count and inspect the beasts. All appeared to be fairly ordinary animals, but when the claims came in, they were invariably described as thoroughbred racing camels; all female and all pregnant! On one occasion, when a deal had finally been agreed and coffee was being served, Major Rigby asked the grieving owner if he'd like us to shoot some more of his camels. It took a moment for the penny to drop before he burst into fits of laughter.

In early November, the first visit by members of the Civil Secretariat took place. These were of great value in ensuring that G5 and other staff branches at HQ FMA were working in line with policies thus far developed, and that records for subsequent submission to MODA when the HNS Agreement was signed, were being maintained. During the first visit, Commander FMA requested that a Civil Secretariat representative be permanently attached. No one could be spared from the Riyadh office, but on 15 December Mr Andrew Moffat, seconded from Defence Lands in the United Kingdom, arrived in Jubail.

Meanwhile, HQ FMA had moved into Old Port Barracks (OPB) and about 20 properties had been leased. Some were on Royal Commission land but, in accordance with the deployment plan, most were to the south and south-west of the town. A major crisis occurred in mid-December when, having negotiated the use of a large area of land at the entrance to the Industrial Port and, having earmarked it for the arrival of 1 (UK) Armoured Division, we were told that it was no longer available. All attempts to notify senior members of HQ FMA of this development failed. They had disappeared on some unspecified urgent business to an unknown destination! Major Rigby was also keeping a low profile for the vessels were being unloaded and approximately 1,000 vehicles were moving towards the Industrial Port. The Royal Commission ordered their immediate removal, which was, in the circumstances, impossible: we had nowhere to move them to and their drivers had dispersed to other duties.

The crisis was to prove fortuitous because a vast tract of land adjacent to the Commercial Port was offered instead. On 20 December, the site was recced and it was decided that it would be perfect for the post-operational concentration of vehicles and equipment. Pictures of the area were to appear in many newspapers during the recovery phase. Further discussion with the Royal Commission followed and it was agreed that we could remain in the Industrial Port, but were to move the vehicles – and the Tank Transporter Regiment headquarters which had appeared overnight – as soon as possible. This we did!

Defence Lands in Jubail

By November it had become clear to John Rigby and Commander FMA that the real estate problem was now a major issue requiring professional support and the Civil Secretary HQ BFME in Riyadh turned to Defence Lands for assistance. The Defence Lands Service are the professional real estate managers for the MOD with offices throughout the United Kingdom and overseas stations. Their work varies from the acquisition and disposal of all types of land and property to management of the agricultural estates which form part of training areas. The situation in Jubail was clearly in need of their expertise. Mr Andy Moffat volunteered to assist and was given military kit, a crash course in NBC survival and some very rapid briefings. He flew out to Riyadh where the Civil Secretary and the staff of BFME briefed him in detail on his responsibilities before the long drive to Jubail on 11 December 1990. He then embarked on what he subsequently realised was to be the busiest but most rewarding period of his life.

The need was pressing since accommodation was needed for the imminent arrival of 1 (UK) Armoured Division. At the same time, the Americans were also building up and the competition for real estate was fierce. Mr Moffat began to experience the problems which had already been clearly identified by John Rigby and soon began to make a vital contribution to the G5 Team. He soon realised that all land, even the desert, belonged to somebody, but it was not always clear who had title. No central Land Registry existed and some individuals even claimed false title with the aim of negotiating a good price with the British Force before approaching the real owner with their own, knocked down bid. Our local agent, Abdul Aziz, proved to be an invaluable ally in resolving these disputes and providing sound advice on the more outrageous prices.

The standard of living accommodation varied from disused workers' camps previously occupied by contract labour through the good barrack style accommodation to the lavish (and expensive) European style houses and bungalows. During the reception phases, some 13,000 bed spaces were required at the peak, but a requirement was stated subsequently for a further 20,000 bed spaces for recovery. In the event, the availability of accommodation was a major factor in recovering the Force through Jubail. If it had not been for the foresight shown in setting up these base facilities, the soldiers would have spent even longer in the desert waiting for call forward to fly home.

The involvement of Mr Moffat began to show benefits quickly. He had the professional expertise to enter into negotiations with local owners and achieved reductions in costs at a time of rising demand for increasingly scarce accommodation. He wore a uniform which associated him with the Force and greatly assisted him in his dealings with both the local authorities and contractors. In effect, he became the local representative of the Civil Secretary and took over much of the routine day-to-day dealings at Jubail, particularly on the developing HN agreement. His expertise was adjudged to extend beyond normal lands matters to the effects of explosions on buildings, vehicle disposal, and other contract matters.

With hindsight, it is clear that a Defence Lands Officer was required earlier in the operation as indeed were contracts personnel. It was, therefore, most unfortunate that Andrew was recalled from the potential combat area to the relative safety of Riyadh when the air war started. Much remained to be done and his removal made links with the Civil Secretary more difficult. Some commitment is required if civilians are to deploy with a force since their support becomes incredible if they are to be removed at the outbreak of hostilities. It is also extremely bad for the morale of individual volunteers.

Forward Operations

The need to deploy and inload an FFMA also required enhancements and a need for another G5 staff officer was identified. Lieutenant Colonel Geoff Hill was despatched from BAOR and after a brief sojourn in Jubail, he moved out with the advance party which was to set up HQ FFMA. The creation and inloading of the FFMA has been described elsewhere but the local population (or the lack of it) was to inhibit G5 activities.

Adjacent to the FFMA was a small Arab settlement that the Americans had charitably christened a three-horse-town. This hamlet was hard pressed to muster three camels let alone three horses, but it soon became an entrepreneurial hotbed with probably the world's greatest sales per head of population for mattresses, heaters and alcohol-free beer. To their credit, this small row of shops never seemed to be without stock, despite the constant demands of the passing American and British trade.

The majority of logistic traffic turned off the road at this point, crossed the tapline and deployed into what had been virgin desert, but rapidly became a hive of activity. Some 10 kilometres to the south lay an ARAMCO (Arab American Oil Company) pumping station and airstrip which was to be home for an American helicopter battalion, but that was it! Apart from three Bedouin camps and a small Saudi Arabian National Guard detachment with ARAMCO, there were no inhabitants in the area and even the nomads had moved on to the south or up into Iraq. The nearest centre of population was Al Quaysumah to the west with its own brand new airport. The Director of the airport had recently arrived with the intention of enjoying the simple life with only two flights daily, but the airport was now handling American fixed-wing aircraft and was to develop into a vital airhead for us in support of the coming land operations. The bewildered Director sensibly took a low profile, but was always willing to assist in allocation of any real estate which the Americans had not already occupied. Apart from the airfield, there was very little at Al Quaysumah apart from small shops, some local government offices and a poor water supply. The real prize for G5 was Hafr Al Batin which was 20 kms further on – but off limits to the G5 staff for operational security reasons. The fact that the British were in the area was to be kept secret, although the constant stream of uniquely British vehicles into the desert would have raised interest from the simplest intelligence agent!

Despite the problems of not being able to deal with local government authorities in Hafr, Geoff Hill began developing local links wherever possible, although in the early stages, this was constrained to discussing matters with the few locals still in the area. However, Hill's Arabic, if not his digestion, was improved by some very basic discussions with a Bangladeshi goatherd. He was also heard to mutter something about the unfairness of being drowned in the desert as he stood on the tail board of a dug-in office truck and watched the rains gradually fill up the great hole which had been so laboriously created.

When the inload of the FFMA began, the G5 staff became busier, resolving the few local problems created by setting up a large logistic installation in what had been an empty space. One unfortunate local was singularly unimpressed when he returned home on his customary route in the driving rain and found that he was trying to cross a ploughed field created by DROPS vehicles inloading the ammunition supply point. He was even less impressed when he sought British assistance to recover his bogged pickup and was promptly arrested as a potential Iraqi agent! He was eventually delivered to the local police post where he was greeted as a long lost friend and, after much coffee, all was forgiven and forgotten.

A further complication for the G5 staff was that the FFMA was in a different Saudi Military District to Jubail and separate liaison channels had to be set up. Links were developed with the Saudi Liaison Staff based in the military complex at King Khaled Military City (KKMC) which was an awe-inspiring military town created in the desert that was now a frenzy of American, French and Saudi activity. Colonel Mohammed Nasir al Qahtani was to lead the Saudi Liaison Team and became a staunch supporter and determined friend, despite the other pressures placed on him by Allied Forces on the spot. As to the Americans, they had brought in the advance party of their own Civil Affairs (CA) Battalion. These individuals were an extremely friendly and enthusiastic group who did not seem to be overemployed. However, some official frostiness developed when the British element realised that one task for the CA Battalion was likely to be provision of military government in any occupied areas of Iraq. Commander FFMA made it quite clear to Lieutenant Colonel Hill that he was not to start developing contingency plans as Governor of Southern Iraq, and it was assumed that other minds were actively addressing the question of civilian government if the Allies were to remain in Iraq.

The route to KKMC actually passed through the suburbs of Hafr Al Batin and it was galling not to be able to contact the local agencies. Eventually, G5 were officially allowed into Hafr, although the gloss was tarnished when soldiers of the American 101st Division politely, but firmly, arrested Lieutenant Colonel Hill as he was recceing a quarry! Work now began in earnest to develop the local links so necessary if the British were to operate effectively in the area. Contacts were established with the Emir, the Police and providers of local utilities. Routes and the construction of new roads were cleared with the local authorities while engineer resources were identified. A reverse charge call facility was generously provided by ARAMCO for telephone calls to Europe, but the greatest success was gaining access to a water pipeline running from Hafr to KKMC which was subsequently used as the main water source for the Division until it was well on its way into Kuwait (see Chapter 3 Part 3). G5 were also closely involved with the Army's own water diviner, Major Tom Ogilvie–Graham of the Royal Army Veterinary Corps. Quite why this officer had become such an expert on water was unclear, but the fact remained that he was extremely successful in finding sources and needed G5 support in liaising with local agencies.

Reflections

Despite the number of tasks and the need to liaise with local agencies, Hafr Al Batin was the only major town in the vicinity of the FFMA and on the Divisional route to the breach. In consequence, the G5 task was not particularly onerous in the forward areas because units and formations were able to move and set up without meeting locals or needing clearance for their activities. However, this would not necessarily be the case for future operations and G5 support must be considered and properly resourced. In particular, the chief G5 officer must have the rank and status necessary to open doors of both the Host Nation and Allies if liaison is to be effective and the force is to obtain the support it needs. Similarly, Commanders and their staffs need to recognise that relations with the Host Nation are a staff function and that the G5 staff have responsibilities beyond interpreting.

A constant concern for all those using HNS was its reliability. In the earliest stages of the deployment, contracts had been negotiated locally and funded nationally in the expectation of eventually recovering some or all of the costs. However, the stated aim was to develop a formal Host Nation Agreement which would define responsibilities and funding arrangements. The Americans had operated under such an agreement from their arrival with mixed success and the British Forces were extremely wary of the effects of such an agreement on the effectiveness of their logistic support. In particular, the scrutiny requirements appeared to be too complex for an operational situation while contractors had little confidence that their bills would be paid as readily by the Saudi Government. In the event, most of the major contractual and logistic activities were achieved before the Host Nation agreement was introduced. A subsequent attempt to test systems by seeking engineer plant under the agreement demonstrated a willingness to succeed, but unfortunately the time taken would not have met operational needs nor was the plant of the required quality. The need to staff HNS bids to the Civil Contracts staff in Riyadh from Jubail and the FFMA also created problems. The communications difficulties were apparent during the build up and it is extremely unlikely that any major requirements for HNS would have been met in a timely fashion if operations had been protracted. The deployment and training of the Defence Lands Officer demonstrated that Civil Servants are willing to volunteer and move up to the 'sharp end', but this support should be formalised. If the Civil Service intends to deploy personnel to operational theatres, they must either be prepared to move forward or delegate appropriate authority to those on the ground.

When land operations had ceased, the G5 staff concentrated in Jubail and began to consider how the hard won resources were to be used and eventually handed back to the Host Nation. Many interesting and varied conversations took place between the G5 organisation and regimental commanding officers as units argued priorities for accommodation in the relative luxury of Jubail. At the same time, there was a pressing need for working accommodation for logistic units involved in the recovery of the Division, its equipment and the enormous amount of ammunition which had not been fired. It was at this stage that the forethought of the planners reaped dividends since units were dekitted, transitted and flown out while the backloading began in earnest.

Many of those involved in the later stages of the operation may argue that the return of the Division to the UK was carried out with indecent haste and without due consideration of the aftermath. There is little doubt that, but for reinforcement by MOD Contracts Staff, the local contractors would have profited from this early departure. The force had assumed that deployment, operations and recovery would take at least one year and estate contracts had been let accordingly. Considerable expertise was required by officials who were despatched to address contractual issues and these activities are covered in greater detail in Chapter 11. However, there is no doubt that contracts would have been better written if Contracts Staff with adequate authority and understanding of the military requirements had deployed initially with HQ FMA.

The recovery is discussed in more detail later, but a significant lesson from the operation was the need for dedicated G5 Staff to support operations outside the homebase. The British Army has often depended upon gifted amateurs available within its establishment, but this can no longer be guaranteed, particularly if future deployments are outside traditional areas of interest. The civil–military interface needs should be defined, sources of training identified and appropriate resources allocated.

Chapter Ten

1 (UK) Armoured Division Logistic Operations

Brigadier G A Ewer CBE
(DCOS, 1 (UK) Armoured Division)

This chapter summarises Combat Service Support (CSS) activities within 1 (UK) Armoured Division from the first warning order to the return of HQ 1 (UK) Armoured Division (Rear)[1] to Verden in April 1991. At the height of the Operation, over 13,000 men and women were involved in the Division's rear area providing CSS to the fighting troops. Justice cannot be done in the space available to the sterling work of each individual or unit who came together to form the complex and extensive team effort required. The emphasis here is upon the orchestration of that effort and the points of history of best value for the future. It goes without saying that without the soldier to do the job, none of this could or would have happened.

The Deployment of 7 Armoured Brigade

In January 1990, the prospect of a full scale Divisional operational deployment seemed, at the very least, remote! Although events in Germany the previous year heralded change, at that time such change pointed more towards a reduced threat and less operational opportunity than to imminent operations. Nevertheless, a full training year was planned and organised, building on the experience gained during the Division's major exercise in the autumn of 1989. The 1990 training year included a work up series of command post exercises (CPX), a two week full logistic exercise (LOGEX), and participation by the Divisional Headquarters in the Corps CPX, Exercise SUMMER SALES[2] in July 1990. Insofar as the logistic activity of the Division was concerned, two important developments were to be examined during the year: first, the introduction of DROPS and the effect this would have on logistic support operations; and, second, further work on the organisation of the divisional Rear Headquarters, in particular, how it should be mounted and its Step Up capability to enable it to move effectively. Amongst other things, mounting divisional Rear Headquarters in ISO containers was under trial. Against this backdrop, all logistic plans were under review and the Division's service commanders were actively involved in reviewing Standing Operating Procedure (SOPs). A change of GOCs was also in prospect, as well as handovers between the principal Heads of Service during the year. It soon turned out that the Division could hardly have had a better programme of preparation for the events that subsequently unfolded. Certainly its logistic staff, in all disciplines, were tuned to change and looking forward to different challenges to those which had been faced in the previous decade.

The planned training year developed well and by the time of Exercise SUMMER SALES, the Divisional Rear Headquarters and its Service[3] headquarters were well worked up with practised procedures and a firm understanding of the feasibility of a more mobile combat supplies deployment, as well as more responsive casualty evacuation and main-tenance procedures. During Exercise SUMMER SALES, Divisional Rear headquarters practised one level up as a Corps headquarters, providing a valuable insight into Combat Service Support (CSS) at the operational level for the G1/4 Operations Staff and the Services alike. Events unfolded quickly after SUMMER SALES in July. Key staff taking late summer leave did so with a slight preoccupation, as the GOC was drawn in to the early discussion of options for United Nations action in the face of Iraqi aggression. By the second week in September, it was clear that the commitment of British armoured forces was a distinct possibility; 7 Armoured Brigade, equipped with Challenger 1 (British Main Battle Tank) and Warrior (British Infantry Fighting Vehicle), with a well practised headquarters, and units well worked up at BATUS (British Army Training Unit Suffield), the British Army's live firing and manoeuvre facility in Canada, was a prime candidate for deployment. On 14 September 1990, the intention to declare 7 Armoured Brigade for Gulf operations was made public. Much had to be done, and in quick time. There were a number of specific areas to be addressed in the logistic field. First, 7 Armoured Brigade was not equipped logistically for independent operations. Its CSS was based upon the standard BAOR framework of the divisional logistic system, within which all logistic resources are controlled at divisional level, with no permanent alloca-tion of CSS resources to brigades. When deployed independently, these would be needed. Moreover, on its own, in a multi-national context, the brigade would need greater depth to its sustainability with a slice of third line support; that which would normally be supplied from Corps level. This Corps level was to be provided by the creation of a Forward Maintenance Area (FMA) under the command of Colonel Martin White,

DACOS Logistics Operations and Plans in HQ BAOR with an ad hoc headquarters raised for the operation. At an early stage, HQ 1 Armoured Division also gave some assistance to the newly forming FMA, providing key staff such as Major Wayne Harber and Major Stephen Howe, the SO2's G1/4 Ops and G1 in HQ 1 Armoured Division. Their accounts appear in Chapters 3 and 8, respectively. Although this was to lead to some turbulence later when HQ 1 Armoured Division itself deployed, such action was vital to set up the FMA HQ quickly. Our immediate problem at divisional level was to establish the right level of second line support to go with the brigade with the appropriate resources, and command and control. This too was ad hoc: command and control was provided by Commander Transport 1 Armoured Division, Lieutenant Colonel Gavin Haig, with a small headquarters. They were immediately put in close contact with HQ 7 Armoured Brigade and included in the work up for the deployment.

The whole question of fleshing out 7 Armoured Brigade to its war establishment, and the proper scale of special equipment for the operation then had to be addressed. Achieving this bears some description.

HQ 1 Armoured Division called two major conferences immediately the operation was notified. One, chaired by the Chief of Staff, Colonel John Reith, examined peace and war establishments and manning so as to identify shortfalls made good initially from within the Division, then by HQ 1 (BR) Corps and HQ BAOR and so on. This trawl for suitable officers and soldiers extended out of theatre, worldwide in some cases. At the same time, I chaired a large meeting to examine peace and war equipment establishments, and actual equipment holdings, with the same intention of making up shortfalls. It was quickly found that equipment scales were in some cases badly out of date with a glut of obsolescent items and a shortage of current ones. Unserviceable equipments were assessed by Commander Maintenance and equipment transfers initiated in conjunction with G3, starting with key fighting equipments, such as Main Battle Tanks. Stores demands quickly became a problem and the division's new Commander Supply, Lieutenant Colonel Tim Cross, in conjunction with Commander Supply 1 (BR) Corps, Brigadier Peter Chambers, had to establish an Indent Clearing Cell in Shiel Barracks, Verden, to monitor and coordinate the standard priority system which was becoming over burdened with top priority demands. Initially, all Operation GRANBY units world wide were authorised to use Priority 1 for all their demands. For a short period of three weeks it was necessary to conduct a manual scrutiny to sort the wheat from the chaff, and discipline the system to identify real priorities.

The work-up to full serviceability was a mammoth task in the face of the need to move all heavy equipment early by sea. It was clear that a modification plan for Main Battle Tanks in particular would be essential to deal with desert conditions, but there was no time to do this before departure. For a start, modification kits had to be created and made ready. Modifications apart, much had to be done to make key equipment serviceable and all first and second line workshops in the Division were flat out on that task from the time the operation was ordered.

The Division's role throughout this period was to act as a mounting base for 7 Armoured Brigade and absolute priority was given to seeing them away in best order. The highest traditions of the British Army came to the fore as a diverse range of capabilities across BAOR were put to bear to achieve this. Activities were wide ranging. In the face of 7 Armoured Brigade's departure, new arrangements had to be made for garrison command and, within that, a new structure for dealing with such G1 matters as casualty reporting and family support was needed. 22 Armoured Brigade in Hohne took responsibility for 7 Armoured Brigade's administrative area and HQ 1 (UK) Armoured Division, in conjunction with HQ BAOR, set up a revised casualty reporting and family support system in those stations providing units to the operation. This varied in scope from, for example, Fallingbostel (7 Armoured Brigade's base), where virtually every unit was committed and a strong family support structure, tailor-made for the task, had to be established; to individual Stations providing detachments to the operation only, and which needed no more than minor enhancements.

Bearing in mind its unique nature, the deployment of 7 Armoured Brigade went smoothly and with expedition. But, they could not be fully equipped – for example, desert clothing was not yet in the inventory, so they had perforce to deploy with tropical combat clothing. Special items like this could only be supplied later in Theatre. Once the deployment of the brigade was completed, it was time for HQ 1 (UK) Armoured Division to take stock and a major reconstitution conference was held on 23 October 1990. This Conference attempted to assess personnel and equipment states post deployment in anticipation either of subsequent roulement[4] of the force or reinforcement. The mood of 1 (UK) Armoured Division at this time can be imagined. Not a man left in the Division would not have given his right arm to have deployed to Saudi Arabia: that wish was shortly to be granted.

Divisional Deployment

The developing situation at this time is described elsewhere. Suffice it to say here that it was soon apparent that more than just a brigade would be needed and that the British Government was prepared to commit a larger force, of divisional size, to operations. By early November 1990, it was clear that 1 (UK) Armoured Division was a prime contender for such a deployment, albeit that the additional brigade required would have to come from outside the Division, if key equipments such as

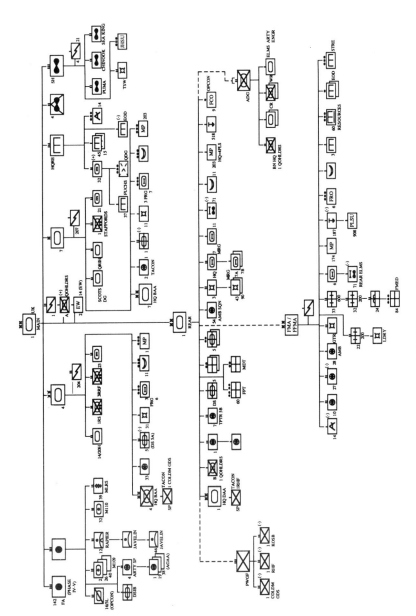

Figure 10.1 Order of Battle, 1 (UK) Armoured Division and FMA/FFMA

Challenger and Warrior were to be provided to match 7 Armoured Brigade, already in Theatre. 4 Armoured Brigade with its headquarters in Munster was selected and, post reconnaissance, the final ORBAT shown at Figure 10.1 became a reality. As notice of deployment reduced, so the tempo of activity in the Division increased. This affected two principal areas – getting the Division's own house in order by bringing the Headquarters onto a full war footing, and dealing with the actual problem of the force to be deployed and the job to be done.

Insofar as the Headquarters was concerned, there were two aspects to be addressed; first, bringing Division Rear Headquarters to a war establishment that would be suitable for operations in the Gulf, and second, pinning down the equipment and men required. As soon as 7 Armoured Brigade deployed to Saudi Arabia, it was realised that local conditions demanded a much higher level of mobility for headquarters than in Germany. The ponderous four tonne box body vehicles established for Divisional Rear Headquarters clearly would be unsuitable, and at a very early stage it was decided to harden Rear Headquarters using FV436s (armoured command vehicles). Moreover, the capabilities of the headquarters had to be increased dramatically: it had neither a step-up capability nor proper manning for 24 hour operations.

After making a quick appreciation, we decided upon an open plan cruciform arrangement using eight FV436s laid out as shown at Figures 10.2 and 10.3. This allowed us to continue to use on operations the well proven and successful bird table[5] arrangement that had been developed on three years' worth of exercises. It capitalised on the mobility of tracked vehicles which, at the same time, offered some protection should that be needed. The major problem was to cover the open plan bird table with a proper shelter to keep the weather out and the light in at night. In very short order, under the driving force of Captain Angus McDonald and Captain Glenn Harwood and his crew of signallers, especially Yeoman Gascoigne and Foreman Plumb, a plan was developed and vehicles prepared ready for early shipment on 29 November 1990. Two additional tracked Secondary Access Nodes (SANS)[6] were agreed to enhance communications: the second provided Rear Headquarters with a proper step up capability for the first time. All this equipment had to be drawn up both from within and outside the Division. In the event, no less than 14 separate units provided men and material as reinforcements.

We had already passed some key staff to the FMA earlier in the year to see them up and running. Thus in Rear Headquarters we had to work fast to fill gaps and bring ourselves up to establishment for operations. The staff reinforcement plan was as extensive as that for signallers and drivers. Rear Headquarters field staff strength rose from its peacetime level of 40 to over 70. It was vital to upscale the Head-

DIVISION REAR HQ LAYOUT

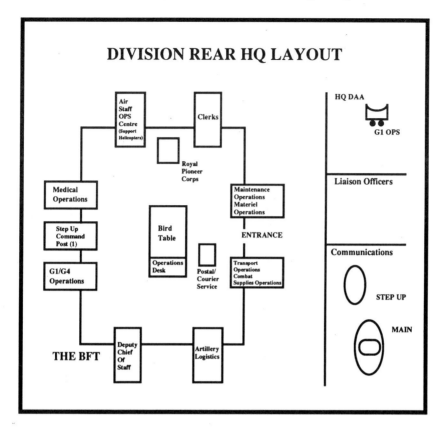

Figure 10.2 Layout, Rear Divisional Headquarters

quarters with proper manning for 24 hour operations and to introduce a G1/4 Plans staff to provide a forward planning capability, over and above the minute by minute control of logistic operations. Early reinforcement included Major Nigel Lloyd as SO2 G1/4 Ops on 2 December 1990 but the plan was not actually fully achieved until quite late in the day with Major Mark Varley arriving in the desert in mid January, direct from his staff course in Australia! Numerous short order postings took place. Nevertheless Captain Angus McDonald, then the SO3 G1/4 Ops, had to shoulder the SO2's burden alone during the early stages of build up until late November. He did so with great success.

Headquarters activity went in fits and starts. Frantic activity was needed to prepare vehicles and equipment in time for shipment in late November 1990. This was then followed by a lull, allowing us to concentrate more upon those units deploying with us before having to turn again to the mounting of the operation and the move of the Headquarters in particular. I formed part of the GOC's reconnaissance with the Chief of Staff from 20 November 1990 to 24 November 1990.

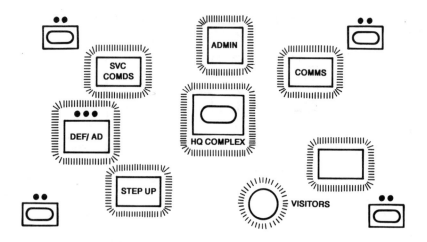

Figure 10.3 Headquarters complex, Rear Divisional Headquarters

Advance parties, with G1/4 Ops led by Captain McDonald, deployed on 4 December 1990.

The full deployment of both the Headquarters and our units went well. There were two reasons for this. First, there was the invaluable presence of the FMA already established in Jubail. They had forged a strong relationship with the USMC and the Host Nation and were able to make vital preparations for our smooth arrival, freeing us of much of the burden of reception arrangements. Second, all involved had the benefit of experience by this stage so that it was possible to arrange the Desired Order of Arrival Staff Table (DOAST) to make our arrival in theatre as coherent as possible, given the constraints on movement resources, and the availability of units in Germany and the United Kingdom. For example, we were able to arrange the early movement of some key logistic units such as transport and workshops, needed to assist with in theatre armoured vehicle modifications.

Divisional Headquarters deployed on 10 December 1990, transiting through camps in Jubail to occupy an office-cum-warehouse complex on the outskirts of the town (Camp 9) with Main and Rear Headquarters deployed side by side (see Figure 3.3). In principle, the deployment plan into theatre was that equipment, moved by sea, and unit personnel, moved by air, were scheduled to arrive together. On arrival, after an initial marry-up, units moved into temporary staging areas in the Jubail area before deploying up country to join 7 Armoured Brigade in the desert to the north.

Some fundamental logistic decisions were made at this early stage.

The framework of the divisional logistic system was set up from the outset. It was overlaid on that already in place for 7 Armoured Brigade with the introduction of Divisional Rendezvous (Div Rv's), an Headquarters Divisional Administration Area (DAA); and divisional logistic troops serving units from the very beginning, even though they themselves were working up and gaining desert familiarisation. This provided the right framework to concentrate all those involved upon preparation for operations and provided essential training for head-quarters, especially since units were quickly committed to real logistic preparation for operations in terms of moving stock, preparing equip-ment, and so on. Priority had to be given to real administration and logistic units had little time at this stage to train.

Divisional Rear headquarters moved into the field on 3 January 1991. Although by this time the overall preparation for operations was in full swing, priority went to preparing the headquarters, working up move-ment drills by day and night, and, above all, practising the transfer of command. Quite a small area was used for this but it was enough to get basics right. Incidents were not infrequent, one particular AFV436, the property of Maintenance Operations, broke down on every move, but ruthless practice was to pay off later!

The tempo of activity at this time was intense. Whilst some elements of the Division had deployed into the desert, units and stock were still arriving as the process of deployment saw 4 Armoured Brigade and the remaining divisional Combat Support and CSS units into theatre. However, more importantly, as Christmas was celebrated, the future role for the division had been decided. To consider this, it is necessary to go back to December 1990, before Divisional Headquarters deployed into the field, to examine how the logistic plan was prepared. GOC 1 (UK) Armoured Division alerted John Reith and I to the plan to deploy the division to the west shortly before Christmas. I then did a rapid assessment of the logistic and medical requirements to match this plan in conjunction with Martin White. A key staff check was conducted and completed by 22 December 1990 to determine the movement require-ment to deploy the combat supplies, materiel, and medical resources required to establish the plan which is shown schematically at Figure 1.5. Subsequently a carefully controlled reconnaissance was conducted. Essentially, by pooling all transport resources from the division and the FMA, it would be possible to deploy the Forward Force Maintenance Area (FFMA) within 21 days and a Divisional Maintenance Area (DMA) beyond there in a further 7 days.

This CSS plan was presented to Commander 7 US Corps on 1 January 1991 at his Briefback on the overall plan. This meeting was a vital early opportunity to establish relations with the US Army, decide on a common currency for logistic matters (US gallons v litres, rounds of ammunition v divisional consumption rates), and start to address interoperability.

The order to initiate the Outload was given on 2 January 1991 by HQ BFME.

Meanwhile, the Division's combat units were training and preparing in the area north of Jubail. In the interest of speed, CSS for the Division in training was minimised to only that essential for its support. The majority of Divisional CSS resources, principally transport, re-deployed in support of the FMA to see the re-deployment under way. The build-up and training of the division in the east was an essential deception measure also for logistic re-deployment perforce preceded operational re-deployment. Deception was re-enforced by extensive and deliberate HF logistic radio traffic in the training area, much of it phoney, subsequently to be re-broadcast as an EW deception measure. Operational re-deployment was left until as late a stage as possible.

This re-deployment of the Division was a sizeable problem which needed a special approach to move the most in the shortest possible time over a crowded two-way multinational main supply route (MSR DODGE). Sterling work was done by Major Jonathan Shorer who, in conjunction with G3 Ops and the Assistant Provost Marshal, developed a movement plan for the Division's tracked and wheeled vehicles. By mid January 1991, after the start of the Air War on 15 January 1991, deployment areas within Area KEYS, as part of 7 (US) Corps deployments, had been selected. This was conveniently North of the by then established FFMA, and not too far removed from the vital MSR, the Tapline Road. An imaginative plan, involving the use of support helicopters for the movement of personnel; tank transporters or low loaders for moving heavy armour; and DROPS vehicles for moving light A vehicles, was developed. DROPS vehicles were particularly successful; pick up times were impressive.

Divisional Rear Headquarters preceded Main Headquarters to Area KEYS on 18 January 1991, a time of quite some uncertainty as a result of the Iraqi attack on Khafji and with a very strong possibility of further Iraqi raids to the south of the Saudi Arabian border, close to Area KEYS. All this preceded the issue of GPS which lead to some interesting encounters. On one memorable occasion, I enjoyed the hospitality of an Egyptian M109 self-propelled artillery battery, the divisional troops DP[7], and a large Main Battle Tank (MBT) tank scrape in the process of a short 500 m journey between the new Rear Headquarters and the new Divisional RV! Rear Headquarters was also very short staffed due to sickness – key staff succumbed to influenza and even pneumonia.

But for Rear Headquarters and for the Division's CSS units, the time spent in Area KEYS was invaluable. First, for the first time, all the Division's fighting units were able to shake out with their logistic system fully established. By this time, the inload of the FFMA was complete and it was possible to turn attention to the realities of supporting the

Division on operations. Divisional study periods, map exercises (MAPEXs), and 'teach ins', organised by my staff and complementary to General Rupert Smith's training, had been a feature from the outset but now plans could be practised. Essential movement drills for the Divisional rear area were developed. This included drills for reconnaissance, with a reconnaissance party lead by the SO2 G1/4 Ops and 2IC of 1 Armoured Division Transport Regiment, Major John May, operating to standard SOP's. A standard layout for the Divisional Rear Area, allowing rapid and parallel movement across the desert where necessary, was designed also. The divisional layout is shown at Figure 10.4, together with that for a brigade administrative area at Figure 10.5. Most important, movement drills for all were designed so that routine could be standardised and, with it, the surety that battle procedure would continue, even in the event of a difficulty, leaving commanders better able to deal with a particular situation which might confront them. Equally important, procedures were refined for the use of forward logistic detachments from divisional troops to brigades to reinforce sustainability forward; for casualty evacuation; and for the necessary link-up with third line (FMA) resources.

Battle Preparations

This was the time to put into practice the detail of the logistic plan necessary to support General Rupert's operational plan, by this stage hardening into detail. The Division was faced with the possibility of a break in battle, and the prospect of a long opposed advance to Kuwait. Distances were going to be large, and the consumption rate of some combat supplies such as fuel accordingly large, even if enemy resistance were to be minimal. In terms of support, the devil was going to be in the distance, with a classic problem of support for the advance. At Divisional level, the essential requirement was to employ logistics like firepower, placing them where they were needed to sustain operations for as long as possible and thus maximise the fighting power of the division.

Five essential principles underlay this general intention:

First, there would be maximum self sufficiency forward for fighting units in terms of combat supplies. This was achieved by increasing first line scales, and increasing the holdings of combat supplies at brigade level, essentially placing more stocks on wheels with brigade administrative areas (BAAs) and in immediate replenishment groups (IRG).[8] Forward Logistic Detachments were also placed with Brigade Administrative Areas to increase holdings and thus speed replenishment by reducing replenishment distance within the brigade. Forward sustainability was repeated throughout, with third line detachments

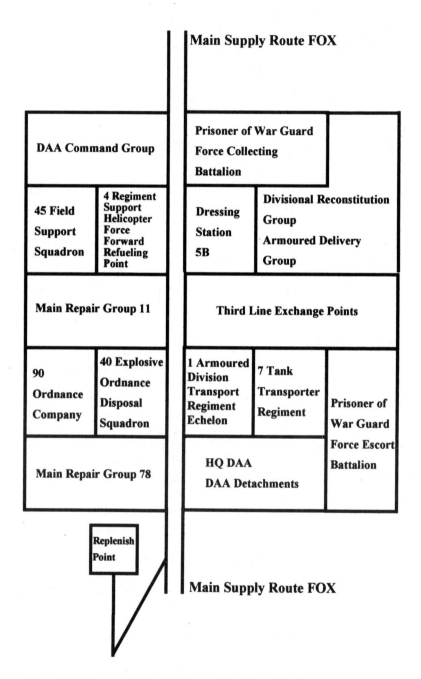

Figure 10.4 Layout of the Divisional Administrative Area

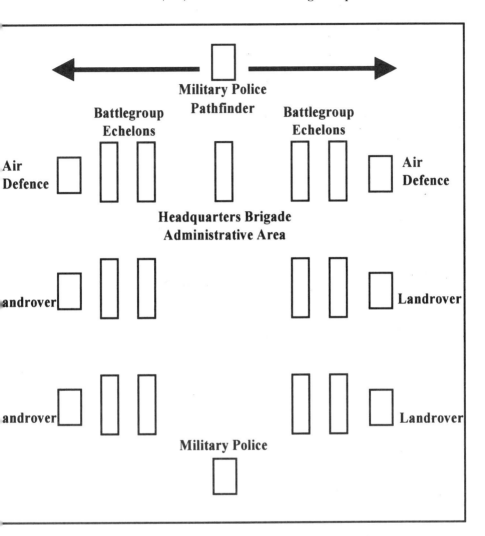

Figure 10.5 4 Armoured Brigade: Brigade Administrative Area

moving with the Division to save time in the third to second line replenishment loop also.

Second, at the same time more materiel was placed forward, particularly power packs, engines and major assemblies, again with the intention of placing resources on the spot near the point of failure so that REME could repair further forward and faster.

Third, stocks were very carefully balanced between the Forward Force Maintenance Area (FFMA) and the Divisional Maintenance Area (DMA) and within the division itself, to cater for the likely development of the battle. Quite clearly, at the operational level, support through the breach and the breakout from the breach would be vital. But the line of communication through the breach would be a very long one as the Division moved towards Kuwait. Thus it was important to keep open the option of a more direct supply route, perhaps up the Wadi Al Batin, direct from the FFMA if circumstances would permit and the Iraqi forces in that area were neutralised. Thus a reasonable reserve had to be held back in the FFMA for replenishment. At the tactical level also, a careful balance was needed to ensure units were not encumbered by unnecessary stocks reducing their agility. The balance between the fighting and CSS elements of the Division was kept under constant review to ensure that logistic drag was minimised and agility was maintained forward. Whilst stocks placed forward could speed replenishment by reducing distance; at the same time, if the brigades' logistic tails were to be too large, the stocks would prove a greater hindrance than help as they could slow down movement, as well as provide a target for enemy action.

Fourth, if logistics were to be deployed like firepower, then a sound Command, Control and Communications plan was essential so that logistic assets could be quickly re-directed to the GOC's point of main effort. The scope of this plan was very broad. It included communication improvements: the provision of encryption devices for high frequency (HF) radio to increase their capacity and utility and additional rebroadcast stations for the Division's VHF Command net to allow Divisional Rear Headquarters to communicate with Divisional Main Headquarters more readily and read the battle for CSS planning. It also included organisational measures in the Divisional rear area, such as the grouping of all heavy CSS units under a single commander with clear SOPs and drills for movement. Essentially, this kept heavy CSS units clear of the battle so that they did not slow down the advance as shown at Figure 10.6.

Fifth, a balanced medical plan was needed. This included placing a dressing station, reinforced by a field surgical team under the operational control of each brigade and the artillery group. The primary means of CASEVAC was planned to be support helicopters to Field Hospitals in the FFMA and FMA. However, an option was retained to fly a 50 bed Field Hospital forward once brigades were operating in depth, if distances and casualty rates demanded it. These two principles were the basis for the Divisional Administrative Order for the Operation, Admin O 4/91. This order enjoyed the straightforward aim 'To maintain 1 (UK) Armoured Division on Op DESERT SABRE' but had to run to 82 pages to tie down the detail! The fundamentals of the CSS plan sprang from an absolute understanding of the essentials of the Commander's intention, and above all, the end game of the operation as a whole, the liberation of Kuwait. From this sprang the disposition of logistic resources for the Division, in the classic

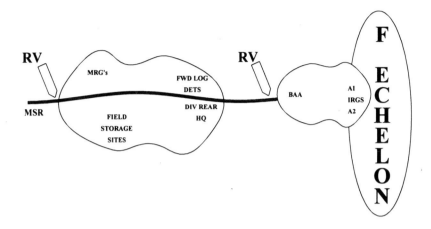

Figure 10.6 Close and General Logistic Support at Divisional Level

posture for the advance with maximum self-sufficiency forward in direct support of brigades and fighting units, complemented by the application of appropriate logistic priorities to support the Divisional Commander's points of operational main effort as he moved his brigades forward.

The overall outline of the CSS plan, in terms of combat supplies, is shown at Figure 1.4. The disposition of combat supplies at the outset of battle is shown at Figure 6.2. By 24 January 1991, the FFMA had been stocked with 18,000 tons of ammunition, 7,000,000 litres of fuel, and 6,000 tons of materiel. On 31 January 1991, the Division's two Transport Regiments started to outload stocks from the FFMA to the DMA 30 kms north-west of Hafr Al Batin. By 15 February 1991, this inload was complete and 10 days worth of all natures of ammunition, and reserve stocks of fuel and materiel, were placed forward in the DMA which formed part of the United States Log Base Echo (LBE). This DMA was to be our ready source for operations in addition to the mobile stocks carried on wheels.

Certain features of the plan deserve emphasis before describing its execution. Throughout the battle, the most critical area remained Command, Control and Communications. The mounting of Divisional Rear Headquarters in tracked vehicles and, above all, the enhancement to its communication capability, were amply vindicated. If the tempo of CSS is to be maintained, then a proper step-up capability for Divisional Rear Headquarters is essential. Botching it just will not do, for only with a proper step-up can the command of CSS activity be maintained. Rear HQ's place on the Divisional Command Net[9] is also vital. Only in this way can the logistician keep a feel for the battle, plan ahead accordingly, and respond more promptly to its ebb and flow. Moreover, it provides an essential contact by voice with the Commander – the hardening of the voice is always a better indication of priorities than the impersonal written order! Increasing communications traffic capacity was equally pressing. The value of IT over Ptarmigan and encryption devices to increase the capacity of HF nets should not be underrated, although the former was never developed as far as it should have been. All these measures contributed to speeding our tempo.

The scale of high intensity conflict and the size of the formations involved quickly proved a salutary reminder of the long established use of liaison officers under these circumstances. Rear Headquarters created a strong liaison officer framework, placing key staff officers in headquarters in 7 (US) Corps, armed with a knowledge of our capabilities and practice, and operating as part of those headquarters, to keep us properly informed of what was going on. Major Pat Callan moved across to 7 (US) Corps Rear Headquarters at the outset and provided a key link throughout the operation of vital importance in a situation where logistic interoperability was subject to serious limitations. Liaison officers (LO's) were equally vital at the tactical level. For example, during the passage of the breach, LOs were placed with US medical units to ensure that our two national CASEVAC systems met without friction.

The value of a strong Command, Control and Communications framework came to the fore time and time again. For example, on the night of the breakout through the breach, 7 Armoured Brigade had some difficulty contacting its BAA. But by manipulating Service HF nets and the passing of messages, it was possible to get the order through via Divisional Rear Headquarters Step Up in spite of the difficult conditions at the time, simply because of the strength of the logistic C^3 framework which offered a number of alternative routings for orders. The enhanced framework was a fundamental basis of flexibility for CSS.

Balance deserves further mention too. Time, space, and opportunity must be created for CSS activity: only the most agile of Combat Service Support units can be near the front line. As Figure 10.6 shows, the logistic tail of the Division was effectively divided, providing strong logistic detachments forward in direct support of brigades but leaving the heavy elements of the Division's tail in the Divisional Administrative Area to be called forward when required. The heavier elements are shown in Figure 10.4. They consist either of units who are not required immediately in support of operations, or those units that need time and space to do their business – for example, workshop Main Repair Groups. Figure 10.4 illustrates the standard layout of the Divisional Administrative Area (DAA) used throughout the operations. The DAA moved on a standard drill as a standard package. This is, of course, easy to implement in the desert, but the drills developed are applicable elsewhere, and, are again part of the business of speeding up CSS procedures. They ensure that activity goes on: it is much better that commanders locally make decisions about actual circumstances on the basis of activity rather than starting from scratch each time there is a problem.

Frugality had considerable emphasis all the way through operations. In spite of increased forward sustainability, there was a vital need to keep down the tail and to stop units encumbering themselves with unnecessary equipment. Trailers proved to be a real hindrance under desert conditions and their scale was greatly reduced. A constant enemy of frugality was our inability to have an overview of our materiel holdings in detail. We did not know in enough detail what we had, and once battle is joined it is vital to know where key spares are so that they can be directed to where they are most needed. The average input of materiel to the division daily before the operation crossed the startline was 200 tons. But for the entire duration of the 100 hour operation, only 30 tons were moved into the division, all by support helicopter. That ability to move 30 tons was a proper reflection of the difficulty of replenishing technical spares during an advance. The real difficulty was knowing whether that 30 tons contained the right spares, those that were really urgently required, allied to a constant difficulty in identifying where particular items might be in the system. This difficulty was greatly exacerbated by the broad and varied nature of the inventory which included support for equipment ranging from the Centurion AVRE, built in the fifties, to Warriors just into service. To cap that, much of our equipment was not as reliable as it should have been and needed more than its fair share of effort to keep it running.

Equipment reliability and serviceability was a constant concern prior to the operation and this is described in detail in Chapter 7. In the early stages of work-up training, it soon became clear that engines and major assemblies for Challenger would be a show stopper unless training mileage was limited. The GOC instituted an equipment management group bringing together Brigade Commanders, COS, DCOS, Commanders Maintenance and Supply, and other necessary specialists, to meet and review the position at least weekly, sometimes more frequently if necessary. At these meetings, the GOC laid down the mileage available to Brigade Commanders for training. His decision on allocations assessed the availability of engines and major assemblies, against current failure rates. A number of hurdles had to be overcome. At one stage, a shortage of quite minor spares – connecting pipes and so on – prevented the mating of engines and gearboxes to produce a replacement serviceable power pack, the essential commodity of battlefield repair. Equally, equipment with a hitherto good reliability record, such as M109 (self-propelled 155 mm gun), proved to have some weaknesses when put to more protracted use – for example, M109 generator drives ran critically short at one stage prior to operations. Elderly equipment also proved difficult to maintain, sometimes with spectacular results, especially in the case of the Centurion AVRE, which had a dangerous habit of catching fire.

AD HOC Groupings

The CSS plan did have a number of unusual features. In particular, the Division adopted a number of ad hoc organisations to overcome the difficulties of distance, and to speed up CSS activity. These measures varied in scope and complexity, but all contributed to this same aim.

For the purposes of the operation, the Division's artillery was brigaded. Whilst there are well established principles for the replenishment of artillery ammunition, second line CSS for artillery units themselves is often glossed over in peacetime training. Once the decision had been taken to form the Divisional Artillery Group (DAG), an Artillery Group Admin Area (AGAA), akin to a BAA, was drawn together using artillery regiments' echelons[10] and re-distributed second line CSS assets. The DAG was also provided with a Field Ambulance and repair elements, becoming effectively as logistically independent as an armoured brigade. In anticipation of heavy ammunition usage, a complete transport regiment, 4 Armoured Division Transport Regiment, commanded by Lieutenant Colonel David Forrest, was allocated to the DAG. His Regimental Headquarters worked direct to the Commander Royal Artillery (CRA), Brigadier Ian Durie, coordinating artillery ammunition replenishment through the divisional area within the overall transport plan run by Commander Transport, Lieutenant Colonel Gavin Haig. This proved effective and responsive. Although artillery expenditure was low, the movement rate for ammunition was high. We could not afford to abandon ammunition pre-positioned for fire plans and subsequently not needed. GPS equipment soon proved a great boon for artillery replenishment, since all those involved could be sure of finding each other quickly with a consequently great increase in flexibility. Brigading artillery echelons has distinct CSS advantages. It is a practice that deserves more work; and inclusion in doctrine with resources to match.

A key feature of the GOC's plan was the rolling commitment of brigades. If this was to be successful, then the brigade out of contact would need to be reconstituted quickly so that it could be re-committed quickly without any loss of momentum to the Division's advance. Clearly a focus and a headquarters was required for this. The commanding officer of 7 Armoured Workshops, Lieutenant Colonel Rod Croucher, and his Headquarters, took on the role as the Divisional Reconstitution Group (DRG). He drew together the mix of replacement equipment, medical, combat supplies, and repair elements (a main repair group) shown at Figure 10.7. He was able to link up with the brigade to be reconstituted, recce a suitable area for reconstitution, and then provide

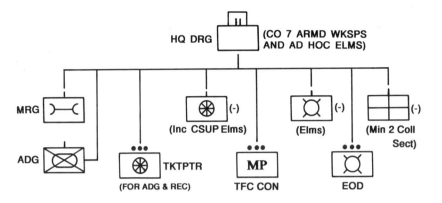

HQ found by CO 7 Armd Wksps, Elms of Gp
matched to task as necessary

Figure 10.7 The Divisional Reconstitution Group

all the support necessary to refit the brigade for recommittal. Once the brigade was recommitted, elements of the DRG could remain in place to repair equipment, deal with casualties and so on. In the event, the DRG was not used during the ground offensive: true reconstitution was not needed and reconstitution, such as it was, was restricted to combat supplies only, using normal replenishment procedures. However, the concept of the DRG proved effective in training and undoubtedly deserves further study with an eye to the future as a means of increasing flexibility.

Leaving aside the whole question of the reconstitution of brigades, the larger question of reinforcements and how these might be organised also loomed large as the administrative plans for the Division were developed. The initial overall plan simply provided reinforcements on the basis of the then current plans with their origins in the practice of the Second World War. Men were to be provided from the United Kingdom in drafts of roughly platoon size; equipment was provided as a War Maintenance Reserve; and only a very limited range of key equipments, principally Main Battle Tanks, were to be provided crewed. Clearly the latter system, that of providing crewed equipment, was far more relevant to the sort of warfare which the GOC envisaged. Moreover, once battle casualty replacements (BCRs) came into the Division, there was no existing organisation which was capable of administering them, training them, and marrying them up with war maintenance reserve vehicles. Some sort of All Arms delivery organisation, capable of keeping up with the fighting echelons, and able to provide a range or reinforcement options, was needed.

216   *Gulf Logistics*

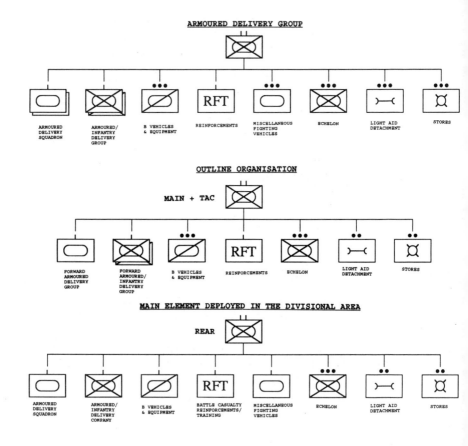

Figure 10.8 The Armoured Delivery Group

As a result, on 4 February 1991, Major General Smith ordered the Armoured Delivery Group (ADG) to form, commanded by CO 1 Queens Own Highlanders, Lieutenant Colonel Seymour Munro, and his headquarters. Men and equipment were formed up into organised and trained units of platoon/troop size and above, manning key equipment. This organisation was then augmented by the provision of 7 Tank Transporter Regiment to carry them to war. The ADG's full ORBAT is shown at Figure 10.8. This would conserve tracked vehicles and speed up delivery. The ADG could be dismounted also, either to act in a reinforcing role or to provide a rear area security force. The GOC gave me authority to dismount the ADG for this purpose if necessary. In the event, the ADG was only twice called upon to provide individual reinforcements during the ground offensive. However, experience on training and during the operation vindicated the organisation as a means of increasing the tempo of battle.

As with reinforcements, there were no clear procedures in place at the start of Operation GRANBY for the handling of Prisoners of War. Three UK Infantry Type B Battalions, each of 520 all ranks, were deployed to the Gulf in the third week of January 1991 to form the Prisoner of War Guard Force (PWGF). The battalion headquarters of 1 Coldstream Guards was augmented slightly to provide a small headquarters under Colonel Ian McNeil for this ad hoc force of near brigade size. Its early days were not easy, since units had not trained together before and unit equipment scales were meagre. The battalions had no troop lift and could not move even their first line combat supplies. The PWGF did not join the Division until 23 February 1991, immediately prior to the offensive. The outline plan was for one Battalion to work in depth under command of the FFMA to run the Prisoner of War Cage, with up to two battalions deployed forward to take on the collection and rearward movement of prisoners. This latter task quickly became very difficult as a result of the speed of the advance, communications difficulties, and, above all, the sheer numbers of prisoners taken (over 8,000). Matters were complicated by the very poor condition of many of the Iraqis captured: most were ill fed, ill clad, and, especially as the advance gathered momentum, very confused into the bargain. Fighting units quickly found the prolonged presence of prisoners on the battle-field an encumbrance. Although, by definition, it is success that produces prisoners, increasing numbers of prisoners in itself produces an humanitarian problem and begins to prejudice the very success which yielded them. All sorts of transportation was used to move them away from the battle area, including support helicopters and returning empty logistic road transport. Arguably, the PWGF was provided too late to do its best for the division. However, given its limited resources, particularly transport, it performed extremely well.

A major concern, in view of the distances to be covered, was whether the Division could be sustained effectively in support of a long desert advance and line of communication. Although CSS mobility at first line was to some degree increased by a limited issue of tracked carriers, the M548, on loan, second and third line CSS was entirely dependant on wheeled vehicles with medium mobility at best. Some key vehicles, notably the 22,500 l. fuel tanker, were low mobility. Something had to be done to ensure that an appropriate main supply route (MSR) could be created behind the division to allow the vital umbilical cord of replenishment to proceed. The solution emerged in the shape of the Route Development Battle Group (RDBG). The Division's engineer group had originally been deployed with the intention of forcing a breach through the Iraqi defence line. Once the full operational plan developed, this role fell almost completely to the US Engineers. Thus additional engineer elements were available for other tasks. Based upon 32 Armoured Engineer Regiment, the RDBG's tasks were to select, build

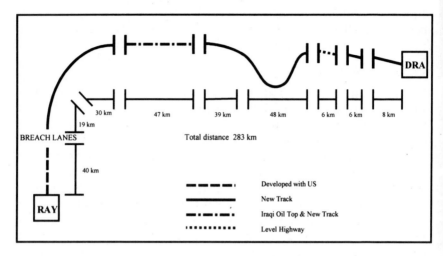

Figure 10.9 Route Development

and maintain the Division's MSR. For this role, the regiment received additional assets, including provost support from 203 Provost Company RMP, mine clearance equipment and a chemical recce capability. Once the advance began, the RDBG moved on a central axis behind the two brigades, marking and developing one of the brigades' previous routes for use as the Division's MSR. Once marking was done, the route was developed to provide a two way wheeled route of sufficient standard to bear the Division's immediate logistic traffic. Figure 10.9 shows the scale of activity needed to provide logistic mobility. This activity was invaluable, given the very poor weather during the advance. Furthermore, the presence of the route development battle group greatly enhanced rear area security for they were available to react to the unexpected and could have escorted logistic convoys, in the true sense of that term, had that been necessary.

Although ad hoc measures were needed, it is worth saying that there were several things in the CSS plan that the Division had going for it from the outset. First, many of the units knew each other well and were accustomed to operating together. Even where this was not so, there was the advantage of common Standard Operating Procedures (SOPs). Indeed, NATO SOPs were shared with US troops as well. Moreover, certain new equipments which were just coming into service quickly proved first rate. DROPS fell into this category and was particularly successful in conjunction with satellite navigation systems (GPS), enabling a large load to be positioned accurately and promptly. Although provided primarily for support of the multi-launch rocket system (MLRS), DROPS vehicles were used extensively by both the Division and the FMA for tasks such as the carriage of water on specially adapted flatracks and the movement of light A vehicles and key stores.

Support Helicopters

No less than 37 Support Helicopters (SH), RAF Chinook and Puma, and RN Sea Kings, were made available to the Division, primarily for logistic tasks. An Air Support Operations Centre (Support Helicopters) (ASOC (SH)) of five officers and three airmen was based at Divisional Rear Headquarters from that headquarters' initial deployment into the desert. Totally integrated with the Headquarters, and linked closely with the Medical Operations Staff, they provided a vital link with both the SH Force and the ASOC at Main HQ. The primary task for SH was to be casualty evacuation and, by the time operations began, drills for this were well practised, especially with medical units. In the event, relatively little casualty evacuation was needed and SH came to the fore as a major enhancement to our flexibility. In particular, SH could speed up critical tasks such as the movement of key stores and key people. For example, in the latter instance, it was Sea Kings of 861 Naval Air Squadron (NAS) who enabled the Divisional Rear Headquarters Command Group to deploy forward rapidly at night to Kuwait at the end of hostilities. The SH Force also played a notable part in the movement of PWs, most of whom were in poor condition and in dire need of early evacuation from the battlefield.

It is in the nature of logistics that the overheads of SH operations should be high, both in terms of fuel and maintenance. Indeed, during this operation, special sand filters for helicopter engines were a necessity: until they could be fitted, engine failure rates were prohibitive. But the overheads are more than offset by the irreplaceable characteristics of the SH on the modern battlefield. SH made a vital contribution to the Division's success because of their unique combination of range, speed, vertical access to the battlefield, and the skill of their crews.

Operations

So much for the preparation for operations. Divisional logistic units remained in Area KEYS until 14 February 1991. Whilst in KEYS, these units took part in Exercise DIBDIBAH DRIVE designed to practise the Division's move through the planned breach in the Iraqi defences. During this exercise, the entire divisional logistic tail was able to get on the move, practising its own move through the breach, and movement drills in the process. By this stage, CSS units were far better practised overall: this was to pay off when the Division moved west to join 7 (US) Corps in Area RAY west of the Wadi Al Batin. This move was conducted as a final work up exercise, Exercise DIBDIBAH

CHARGE, and provided a vital opportunity for logistic units to shake out in role. This was especially true of the ad hoc organisations, such as the DRG, who were able to practise their task with brigades during the advance. Best of all, it gave CSS units and their commanders a realistic feel for the sheer complexity of operations at this scale and the need for confident command within the fog of war and its uncertainties. This was to pay off during the operation itself also.

Area RAY provided the final opportunity for the shake out of units prior to the operation. It was a large and generally featureless area, previously occupied by Syrian forces, and a true test of navigation without the use of GPS. A forward airstrip was built so that C130 Hercules might be used direct into the area and all logistic procedures got an airing, including air despatch. This was a tense time. Saddam Hussein was prone to making peace overtures. Just as men became accustomed to the idea that the operation was on, things looked as if they might not be. For soldiers in CSS units, this was in many ways the most difficult time since all real work towards the plan had generally been done. Further logistic preparation had to be matched exactly to the start of operations, so for a very brief period it was necessary to wait with time to think!

Meanwhile, the GOC's final Orders Group took place with follow on Orders Groups as necessary. There were not many necessary, since the plan was now known and rehearsed, and people were ready for it. In essence, the CSS plan could now unfold with forward logistic detachments and second line units assigned to brigades moving under operational command of brigades as part of their BAAs; and with the bulk of divisional CSS units moving as an entity, in the DAA, as follow up.

Figures 10.10 and 10.11 illustrate the main moves of the CSS element of the Division. Once the move forward to the breach was ordered, Division Rear Headquarters moved forward to the Border Berm on 25 February 1991 at 1630, taking over an headquarter site from Main Headquarters who by this time were to move on through the breach. In this way, Rear Headquarters provided a communications bridge between the DAA, which remained at this stage in Area RAY, and forward logistic units already pouring through the breach with brigades. The battle developed according to plan; or rather better than the plan! The breakout from the breach was fast, in spite of the appalling weather, and it was quickly necessary for Commander 7 (US) Corps to alter his logistic priorities. On the morning following the breakout, just as our brigades were pushing forward and the distances for resupply and CASEVAC were lengthening, 2 Armoured Cavalry Regiment, and the logistic tail of 7 (US) Corps had to swing left and north directly across the route that the DAA should have taken as part of a logical step forward to keep up with the Division. A halt to our DAA was essential to give them passage.

At 0800 on 26 February 1991, the DAA was on the move at last, to

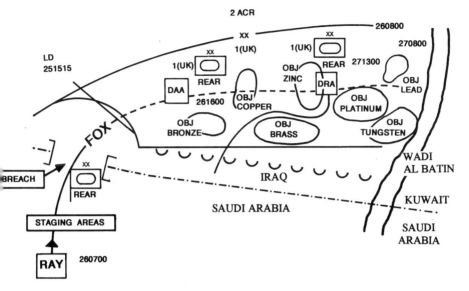

Figure 10.10 Battle Sketch I

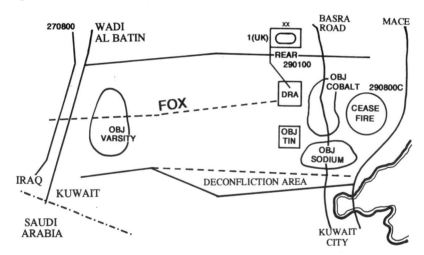

Figure 10.11 Battle Sketch II

enter a new Location DAA that night. This went well but had its moments. The Iraqis were by no means acquiescent. Iraqi armoured forces, by this time cut off by the Allied thrust behind them, sought to return home by the most direct route, as quickly as possible. That direct route lay across the MSR. Tank sightings were frequent and it was fortunate that this enemy armour did not press home any attacks. But to a degree the sheer volume and size of our operation was a deterrent to an enemy who was rapidly losing the will to fight and who would therefore seek to use the space of the desert to find a route home rather than fight it out. As it was, C Company 1 Queens Own Highlanders, at this stage the only Rear Area Security Force, scurried about the battlefield to deal with contacts. The judicious use of indirect fire on Iraqi forces to the south made a vital contribution to the security of the rear area. Command and control, and the analysis of contact reports, fortunately proved to be more demanding than the contacts themselves. But even this quickly put Rear Headquarters under pressure since G3 matters were pressing, precisely at a time when G1/4 matters were also beginning to need attention in the shape of forward planning to deal with the lengthening of the L of C. A separate headquarters to coordinate rear area security would have been invaluable; this was remedied within 24 hours when the GOC was able to allocate the Queen's Dragoon Guards (QDG), the divisional reconnaissance regiment to the rear area to boost rear area security and take on the divided command, control and security over the lengthening L of C, thereby easing the load on my headquarters.

On 27 February 1991, at 0630, Rear Headquarters moved again to reestablish itself on Objective ZINC at 1300 that day. We had planned to establish a new DAA here but events had by this stage begun to move very fast indeed. Iraqi resistance was clearly collapsing and by 1130 on that day 7 Armoured Brigade were already on objective VARSITY. There then began a period of planning options before it became clear that a rapid dash to Kuwait would be required. 7 Armoured Brigade was reconfigured to carry out a rapid advance as a Forward Detachment, replenished as far as possible. They dashed for the Basra road, leaving at 0545 on 28 February 1991 and arriving there at 0725 that day.

This dash outpaced any plans for a new DAA and it was decided to continue the movement of CSS units forward direct into Kuwait to a new DAA north of Kuwait City adjacent to the Basra road. Rear Headquarters Step Up moved forward fast behind Main Headquarters during the night 28/29 February and at 0100 on 29 February 1993 the Rear Headquarters Command Party flew by Sea King helicopter to take command in the new DAA. CSS units closed up non-stop all night and most of the following day. By the morning of 29 February 1993, replenishment of both 4 and 7 Brigades had been completed, giving enough fuel to see the division to Basra if necessary. But this left the Division's second line fuel stocks exhausted, with the balance of stocks still on their way to us up the long MSR area. Figure 10.12 shows the expenditure of Combat Supplies during the operation. Had a very rapid redeployment towards central Iraq been ordered, this could have proved a problem since it was not for a further 24 hours that stocks were back in balance. However, the question proved academic since the temporary ceasefire held and we turned our attentions to the clearance of Kuwait rather than to operations.

COMMODITY	USED	TOTALS
DIESO	1,500,000 ltrs	
CIVGAS	500,000 ltrs	
PACKED FUEL	200,000 ltrs	2,200,000 ltrs
WATER	708,000 ltrs	5.6 ltrs per man per day
AMMUNITION		
155mm All Natures	6736	
8 inch	1522	
MLRS	317 RPC or 1902 rockets	
120mm J1	651	
120mm J2	80	
120mm HESH	849	

Figure 10.12 Usage of Combat Supplies

There followed a period of difficult post-combat activity. The area established as the DAA was liberally littered with the debris of war and a fair number of dead had to be buried. Much live ammunition was scattered about, some of it in a most dangerous state and, of course, the MSR had to be cleared of the various equipment casualties that had occurred during the advance. This route clearance took some four days and 143 equipment casualties of one kind or another had to be recovered. Once our own casualties were cleared, Iraqi equipment was also cleared off the battlefield if it looked at all useful.

We were also faced with the shambles of the Basra road, by this time made notorious by the media reporting that had surrounded the Iraqi withdrawal from Kuwait City. The Mutla Pass resembled a shambolic multiple motorway traffic accident some five kms long. On 1 March 1993, the GOC ordered Lieutenant Colonel Alwin Hutchinson to take 32 Armoured Engineer Regiment to the jam and use his AVREs to clear it. This they duly did, forcing a path through the wreckage, initially one vehicle wide, subsequently cleared properly for two-way movement. His regiment was accompanied by Royal Pioneer Corps burial teams who were faced with the grisly task of clearing the wreckage of the dead where necessary. Rather to our surprise at the time, this task turned out to involve rather less dead than we had anticipated. Once the way into Kuwait was clear, we began to look to humanitarian aid and more general clearance. In early March, Divisional Main Headquarters moved closer to Kuwait City but Rear remained outside to take command of the DAA, which was placed between 7 Brigade and 4 Brigade, who were deployed further to the west in the desert.

A busy month ensued until Divisional Rear Headquarters withdrew from Kuwait at the beginning of April. By this time, a headquaters and base for the follow-on Kuwait Occupation Force (in itself a tale yet to be told!) had been set up. Divisional troops also assisted with the re-opening of Kuwait Airport, removing a burnt out and disabled airliner, using recovery vehicles for that purpose. Amongst other things, divisional logistic units assisted with the restoration of bread-baking facilities for a large part of north west Kuwait, the provision of water, support for the restoration of power generation supplies in Kuwait City and, of course, the return of our forces to Saudi Arabia.

7 Armoured Brigade were early movers in all this as a result of a direct initiative by the Prime Minister, John Major, himself. Heavy equipment was moved by road south to Jubail: personnel moved by C130 and heli-copters. In the early stages, road movement was punishing, especially for tank transporters. Oil fires burnt all over Kuwait, the roads were littered with puncture-making shrapnel, and little infrastructure existed. The latter was remedied later with the provision of formal convoy harbour areas. 4 Armoured Brigade followed on later in early April with Rear HQ as almost the last elements of the Division to leave Kuwait on 6 April 1991. Divisional Rear HQ transited through Jubail and returned to Verden on 11 April 1991.

During Operation DESERT STORM, the strength of 1 (UK) Armoured Division exceeded 25,800 men. Some 13,000 of these provided the CSS needed by the Division to sustain combat. In scale and scope, the operation rivalled those in Korea and Suez. Many old lessons were re-learnt and the apparently easy success of the operation has misled many to overlook the key lessons of its execution, especially in terms of the support area. Even though the casualty evacuation system and the ammunition provision organisation were not fully tested, the remaining disciplines were realistically committed. The key need to use logistics like firepower is demanding of all resources, especially Command, Control and Communications but it pays off as a means of generating tempo. CSS Command, Control and Communications are fundamental, and a real challenge for the future British Army.

Chapter Eleven

The Recovery Operation

Brigadier N Muddiman CBE
(Commander, Logistic Support Group)

As Commander Transport and Movements BAOR, I had been involved with Operation GRANBY from a very early stage. At General Sir Peter Inge's 'What If We Go?' round table for his commanders and staff on 6 September 1991, I had pressed the case for the deployment of DROPS to the Gulf, and obtained his agreement. On 14 September, the day that Mrs Thatcher ordered British deployment, I was on the road to Bielefeld at 4-30am. Later that morning as one of the three briefers facing BAOR's C-in-C, Corps Commander, Divisional and Brigade Commanders and senior staff, I had to outline how I intended to move 7 Armoured Brigade from Germany to the Gulf. As I rose to speak, Brigadier Mike Taylor, then Commander Communications 1 (BR) Corps muttered: 'Looks like your trade test Noel!', and indeed it was. Lieutenant General Sir Charles Guthrie asked how we intended to carry out the move, and my reply: Vehicles, Ammunition and Equipment by sea from the North German ports, the men by air from the most convenient airfield, seemed to answer the immediate question. What do you need from my staff?' he inquired, 'A DOAST 48 hours after the recce party returns from Saudi Arabia. Given that, my staff will do all they can to meet the deployment timetable'.

The Desired Order of Arrival Staff Table (DOAST) took much longer than the promised 48 hours, and it ran into many versions during the subsequent deployment (7 Armoured Brigade alone had 15 editions). Changes, particularly once the decision to deploy 1 (UK) Armoured Division had been taken, became commonplace and I am not sure that the G3 staff ever really appreciated the difficulties of the movements staff who had to tailor the loads to ships to ensure that vehicles and equipment arrived at Jubail in the correct order and on time.

However, the experience of moving the force from Germany was invaluable. The move of 1 (UK) Armoured Division and 4 Armoured Brigade, although larger, more complicated and against a tighter timescale than that of 7 Brigade, ran more smoothly as we all learnt on the job. Vessel loading times could be predicted with some accuracy and, by the end of December, we knew that sustained ship loading operations of 500 tonnes of ammunition daily, or 2000 linear metres[1] of vehicles on RO/RO ships were achievable for an indefinite period.

Preparation

On 20 February 1991, just four days before the ground offensive was launched against the Iraqi forces in Kuwait, General Inge quietly informed me that I had been selected to plan and execute the in-Theatre Gulf recovery operation and to be prepared to deploy to Saudi Arabia – some time in April.

I spent most of the ground war period at the Joint Headquarters (JHQ) at High Wycombe discussing how the withdrawal could be executed, and planning the priorities for the return of men, aircraft, vehicles, ammunition and materiel. The scale of the task could only be guessed-at at that stage, but it was possible to sketch an outline plan with theatre control of the operation to be undertaken by the Headquarters of 4 Armoured Division, which was stood by to deploy from Herford to Riyadh. The detailed execution of the recovery was to be undertaken by a new formation entitled The Logistic Support Group (Middle East) (LSG (ME)), which I was to establish in Saudi Arabia.

I was fortunate to have Air Marshal 'Kip' Kemball, the Chief of Staff of JHQ, as my boss. I had been his Assistant Chief of Staff (ACOS) in the Falklands in 1985/6 and we knew one another well. He accepted my proposal that we make shipping and ship-loading drive the recovery operation, based initially on half the loading rates which we had achieved at Emden (North Germany) during the outload. This would of course considerably increase the shipping bill, but if speed was paramount there could be no quicker way of ensuring that our forces were out of the Gulf at the earliest possible date. He broached this with the Prime Minister (by now John Major), when he visited JHQ on 27 February, and it was approved. The first step in the planning process had been agreed; recovery would be based initially on planning to load 250 tonnes of ammunition or loose cargo daily, together with 1000 linear metres of RO/RO shipping.

The abrupt ceasefire on 28 February accelerated the withdrawal planning process, and just three days later on 3 March, the JHQ staff issued the withdrawal planning guidelines. In brief, planning was to be undertaken on an 'R Day' basis i.e., the day on which redeployment and withdrawal were ordered. Against that:

- All of 1 (UK) Armoured Division's equipment was to be concentrated in Jubail by R + 38.
- All of the Division's personnel were to return to Europe by air by R + 38.

- LSG (ME) replacement personnel were to be in theatre, and the formation reduced to 3000 all ranks by R + 42.
- All logistic stocks were to be concentrated in Jubail by R + 60.
- The return of equipment and materiel to Europe by sea, and the commensurate rundown of LSG (ME) was to be completed as early as possible.

We did not get too far with priorities of return, apart from first in, first out, before the pace of events led to my deployment within a week. I was very fortunate to fly to Riyadh with Colonel Roy Lennox, the QMG's[2] logistic operations planner, who had already done an enormous amount of work coordinating with United Kingdom Land Forces (UKLF) and BAOR their priorities for ammunition and materiel return. Essentially the Individual Training Organisation in the UK had to be re-equipped as the first priority, followed by the reconstitution of 1 (BR) Corps. That governed the vehicle and materiel recovery plan. On the ammunition side, priority was given to those natures likely to be affected by the heat, such as the guided weapons, and then those which were purchased from allies on a 'shoot or return' basis. This put another firm link in the plan, but the scale of the overall task was still unknown. However, the command and control of the operation changed markedly. The plan to deploy Headquarters 4 Armoured Division was cancelled, and the LSG (ME) was to work initially through a reducing Headquarters British Forces Middle East (HQ BFME) in Riyadh, before eventually standing alone and reporting direct to the JHQ in High Wycombe.

Deployment to the Gulf

I arrived in Riyadh on 5 March 1991, and joined General de la Billière's staff in HQ BFME to coordinate the theatre withdrawal plan. This incorporated the movement of ships out of theatre and the rundown of our air bases in addition to the more complicated operation to withdraw the land forces.

The declaration of 'R Day' on 7 March put firm completion dates onto the recovery phases; the Division was to be home by 14 April, and all the stocks out of the desert and back into Jubail by 6 May.

There was little time to spare, if such an exacting timetable was to be met. I had a final meeting with General de la Billière on 8 March and then flew to Jubail to get together with Martin White to start the transfer of command. The LSG (ME) was formally established on 10 March incorporating the logistic staff of HQs BFME and FMA, all FMA units and (from 16 March) the three Prisoner of War Guard Force (PWGF) battalions. Colonel Mike Lake remained as the sole logistician in Riyadh, overseeing the Joint Transport and Movements Staff, whilst Commander Supply (Colonel Frank Steer) and Commander Maintenance (Colonel

Peter Gibson) joined me in Jubail. Such a concentration of staff very soon sorted out who was and was not required and it only took two or three days for the staff to thin out and delegate their responsibilities.

In the immediate aftermath of the war, we were still collecting enemy prisoners of war (EPWs), and the FMA and 1 (UK) Armoured Division staff had already put in train the concentration of several thousand tonnes of ammunition, materiel, rations, water and fuel either forward into the Divisional Administrative Area (DAA) north-east of Kuwait City, or back into the FFMA around Hafr Al Batin. This task, using every available transport asset in theatre, was completed on 14 March.

Whilst this operation was underway, I was on a vertical learning curve, very aware that I was the sole 'GRANBY 2 Reinforcement' in theatre. However, my arrival provided more satisfaction than resentment because it meant those who had fought the war would very shortly be going home.

Martin White briefed me well, introduced me to useful USMC contacts like Jim Brabham and Tom Stouffer and helped me find my feet in Jubail. I was not really prepared for the size of the place nor did I appreciate that the construction of Jubail and its three ports had involved the greatest earth moving operation in history amounting to some 450 million cubic yards – the equivalent of a road around the Equator nine metres wide and one metre deep. I only note these 'gee-whizz' statistics to give some idea of the available space. With a population of only 8,000 in an area the size of Greater London, Jubail also had a wealth of construction camps, many of which were being put to very good use by ourselves and the Americans.

By 11 March, Jubail was already a very busy town with hundreds of American and British troops preparing for the great return home. The first unit to be withdrawn from Kuwait was 32 Armoured Engineer Regiment, (under the command of Lieutenant Colonel Alwin Hutchinson) and it established the Division's Assembly Area on the outskirts of Jubail, preparing harbour and administrative areas together with all the facilities required to brief and look after incoming units as they gradually disposed of their equipment and lost their ability to function independently.

The outline plan to receive the Division in Jubail was well made and I had only to inherit it and let it run until changes became necessary. There was naturally some confusion on when responsibility was to devolve onto the fresh LSG troops who started to arrive in increasing numbers, and there was a not unnatural reluctance to 'let go'. But by the time it had sunk in that you were actually flying the next day, it did not take too much persuasion to let your 'GNG' (Gulf New Guy) step into your shoes.

Martin White and I were old chums and we knew one another too well for any difficulties in this area. After giving me a 'whistle-stop' flight up the Tapline Road to the FFMA, and on through 'The Breach' into Iraq, along the length of the Iraqi lines into Kuwait and back to Jubail through the oil fire smoke and across the oil lakes of the wrecked installations, Martin packed his desk, bade farewell to his staff and headed for the pool at the Holiday Inn. I bothered him a dozen times in the next two days and was very sad to see him fly off with Dick Hardie, the Commander Medical, late on the 14th. However, not before we had an excellent dinner with CGS, AG and DMO³ (who just happened to be passing through) and certainly not before Martin handed me his trusty and unbroached bottle of claret which he had kept hidden for the previous six months.

The Operation

Once I was happy that the reception arrangements at Jubail were working, my immediate task was to see Major General Rupert Smith and to take his concerns and priorities into account. This was not easy because a non-stop list of visitors, including ten members of the House of Commons Defence Committee, were demanding much of my time. However, as soon as Michael Mates and his team departed on 18 March, I headed north along Routes AUDI and DODGE to visit the far flung units of my command, and then on into Kuwait.

I was not unhappy to be out of Jubail and it gave me the opportunity to see 7 and 27 Regiments on the road, and to visit 32 Field Hospital and the Forward Armoured Delivery Group (FADG) in location. It was quite clear that Lieutenant Colonel Chris Bradley and Major Malcolm Hood were enjoying masterminding the recovery of equipment from the desert. They were a little optimistic on the completion date, but certainly they and their troops needed no external motivation to get the job done.

My abiding memory of that period was standing on a sand berm at 2200 hours one night and seeing nothing but lights from horizon to horizon as 139 tank transporters, DROPS and low loaders picked up the entire FADG in one lift. In the morning one lone Scimitar (light armoured recce vehicle) was found in the desert – not spotted in the dark!

The following day, I came upon my first dead Iraqis (in the Mutla Pass trenches), as I made my way to the Divisional Headquarters set up in an olive grove north east of Kuwait City. I spent one and a half days with General Smith, Colonel John Reith and their staffs to finalise the way in which the Division was to move and prepare vehicles for the voyage to Europe. We agreed that as accommodation in Jubail was limited, Rupert Smith would retain his Battle Groups in Kuwait until it was their turn to move. Once they did move it would be a smooth flow through the system from field location to flight home. In brief:

- 'A' vehicles would be transported, and 'B' vehicles driven, from Kuwait to the Assembly Area. All vehicles would move 'bombed up', and the first procedure on arrival would be to hand in all ammunition at a site designated the Returned Ammunition Group (RAG).
- 'De-bombed' vehicles would then move along the Assembly Area circuit to designated unit harbour areas where they would spend up to 48 hours handing over their surplus equipment and 'desert specials' (such as GPS, local maps and desert camouflage nets), before preparing their vehicles for the sea journey to Europe.
- Unit personnel who were not required to crew vehicles would be flown from desert airstrips in Kuwait aboard C130 Hercules. On arrival in Jubail they would be bussed to their unit harbour areas to prepare their vehicles.
- Once vehicles were declared by the unit as 'ready for shipping', they would drive to the Convoy Marshalling Area (CMA) close to the port.
- Soldiers would be bussed from either the unit harbour area or the CMA to Camp 4 to spend 24 to 48 hours before flying home from the airport at Jubail or Dhahran.
- The LSG (ME) would be responsible for securing vehicles at the CMA, and subsequently loading them onto the ships.

This plan worked very well. The only major change I had to make was over the location of the RAG. Before deploying from JHQ, I had asked for the Army's best Ammunition Technical Officer to be my technical adviser on the ammunition recovery. Lieutenant Colonel Alan Glasby GM arrived from Command Ammunition Depot Longtown on 17 March and set to work straight away. His arrival coincided with 32 Armoured Engineer Regiment establishing the Assembly Area, and their ammunition and explosives were removed and placed in the RAG adjacent to Ammunition Supply Point 2 (ASP2) – the joint ammunition depot we shared with the Americans on the outskirts of Jubail. When Alan saw the state of some of the home-made explosive devices put together for the 'breaching operation', he nearly had a fit and was not slow in telling me that unless we stopped the Division's recovery and established a new RAG a long way away from ASP2, we could have a very embarrassing incident which might end the recovery operation somewhat earlier than planned – and also require a major rebuild of parts of Jubail! This was not the sort of news I wanted so early on in the recovery. The first ship was ready for loading with ammunition, and to delay everything whilst a new RAG was sited and established would not be a popular move. It was with some trepidation that I called General Rupert and told him that the move of his Battle Groups would be delayed by two or three days whilst a new RAG was found, but he let me off quite gently. I gave Alan an Engineer Field Squadron and set him two days to complete his task.

The new RAG was established 8 kms away from ASP2. It was akin to 'mountains on the moon' with huge pits dug for different ammunition natures, each pit surrounded by a substantial compacted sand blast wall. Within two and a half weeks of its completion, Alan Glasby's insistence was proven correct; on 4 April several tonnes of white phosphorus exploded destroying all stocks within its sand safety wall. The incident was contained and there was no sympathetic detonation affecting adjacent stocks. The new RAG gave far more space to recover 1 (UK) Armoured Division's ammunition than we originally had available in ASP2. This speeded up the removal of unit ammunition and the two day break in the flow of Divisional units was steadily made up.

Back in the JHQ at High Wycombe, some of the staff considered that it might be possible to execute part of the recovery operation from Kuwait itself, and so, after leaving Headquarters 1 (UK) Armoured Division, I had taken the opportunity to recce Kuwait Port and Airport to ascertain whether there was any scope for using them. The airport was suitable for C130s but nothing larger on the fixed wing side. The port, on the other hand was an utter disaster. The sea approaches to Kuwait were mined, ships had been sunk in the harbour and even at the base of the main RO/RO ramps. The quayside facilities and cranage had been totally destroyed by the Iraqis. One thing was clear, Kuwait port would not be back in use for many months, and so all our vehicles, equipment and materiel would have to be recovered back through Saudi Arabia. That meant reversing the outload and moving everything and everyone the 350 km or so to Jubail.

The amounts to be moved back to Jubail were in the region of:

- 34800 tonnes of ammunition.
- 18 million litres of fuel.
- 2.5 million litres of water.
- 3400 tonnes of rations.
- 1,100 tonnes of engineer stores and loose freight.
- Over 1,000 containers of stores.
- 189 Armoured Vehicles in the Forward Armoured Delivery Group.

In addition the PWGF, comprising of 1 Coldstream Guards, 1 King's Own Scottish Borderers and the Royal Highland Fusiliers had over 8,000 Enemy Prisoners of War (EPWs) to contend with.

The task could only be undertaken with a transport operation as large as that required for the initial build up to the war, and for five weeks convoys of vehicles on round trips of between 24 and 48 hours moved up to 1500 tonnes each day. Every RCT unit in theatre was involved in the operation, only stopping two or three days before they were finally due to leave theatre. General de la Billière and I were adamant that safety and not speed was the order of the day for the recovery. The roads were heavily congested with the traffic of all the Coalition forces doing a similar job and the campaign had already claimed seven British lives in traffic accidents, and several times that number of American road casualties.

Enforced rest and frequent halts for servicing, refuelling, sleep and feeding eased some of the strain of the drive, and few drivers required a route card for the Tapline Road. Standards of driving, convoy discipline and vehicle maintenance were excellent and availability figures were consistently high. Of course few drivers relished the thought of guarding REME installations whilst their vehicles were being repaired, and such a prospect proved quite a motivator to keep vehicles running.

Loop times for the journey varied from 24 hours with DROPS to 48 hours for the Host Nation Support (HNS) vehicles, with 14 tonners and tank transporters taking around 32–36 hours. This part of the operation was completed on 2 April when the last 200 flatracks were moved by 27 Regiment RCT out of the old 12 Squadron location in the FFMA.

Completion of the desert recovery operation one month ahead of schedule provided quite a morale boast to the LSG, but the incoming 5 Ordnance Battalion, which relieved 6 Ordnance Battalion, were faced with the monumental task of sorting out the materiel mountain. 41 Ordnance Company ran the Return Stores Group (RSG) which comprised some 5,000 container loads of unissued stores, issued and subsequently returned stores, stores recovered from the desert and finally the de-kitting recoveries from 1 (UK) Armoured Division's units as they passed through the Assembly Area. All through March and the first few days of April the task grew and grew, and no matter how many men were employed sorting, accounting and repacking this enormous pile of stores, we seemed to be making little headway. However, with the desert recovery operation completed and the move of 1 (UK) Armoured Division's units still on schedule to meet the 14 April deadline, it appeared that the stores mountain was approaching its zenith.

Real estate space in Jubail was at a premium as the US recovery was also under way. US convoy parks and washdown areas appeared at roadsides and camp living accommodation was in short supply. A little delicate negotiation was necessary with Lieutenant General Boomer, commander of the USMC, whose deputy, Major General Hopkins, had ordered, 'No walking out in Jubail', for all soldiers. Up until mid-March, we had generally followed US practice on relations, liaison and the profile to adopt when dealing with the local Arab community. However, with only one or two days to purchase any souvenir of the campaign from a local shop, I felt that the USMC order was impractical – and certainly not appreciated by the local traders! I could not persuade Major General Hopkins to lift his blanket ban on walking-out, and so as diplomatically as I could, I informed Lieutenant General Boomer that I would be allowing British soldiers to 'walk-out' in Jubail, subject to all the necessary caveats on dress and behaviour. We agreed to differ, but the British soldiers certainly made full use of the shopping opportunity. Apart from a couple of minor incidents concerning price disputes, our soldiers behaved impeccably towards the locals.

The day or two of freedom before the flight home also led a number of soldiers to avail themselves of the hospitality offered by the Holiday Inn. After several months in the desert, the splendour of a luxury room complete with TV and en suite bathroom was too good to miss, especially for the many married couples serving together in the Gulf, but in reality apart, as they were nearly always in separate units. My own driver from Rheindahlen saw his wife off to war in December, joined her in the Gulf six weeks later, but only saw her once during the ensuing ten weeks.

Transport units were key to the desert recovery operation, but the withdrawal of RCT units was fully integrated into the plan, even though they each had a major part to play in the inload. 1 Armoured Division Transport Regiment flew on 21 March, closely followed by the first troops of 7 Tank Transporter Regiment and then 10 Regiment. That left 4 Armoured Division Transport Regiment and 27 Regiment to complete the backload plan. 29 Transport & Movement Regiment deployed in mid-March to run the LSG port and movements operations and later (on the withdrawal of 27 Regiment), the residual transport operation. This necessitated a lot of regrouping as the drawdown continued, but caused no major problems.

The final phase of the 1 (UK) Armoured Division move covered the withdrawal of 4 Armoured Brigade and the Division Rear Headmasters. The plan was going well and the final unit, 3 Royal Regiment Fusiliers (3RRF) Battle Group, was scheduled to pull out of Kuwait on 6/7 April. However, the halt in the US withdrawal from Kuwait, their subsequent decision to retain troops there for an indeterminate period, and a request to the British Government to do the same, led to a rapid change of plan. Some excellent staff work saw the establishment of a forward head-quarters of BFME under Colonel Ian McGill and the deployment of a fresh Battle Group (based on 2 Royal Anglian Regiment) from Germany to Kuwait by 11 April. When 3 RRF flew home on 13 April, although four days later than their originally planned date, they still met the R + 38 deadline.

Throughout the Divisional move, FMA units and Battle Casualty Replacements had been inserted into the plan, with few problems. The movement of air passengers from Jubail was fairly straightforward. HNS coaches collected soldiers and baggage from their camps and took them to the MCCP (Movement Control Check Point) being run by 59 and later 50 MC Squadrons. Cleared baggage was then driven by the all female troop from 68 Squadron RCT to the airport in Dhahran, about a one hour journey, and later the passengers were conveyed to the airport to arrive within an hour of flight departure.

The final units to move were the PWGF battalions. At the beginning of the recovery plan the PWGF was established in Maryhill Camp, north of the FFMA, guarding over 8,000 EPW. I anticipated that EPW would pose a major problem, but in the event their repatriation proceeded swiftly and smoothly. Moving mainly by air, all the British held EPW had been moved out of Maryhill into the main US PW camp (Brooklyn) by 18 March. Condemned stores were burned, the camp levelled and all three battalions were back in Jubail by 19 March. They then carried out training and security duties. By 15 April 1 Coldstream Guards and 1 Royal Highland Fusiliers had returned to the United Kingdom, leaving 1 King's Own Scottish Borderers as the LSG Security Battalion until they in turn were relieved by 2 Royal Anglians in mid June. This gave the Borderers the dubious honour of being the final GRANBY 1.5 unit to leave the theatre, outlasting 66 Squadron RCT by one week.

The return of the soldiers by air went remarkably smoothly. A joint recovery cell was established in HQ LSG staffed with representatives from the Division, LSG, HQ UKLF and HQ BAOR. The order of return allowed 7 Armoured Brigade and the early FMA troops to leave first, followed by Divisional troops, 4 Armoured Brigade and the balance of the FMA, BCRs and the PWGF. The joint cell worked well and was seen to be an equable way of resolving the many competing demands and priorities. There were initial difficulties over getting units to plan exactly who was to go on which flight 72 hours in advance. However, these were soon resolved and there were mercifully few flight delays. By mid April 34,000 soldiers had flown home to Europe.

The Clear-up

Once the Division's soldiers had flown, the LSG was left to get on with its main task – sorting out everything which was left behind. There was no accurate database on what had arrived in theatre, what had been lost or expended before, during or after the war, or indeed exactly what had to be recovered. In the pressure of moving, many units had abandoned equipment in the desert or in their camps at Jubail and some failed to notify anyone who could recover it. As a result the size and complexity of the task could only be estimated and initial bids for additional containers were made on this basis. Shipping bids were made in the knowledge that there were thousands of vehicles, containers and tonnes of ammunition to be moved so there was time to modify the detailed shipping requirement at a later stage in the recovery.

The recovery shipping was based initially on the loading rates agreed in JHQ, and the Defence Operations Movements Staff (DOMS) booked the first ship on 1 March 91. The MV Baltic Eider sailed from Jubail on 20 March 91 as the first of the planned recovery ships. (Six other vessels overtaken by the rapid ending of the war were despatched between 2 and 14 March 1991.)

There were two distinct categories of equipment to be returned to Europe. First, that received from 1 (UK) Armoured Division units such as the ammunition in the RAG, the returned stores in the RSG and the unit vehicles in the CMA. The second category comprised the theatre logistic stock holdings in the Engineer Park, ASPs, Bulk Fuel Installations, Ordnance Supply and Vehicle Depots. Much of this had been outloaded to the FFMA and the Division, and some had been issued to units. Many items in the Ordnance Depot had been demanded by units but not issued due to the rapid conclusion of the campaign, the speed of return of units and the inability to identify the location of the stores.

The LSG Engineer, Medical and Supply units had to inspect, condition and if not already on account, bring to charge all equipment before it could be packed and declared for shipping. This painstaking operation began before the GRANBY 2 units arrived in theatre, but they brought a fresh impetus to the task, replanned it and saw it through to completion.

By mid-April there were over 11,000 unit vehicles in the CMA awaiting shipment. 63 Vehicle Company, together with Royal Armoured Corps (RAC), Royal Artillery (RA), Engineer and Infantry soldiers of the Combined Arms Group (CAG) were responsible for running the CMA and subsequently driving the vehicles onto the ships. Following a request from HQ BAOR, the LSG Workshop carried out a road worthiness check on all vehicles prior to loading, and marked them either 'F', fit (roadworthy to European standards), 'R', (repairable at the port of entry), or 'U' (unfit and requiring road or rail carriage from the port of entry). This considerably eased the subsequent unloading and movement of vehicles in Europe.

Apart from unit vehicles, there were the War Maintenance Reserve and Peace Maintenance Stock vehicles to be returned. A total of 14,744 vehicles of all types were eventually returned to Europe. 231 vehicles were disposed of in theatre, and from these the LSG (ME) Workshop recovered some 70 vehicles-worth of assemblies which were returned to UK depots. The resultant carcasses were sold locally as scrap.

In addition, some 1,200 civilian vehicles were leased or hired during Operation GRANBY, ranging from small cars to heavy equipment transporters and plant. The majority of coaches and heavy trucks were hired with drivers and they made a significant contribution to the recovery operation. As the LSG began to recover the smaller self-drive vehicles, it became apparent that little management control had been imposed upon their use. On completion of recovery 19 vehicles remained untraced, seven were totally destroyed and damage claims were registered against a further 111.

Over 3,500 tonnes of 'de-bombed' ammunition had been collected in the RAG ranging from grenades (taped for throwing) to Rapier missiles, millions of loose small arms rounds and to huge explosive pipes specially manufactured by the RE for the breaching operation. The ammunition was covered in dirt, sand and even paint; it was without its packing (used for fires during the campaign), and its value running into tens of millions of pounds meant that it had to be recovered if at all possible. The unbroached stock amounting to a further 53,000 tonnes was relocated in the two ASPs on the outskirts of Jubail; its value was over £800 million.

The ammunition stock in the two ASPs was in generally good condition, having remained under RAOC control throughout its time in theatre. However, a major refurbishment task was required before the ammunition could be returned to UK. Over 18,000 pallets required some degree of repair work ranging from replacement of banding to the complete repalletisation of 3,500 pallets of 155 mm charges.

The recovery of ammunition was a very successful operation, and over 90 per cent of the stock was recovered to Europe, or handed back to US forces in the Gulf. Over 47,400 tonnes were shipped back to Europe, including 2,839 tonnes of the ammunition taken off the Division's units in the RAG.

It was the materiel recovery which concerned me most, and as the recovery progressed the LSG required a number of operationally vital items such as banding machines and wire, DROPS, MHE and Container Handling spares to ensure that the materiel recovery operation did not falter. Materiel issues were also being made as the LSG's remit extended beyond the Operation GRANBY recovery operation. Developments in Kuwait, in particular, posed an increasing logistic burden. Once it was decided to leave a Battle Group in Kuwait, a logistic support company was formed from the LSG to provide Kuwait with second line logistic support. The UN activities establishing first UNIKOM (UN Iraq/Kuwait Observer Mission), and then Operation ROCKINGHAM – the monitoring of Iraqi nuclear assets – entailed the LSG providing initial administrative and logistic assistance. Rations, vehicles and operational equipment were also flown and shipped to Cyprus to support Operation HAVEN – the Kurdish relief operation. Finally, in Kuwait, the deployment of 49 EOD Squadron RE on contract to Royal Ordnance Plc for the Battle Area Clearance task, saw the LSG again heavily involved in providing initial and longer term logistic support. So amid the pressure to receive and despatch, the flexibility to make issues continued.

As the soldiers of 41 Ordnance Company continued their task, their container sorting and packing speed increased. From 20 containers per day in late March they were achieving between 30–40 daily by mid May, and this effectively brought forward the completion date of the entire recovery operation by some two months.

Much of the packaging had suffered whilst in unit hands, due to repeated movement and heavy rain, and so the RSG task involved a lot of repackaging and redocumentation before stores could be accounted for and subsequently containerised for shipping. Where the necessary expertise for conditioning materiel was lacking, other equipment managers, especially REME, were called upon for advice. A timely decision to destroy a large number of desert camouflage nets saved the RSG one month's work and released manpower for other tasks.

To prime the base workshops, 229 engines and major assemblies (E&MAs) were airfreighted to Europe in early April. A total of 2,600 E&MAs were recovered. In May £2m worth of E&MAs were issued to 2 Royal Anglians to keep them operational in Kuwait for a further three months.

In mid March, the AMF(L)[4] Ordnance Company took over the supply depot operation. They inherited over four million man days of operational ration packs (ORPs) and 550,000 EPW (Halal) rations. The decision to dispose of most rations locally was swiftly made. However, decisions on where they were to go were far from timely. In the meantime, stock deteriorated through heat when it could have eased the plight of many starving refugees. Operation HAVEN received 600,000 of the ORP (167 containers + eight refrigerated containers and six generators), a small amount was given to UNIKOM and the remainder were gifted to famine relief organisations. A plan to gift 50,000 rations to the Somali government did not come to fruition. Despite attempts to send the Halal rations to ease the plight of the Kurds, they were eventually returned to the original supplier (ASTRA Farms) for disposal. As the LSG task reduced, we deliberately gave up camps where we were responsible for both ration supply and catering, and concentrated in those camps (like Camp 4) where there was a contract catering system. This worked well and enabled the early release of the AMF(L) Company, the majority of the catering staff, and the local disposal of the remaining fresh rations. Pork products were sold to ARAMCO.

Bulk fuels were supplied by the Saudi Government. As the LSG (ME) operation progressed, we ceased taking fuel deliveries and negotiated a coupon system to use local filling stations. 18 fuel tanks and 8 pump assemblies were then drained and recovered to UK. All serviceable specialist oils and lubricants were returned to UK, along with all sound containers. 63,000 jerrycans manufactured before 1970 were sold locally.

The engineer plant and materiel recovery task was undertaken by 61 Field Support Squadron who arrived in theatre on 16 March. In addition, 50 Field Squadron provided field engineer support to the LSG until late May. Regimental Headquarters 36 Engineer Regiment provided the Headquarters' Engineer branch. The programme included 10,000 tonnes of bridging, engineer stores and even 70 miles of PLOD (Pipeline Over the Desert) as well as the temporary camps. The task was a complicated one and not helped by a lack of records on camp structures and locally purchased and hired items such as power generators. In addition 220 'C' vehicles and items of construction plant were serviced, inspected and repaired before being shipped home.

All equipment recovered to the Engineer Park was repacked, apart from some specialist items such as Reverse Osmosis equipment, where no in-theatre expertise existed. 7,620 tonnes of Engineer stores were containerised or palletised for shipping. Some equipment such as the 70 miles of victualic pipeline required washing before palletising. HNS labour set to this task only managed to make seven pallets each day. RE and RPC labour achieved seventy pallets per day and completed the entire task (713 tonnes), ten days ahead of schedule.

The composition of the LSG(ME) from both its headquarters staff element and its component units continually changed throughout the recovery operation. On 17 March, the three PWGF battalions brought the LSG strength to 14 major units under command. However, within a month this had been reduced to a more manageable level of four major and eight minor units (see Figure 11.1) which then changed little until early June.

The key staff and service branches required to plan and oversee the recovery differed from those established in the FMA and BFME to prosecute the war. Transport & Movements and Supply were key to the entire recovery, whilst the Engineer and Medical branches were very busy for the specific phases to recover engineer equipment and effect the withdrawal of the medical units. The accounting and conditioning of combat supplies and materiel determined the requirement for a Commander Supply at Colonel level, and Colonel Graham Cowell (late RAOC) arrived at the end of March to take on the job from Frank Steer. Graham also assumed the appointment of Deputy Commander LSG, thus releasing Colonel Tony Welch. Because the maintenance load reduced markedly the final Colonel, Peter Gibson, was also able to leave the theatre before the end of March.

In early April Major Stuart Carruthers REME arrived as SO2 G4, and became *de facto* Chief of Staff. He and Graham Cowell made an excellent team and worked tirelessly to plan the detail of the recovery whilst continuing to support our soldiers in Kuwait. There was no blueprint for planning the total withdrawal from a theatre on such a scale. With no residual British force being left in Saudi Arabia, the planners virtually worked back from closing the RO/RO ramp on the final ship. This focused minds on exact ship loads, dates for ending contracts, handing back camps and of course the LSG's own unit and individual order of departure.

As the recovery progressed we had more and more contact with the local population, particularly over contracts. The G5 staff were kept fully employed. In early April, Lieutenant Colonel Geoff Hill handed over the baton to Major Willie Nichol, who built up a fund of amusing tales.

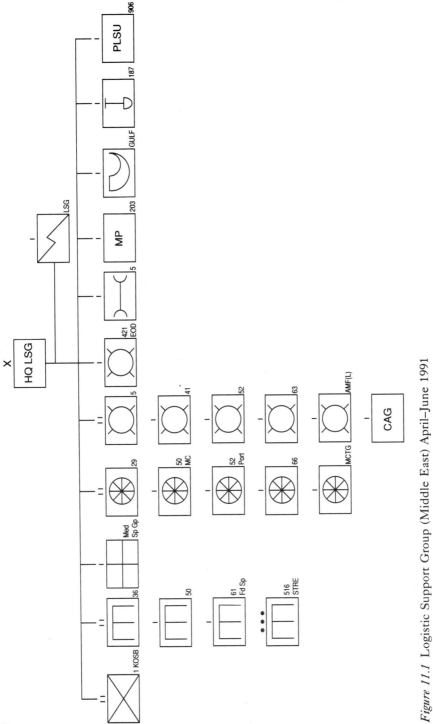

Figure 11.1 Logistic Support Group (Middle East) April–June 1991

One day he was called to a small Arab camp on the outskirts of Jubail where a local man claimed that we had killed one of his camels in a traffic accident. The proof was that he had seen military vehicles on the adjacent road the previous day, and that whoever had run-over his camel had been thorough enough to drag it off the road and hide it behind a sand wall. He argued that only a soldier would have done that. Not too convincing a claim we felt, and when Willie found one of our missing three-quarter tonne trailers hidden behind the man's tent, that was taken away from him and the camel claim rejected.

Medical support during the recovery was continually changing. On 10 March 91, the LSG had the FMA's six Field Hospitals under command including one each from Norway, Canada and Romania. Apart from 32 Field Hospital, casualty loading was light and there was an urgent desire to get medical personnel back to Europe to reconstitute closed military hospitals such as BMH Hannover and the Cambridge in Aldershot. In addition, there was political pressure to get the reservists back to their civilian employment.

The Norwegian Field Hospital provided the theatre second line medical support from 21 March 91 until 14 April 91 which enabled the three UK Field Hospitals, the LSG (ME) Field Ambulance and the Canadian and Romanian hospitals to leave the theatre. During this period, the Norwegians treated over 700 British patients.

From mid-April, a Medical Reception Station was established in Old Port Barracks for routine medical cover. Trauma cases were treated by a British medical staff element in the USMC Hospital in Jubail. The USMC Hospital closed on 12 May 1991, and I then approached Prince Abdullah, the President of the Royal Commission for Jubail, to see whether or not we could make use of the Royal Commission Al Fanateer hospital. The Prince was very accommodating, and thereafter trauma cases were treated at the Al Fanateer, whilst the MRS moved to Camp 4 until it disbanded in mid-July.

Many of the other activities undertaken by the LSG were continuations and reductions of the operations initiated by the FMA. Huge volumes of mail (16 articulated trucks daily) were still arriving in mid March, and as the distribution service reduced the tracing and redirecting service increased. The EFI reduced rapidly and sales fell from £200,000 weekly in March to £35,000 weekly in May and June. The quick end of the war and the low priority afforded to EFI containers led to many goods arriving after the Division's troops had left. BFPO 3000 parcels also had a significant affect on sales. The result was that £300,000 of goods with a short shelf-life could not be returned to UK and the EFI operation in the Gulf netted a £250,000 loss. However, it was an invaluable service and continued to function in Kuwait until 15 July and in Jubail until 20 July.

Increasing use was made of HNS as the recovery continued, thus releasing soldiers to return to Europe. However, civil labour in Saudi Arabia is provided by TCN (Third Country Nationals), primarily from the Indian sub-continent which has a different work ethic. There were numerous frustrations caused by prayers, religious holidays and general idleness. They had to be constantly supervised and were unsuitable for urgent, difficult or dangerous jobs, or any involving physical strength; for example two men were needed to carry one full jerrycan. This precluded them from many of the LSG tasks involving ammunition and shipping. However, they provided an asset for low grade tasks requiring little physical strength and thus released soldiers for other duties.

HNS transport provided low mobility, high capacity lift. Without it we would have required two additional in-theatre transport regiments. However, many of the drivers came from Turkey, Syria and the Sudan and lacked the necessary documentation to cross the Saudi border into Kuwait and Bahrain. There were obvious language and culture difficulties, but one unexpected development was when 15 of our civilian coach drivers drove their coaches to Mecca in a 'moonlight flit' to gather richer pickings during the Haj (Pilgrimage), leaving several hundred LSG soldiers unable to get to work, or catch their aircraft home!

However, these frustrations were accepted pragmatically by the soldiers who continued to work 'around the clock' to complete their task. The hardest working conditions were in Kuwait and in the desert, where the ammunition technicians were destroying degraded stock. The port operators, who were 'the cutting edge' of much of the LSG operation, were also working in harsh, noisy and hot conditions in the holds of ships. Temperatures were often 55°C, and frequent breaks and copious fluid intakes were essential to maintain the momentum of the loading operation, which continued for 24 hours a day when necessary. The small industrial fork lifts used in the ships' holds often overheated and we were fortunate that our US allies were generous with their equipment loans.

During the final two months of the recovery operation, the LSG (ME) sold over 640,000 items of equipment, 600 tonnes of food, 1½ million litres of water and some 1,300 tonnes of scrap. This involved seven separate tender sales comprising some 250 lots and a running scrap contract with the local steel works (at two and a half times the European scrap price). Receipts amounted to over £1.5m. Additionally, 1,850 pallets of ORP were gifted to charity for famine relief.

A wide variety of items were sold including Blackadder Camp, which just as the BCRs departed had living and dining accommodation for 2,000 men. Vehicles, chairs, generators and even 4,000 body bags were included in the sales, which generated enormous enthusiasm from local Arab traders.

Uncertainty over the future of British Forces Kuwait (BFK) was the most significant complication in the LSG withdrawal operation. From the outset, it was clear that retention of troops in Kuwait and total withdrawal from Saudi Arabia as soon as possible were incompatible. However, the rolling nature of the lack of a firm decision on the role, size and future of our forces in Kuwait effectively prevented the establishment of an alternative support structure. The LSG (ME) remained in support of BFK throughout, even though earlier planned air links were withdrawn and the 350 km L of C was made even more tortuous once post war 'normality' returned to the Saudi-Kuwait border.

Six different withdrawal dates were planned for, before the definitive decision was made in early June to retain an Armoured Infantry Company in Kuwait until the end of July, and to withdraw it in conjunction with the LSG. By then it was clear that the LSG task would be completed before the end of July, but a plan to withdraw BFK and to load their vehicles onto the penultimate RO/RO ship on 18 July 91 was vetoed. However, a devastating US ammunition explosion at Doha on 11 July 1991 made the British camp untenable, and the withdrawal of BFK equipment and vehicles was brought forward to 23/24 July 1991. In turn this enabled the LSG (ME) to close on 27 July 1991.

The recovery operation presented an enormous challenge to all units and individuals in the LSG. In the immediate post-war period no one knew just how large the task would be. In the run-up to the ground offensive, the RAF had airlifted more stores into theatre than were moved during the entire Berlin airlift. There was no time to take these stores to account, and no records were made of consumption during the campaign. So it was only when everything had been recovered to Jubail by mid April, that realistic assessments of the entire task could be made. As the sorting out progressed and the ships left fully laden, the estimates were further refined and the withdrawal of the elements of the LSG could then be planned.

My initial estimate on how long the recovery operation would take was made in HQ BAOR before I deployed, and was based on what I knew had been moved from Germany to the Gulf. Optimistically I opted for an end of July 1991 completion date. The logistic planners in MOD were estimating completion by March 1992. On arrival in theatre and seeing the enormous volume of equipment to be moved, I felt that the MOD had probably got it about right, but I hoped that we could be finished by Christmas 1991. However, as the soldiers in the LSG got to grips with their enormous task, it developed a momentum of its own which in turn became self-motivating. Each and every unit took immense pride in completing its particular part of the jigsaw. It started with the RCT physically moving tens of thousands of tonnes out of the desert into Jubail, the sappers and RAOC supported by the RPC and a Combined Arms Group of cavalry, gunners and infantrymen then tackled the detail of cleaning, packing, accounting and preparing for shipment. Finally the RCT finished off the job by loading and despatching the ships.

The total stock recovered to units and depots in Europe on completion of Operation GRANBY was:

- Vehicles and Trailers 14,744
- Ammunition 47,477 tonnes
- Engineer Stores/Loose Freight 11,600 tonnes
- Containers 7,188
- Flatracks 2,214

The 92nd and final ship *Salar* sailed from Jubail on 27 July 1991, and later that day the LSG (ME) officially disbanded. I flew back to Germany leaving Graham Cowell and a small rear party to close the final contracts and hand over Camp 4 before flying home from Bahrain.

It was not quite the end of the story because on 28 July, the day after the last ship had sailed, six containers and two flatracks were found in Camp 9 which had not had any British unit in occupation since February! On the return from the war, the unit owning them had just forgotten that they had left anything behind.

The LSG (ME) soldiers were proud to have worn the Blackadder on their sleeves. Their task was very different to that of their predecessors in the FMA and was undertaken without the uncertainty of war hanging over them. However, it was not without its pressures; many of them financial.

Every aspect of the Operation GRANBY recovery operation was looked at in value for money terms. If it was more cost effective to recover materiel and ship it to Europe then that was planned. If it was better value to dispose of it locally, then we went ahead on that basis. Such an approach was unique in my experience, and it produced a number of interesting by-products. From the military vehicles cast during and after the campaign, the LSG workshop recovered over 70 vehicles-worth of assemblies which were containerised and shipped back to UK depots. The resultant vehicle carcass (less its reclaimed parts) was sold locally as scrap to the local iron and steel foundry with whom we negotiated over twice the European scrap price.

On 25 July, Prince Abdullah sent for me so that I could report on the withdrawal of the British troops from Jubail. I took the opportunity to present him with the FMA/LSG shield featuring the Black Adder. 'Ah thank you', he said, 'I studied in your country and I know that the Black Adder has a long military tradition with you, I have even seen stories of it on your television!' 'Not quite Highness', I replied, 'I think you will find on this occasion that military tradition has been born out of a television comedy – my friend Martin White is to blame'. 'I do not believe you', he retorted 'This cannot be, however I will keep this little memento for myself, just in case . . .'

And what happened to Martin Whites's bottle of claret? Believe it or not, it remained unbroached and hidden in my cupboard until 26 July.

On the eve of the LSG's closure Graham Cowell, Stuart Carruthers, Willie Nicholl and I drank it reverently, as we reflected on not just the recovery, but the enormity of the entire Operation GRANBY logistic operation.

Chapter Twelve

Conclusions

Major General M S White CBE
(Commander Force Maintenance Area)

The Gulf War was unique in many ways, fought in a country able to provide a rich infrastructure of ports, airports and resources for the coalition forces. Time was on our side, facilitating a deliberate build-up of military power, at a time and place of our own choosing and at a political watershed in the 20th century which allowed the United Nations Security Council unprecedented freedom of action. Arguably it is a freedom that they have not enjoyed before or since. We must therefore set any logistic lessons and conclusions against this background and in the certain knowledge that there will never be an exactly similar campaign, but that nevertheless there is much we can learn as military men for the conduct of future conflict; be it at the high intensity end of the warfighting spectrum or engaged in peace support type operations with the United Nations.

Each chapter in its own way has produced many indications for the future, but I would like to draw out some of the main lessons from my perspective as a logistic commander on the ground in the Gulf and perhaps point the way for logistic support (at the operational level) in largely multinational formations having to deploy over long distances and liable to be engaged in a variety of military options.

Lessons from the War

I shall start by considering command, control and communications. Whilst the Army provided the major contribution in terms of men, all three Services placed heavy and concurrent demands on their own respective logistic chains. There was, initially, an absence of, but an obvious requirement for, a single organisation (ideally joint-Service) to categorise and put demands into priority in order to avoid duplication and confusion and to ensure that airframes and, if necessary, shipping were allocated appropriately. The ability to track assets and to control stores within the system also proved limited and, whilst units generally received everything they demanded, it occasionally proved quicker and more expedient to re-demand than to try and locate an item that might have been delayed or temporarily 'lost' in the system. At the divisional level, Graham Ewer has brought out the vital need for effective logistic command, control and communications on the modern battlefield.

We had no standing structure, designed for the support of such a sizeable armoured force operating so far away from the support base in north-west Europe. Looking specifically at our ground forces, the problems encountered in the preparatory phase, particularly the shortage of time to structure HQ FMA, to confirm the logistic ORBAT and to assemble the many individuals and mass of equipment for operations, have led us to look again at the case for some sort of HQ FMA in peace; it must also be provided with adequate communication and computer support. A point equally applicable at divisional level.

The responsibility for controlling the resupply chain needs to be clearly defined. Planning should be joint from the earliest opportunity. At the same time, the ability to ensure the timely delivery of stores and assets requires that they be tracked accurately throughout the resupply chain and not end up as we did with hundreds of tons of unidentified priority stores for fighting units dumped in Jubail. This could be achieved best by developing a comprehensive, robust and flexible logistic management information and tracking system. This would also have the possibility of NATO-wide application for the use of multi-national or combined forces.

A significant aspect of our logistic operations was the unprecedented reliance on Host Nation Support in spite of the large number of our own logistic troops deployed in theatre. Over the total Coalition, this was a massive exercise which represented a welcome reduction in the size of the military support operation. There are, however, a number of points which it would be worth noting for the future. Negotiations and contractual arrangements often proved time-consuming and complex for our small liaison staff. Delays were encountered as requests and paperwork were referred up the chain-of-command for agreement by higher authority. Valuable time could have been saved if greater authority could have been delegated to a lower level.

Whilst all the civilian contractors made a significant contribution to our own efforts, they were, inevitably, less predictable in terms of availability, workrate and reliability than would have been personnel under military discipline and this required us to remain rather more flexible than normal. Sensitive issues are involved, but tighter control of local contractors would have made life a little bit more structured and could have been of major importance had we experienced any setback affecting the morale of the civilian workforce.

The importance of Host Nation Support, particularly in this sort of operation, cannot be over-emphasised, but it requires an extensive, capable and flexible liaison organisation at all levels, with executive powers devolved to local liaison officers. It also requires a robust approach with firms and contractors to be maintained. This, I believe, is an important aspect for future operations and has an international dimension. Given time in Saudi Arabia, we could have developed a much more effective international Host Nation operation at the grass roots level in conjunction with our Saudi Arabian hosts, and our Coalition partners, particularly the United States. The budgeting and financial aspects are also important and do not sit easily with military operations; there is a need for properly trained staff deployed forward early to deal with the financial aspects of all these matters.

The deployment of a force to the Gulf highlighted a number of gaps in the UK logistic capability. Many were as a result of having to adapt and equip our vehicles, aircraft and men to operate in an unfamiliar, harsh and somewhat hostile environment. Demands were placed on the Defence Industry to respond at short notice to vital procurement and resupply requirements, and Service technical branches were placed under enormous strain to take on the major modification and maintenance tasks that such operations generate. A number of new equipments and vehicles were deployed with only limited time available to train operators. The success of our palletised load system, DROPS, re-emphasized the importance of flexibility and mobility. It was, however, necessary to procure or borrow vehicles to achieve the same degree of mobility in other areas. There were also benefits which could have been derived from greater use of containerised stores and equipment. However, this would have further stretched our limited container handling capability which was pressed to meet the existing commitment and, therefore once again, would have required significant Host Nation and Allied support to assist.

Turning to the organisational and manpower aspects of logistic capability, we had a major problem in providing adequate support for one division in battle without recourse to the reserves. That situation has not improved since the end of the Gulf War and must be one of the highest priorities to put right. It is also vital that logistic planning takes account of limitations in the Defence Industry's ability to respond to procurement and resupply demands. A clear indication of response times, whilst often difficult to predict, should be reflected in contingency plans.

As has been described, our medical system was eventually robust and well set up. Cooperation with our allies and the multinational medical services deployed in theatre provided invaluable support and were a great boost to confidence and morale. However, it presented the staff in the field with a major management and coordination task. As a bonus, I understand that contingency planning with our own National Health Service resulted in an extremely flexible response in making arrangements for the reception of casualties in the United Kingdom.

Medical planning must be an integral part of the force build-up. If a threat exists, adequate facilities must be made available for chemical and biological casualties and for operating in such an environment. Realistic casualty estimates, including likely enemy casualties, are vital, and close cooperation and liaison with Allied medical services must be maintained to ensure procedures are, where possible, standardized and integrated.

Finally, a word on Cooperation, Standardisation and Integration and I have already highlighted some examples. All three Services operated closely with the respective Services of our Allies. Few unexpected problems were encountered but the close cooperation did reconfirm the value of interoperability and the advantages of equipment standardisation, long paid lip service to in many areas. Ammunition shortfalls were met from American, Belgian, Dutch and German sources. The need for cooperation and standardisation of operating procedures, treatment régimes and equipment scales is obvious but for 40 years in NATO it has never been fully faced. However, perhaps we now live in a different environment where lack of resources will force a realistic approach to this subject. I hope so.

Because of the short and successful nature of the ground war, the logistic system was not put under great and enduring stress. Nevertheless, I firmly believe that it was sufficiently balanced and robust to have coped with more sustained operations; the preparatory phases were, of course, equally demanding and a valuable measure of the system's competence and capability. Had the NBC threat materialized it would have impeded our logistic operations. The absence of air attacks also allowed us substantial freedom of action. Throughout all phases of the logistic support effort, the principle of flexibility, the recognised response to the unpredictability of the battlefield, was both necessary and well demonstrated.

A number of the problems we encountered were unique to the desert environment and to the distances over which we had to operate. The extremes of temperature, coupled with the tempo of logistic operations, might have had both a physical and psychological effect on our soldiers if hostilities had continued for much longer. There were also the organisational shortcomings which I have mentioned. In the end, there was a concern that the very speed and degree of our success might have unbalanced our logistic support. Fortunately, the logistic balance which we had established and the flexibility of our distribution system were more than adequate for the task. Indeed, with hindsight and knowledge of the enemy, there was over-insurance in some areas.

I believe that our success in establishing the strong and balanced logistic base demonstrated, as much as the thorough training of the combat arms, that the British forces were fully prepared for battle. The strength and robustness of that base was a product of sound planning and good leadership backed up by the excellence and determination of our soldiers.

The Future

Finally, I would like to briefly review the new challenges for logistics in the changed political military environment. The dramatic developments which finally led to the reunification of Germany and the breakdown of the Warsaw Pact are well known. And, more recently, new threats to security throughout the world in such places as the former Yugoslavia and Somalia outside the NATO areas of responsibility have caused a revision of political and strategic thinking. This encompasses the likelihood of UN (possibly also WEU and CSCE) operations, including humanitarian aid through peacekeeping to peace enforcing. Armed forces are reducing as budgets reduce and we see a growth of multinational formations at corps level and below.

Implicit in the greatly extended scope of possible operations for multinational forces is the need for a real change of direction and emphasis for logistic support. For, moreover, there is a need for an effective NATO movement control organisation, for instance to direct and monitor the deployment of multinational formations in accordance with the commander's plan. I believe it should also be linked to an in-place logistic headquarters able to control the many other aspects of the international build-up and support organisations. In particular, the proper coordination of lines of communication and liaison with host nation and non-governmental agencies (if appropriate) is essential.

One of our greatest failings in the Gulf was our inability to 'track assets' and this is even more critical for the support of future operations. What is needed is a cheap, user friendly computer system which can track our supply items and also be used for other logistic operations such as movement planning, field (personnel) records and casualty evacuation control.

Again, there was much duplication of logistic effort in Saudi Arabia and this could be partly overcome by international (multinational) logistic coordination. Even with our lamentable record of standardisation and interoperability, there are still areas of common supply which could be provided on a 'lead nation' basis, such as fuel, water and transport for certain operations. There is also a great deal of scope for harmonising the medical evacuation chain.

The 'new' military environment has kept logistics in the forefront of the military planner's mind and it is essential that it remains there in the future. The need to deploy armed forces throughout the world rapidly will remain and for those deployments to remain credible and sustainable they must be properly supported with logistic troops that are at least at the same state of readiness as the fighting troops.

For all of us the Gulf War was a unique and unforgettable experience and life will never be quite the same again. We all felt very privileged to be part of one of the most effective military campaigns in modern times and to have made a contribution to the liberation of Kuwait.

Chapter Notes

Foreword

1. See campaign map at p. 11.
2. Details of contractor support at Chapter 7.

Chapter 1: The Support of the War in Perspective

1. The Gulf War 1990/1991 was known by a variety of codenames amongst the coalition partners including:
   a. Operation GRANBY 1 (UK) – the deployment of 7 Armoured Brigade Group
   b. Operation DESERT SHIELD (US)
   c. Operation DESERT STORM (US)
   d. Operation DESERT SABRE (US/UK)
   e. Operation GRANBY 1.5 (UK) – the deployment of 1 (UK) Armoured Division
   f. Operation GRANBY 2 (UK) – the recovery operation
2. A number of possible British deployments were considered including the deployment of an armoured brigade from Germany; this was the eventual option chosen, the brigade being 7 Armoured Brigade.
3. The UKMF, now defunct, was a UK-based brigade-sized formation with integral logistic support with deployment options in Denmark and Northern Germany.
4. Individual reservists are ex-regular soldiers with a residual commitment once they have left the Colours. These should not be confused with TA individuals and units who are all volunteers.
5. Combat Supplies. Those items critical to the immediate sustainment of the battle, i.e. ammunition, fuel, rations and water. For logistic planning purposes, combat supplies are quantified in days of supply. That is the average quantity of combat supplies which a given formation would be expected to consume on a normal day of combat. For example, an armoured division's consumption, i.e. one day is approx 2,000 tons (mainly ammunition). At the height of battle an intensity factor of three is applied, i.e. for an armoured division 6,000 tons. Strategic logistic planning is based on these quantities but clearly a great deal of refinement is needed further forward in the chain.
6. 30 days at normal rates.
7. Logistic support is broken down into lines:

a. First line. Support integral to the unit and provided by the quartermaster.

b. Second line. Support provided by logistic units (transport supply, maintenance, medical) integral to the fighting formation (division or brigade).

c. Third line. Support behind the division (or brigade) but forward of the port or airport of entry into the theatre of operations.

d. Fourth line. Base support (usually the United Kingdom).

8. Combat Service Support (CSS). CSS, a relatively new term, is defined (in UK Army Field Manuals) as the support provided to combat forces, primarily in the field of administration and logistics. In the context of this book, CSS will be limited to the support provided at divisional level and forward.

9. DROPS. The DROPS fleet (US PLS system) had only just entered service in the United Kingdom. It is a modern, reliable load handling system consisting of Leyland Daf trucks with dismountable platforms (flatracks) designed to carry logistic loads.

10. MLRS. A modern, highly accurate, mobile tracked rocket system jointly developed by UK, US and Germany with a range of up to 30 km.

11. A mix of RAF Chinook, Puma and Royal Navy Sea King helicopters.

Chapter 2: The Commander's Role

1. The whole episode of what was known as rate capping caused immense frustration in the field. This process set a manpower ceiling on the Force despite military advice to the contrary. In one extreme case, part of an infantry battalion was deployed to the Gulf (the Queen's Own Highlanders) only to be returned to Germany, leaving much of their equipment in Jubail. They returned a matter of days later!

Chapter 3: The Force Maintenance Area
Part One: The Logistic Structure

1. In peacetime, the men and equipment in a unit form the peace establishment of that unit. On transition to war reservists and equipment are added to bring it to a war establishment to enable it to sustain operations. The increase is between 10 and 20 per cent.

2. The staff of a headquarters are divided according to their responsibilities in support of the commander.

a. G1 Personnel matters

b. G2 Intelligence

c. G3 Operations

d. G4 Logistics (Combat Service Support)

e. G5 Civil-military cooperation and host nation liaison

f. G6 Communication matters.

g. Arm and Service branches. Responsible for functional matters e.g. artillery, engineers, medical, transport, etc.

3. The home in Germany of 1 (UK) Armoured Division. The 'Options for Change' exercise has closed Verden and the reorganised Divisional Headquarters is now in Herford.

4. In general terms, in the British Army, staff officers are categorised as staff officer Grade 1 (SO1), a lieutenant colonel, staff officer Grade 2 (SO2), a major, and staff officer Grade 3 (SO3), a captain.
5. The British contribution to the Gulf War was commanded by Air Chief Marshal Sir Patrick Hine from his headquarters at High Wycombe. He and his staff provided the strategic political interface and issued direction and guidance to deployed forces.
6. A derogatory description linking it to the house of an infamous murderer.
7. The ability of a headquarters to leap frog forward in support of operations is known as stepping-up.

Part Two: Rear Area Operations

1. Although somewhat limited in its capabilities the cell produced excellent and timely information and assessments for the logistic units.
2. The chemical monitor that we had deployed included:
NAIAD – Nerve Agent Detector
CAM – Chemical Agent Monitor
RVD – Residual Vapour Detector
In addition troops took other personal protective measures.
3. Both Camp 4 and the large sheds (4, 5 and 6) in the port loomed large in our lives. In the former case Camp 4 provided a respite from the desert and the sheds provided somewhere to live whilst waiting for ships to arrive with vehicles and equipment.
4. The authorised level of vehicles, weapons and equipment belonging to an army operational unit is known as its G1098, which is the number of the printed form in which the details are contained.

Chapter 4: Transport And Movements

1. The DOAST is the key document for the deployment of a force. It is confirmed by the commander following a reconaissance and sets the flow of men, equipment, ammunition and stores into the theatre of operations. It stands for the Desired Order of Arrival Staff Table.
2. Transport to clear ships, move equipment and men and under the command of HQ FMA.
3. R and R (rest and recuperation). Troops were able to enjoy a brief respite from preparations for war in Bahrain, away from the immediate threat from Iraq.
4. The Mobile Civilian Transport Groups (MCTG) formed at the end of the Second World War were originally a wide mix of European nationals who manned transport for garrisons in Germany. A TSU is a similar all military unit.
5. 27 Regiment, based in Aldershot, provided reinforcement for the FMA. They had a similar organisation to 10 Regiment (see Figure 4.1).
6. A staff check is a tool to test the feasibility of a plan. In essence it is an overall calculation of, for example, time, quantities and available transport to check whether we could support 1(UK) Division in their operation with 7(US) Corps.

7. See ORBAT at Figure 3.4, Page 39.
8. The reason for the presence of MOD officials (Civil Secretariat) in Riyadh was to provide financial and contractual advice to commanders, an area where many service officers have little experience. They were invaluable.

Chapter 5: Medical Support

1. Field Ambulance. A second line (divisional or brigade) medical unit stabilises and evacuates casualties to a field hospital. Surgery is not normally carried out at this level. Typically an armoured division of two brigades would have two tracked field ambulances (one per brigade) and a wheeled field ambulance for the rest of the division.
2. Regimental Aid Posts (RAP). The first line of medical support at the unit level. All casualties begin the process of evacuation through the RAP. Run by the Regimental Medical Officer (RMO) it is sited close to the front line. The regimental chaplain is often to be found here during battle.
3. Soldiers, NCOs and warrant officers of the Royal Army Medical Corps (RAMC) operating in the field army are known as Combat Medical Technicians.
4. The wartime role of army musicians is as stretcher bearers in medical units.
5. The Global Positioning System (GPS) is an American military satellite system enabling military units to pin-point their position with a high degree of accuracy. It was of the utmost importance to operations in the desert, where maps are notoriously inaccurate.
6. A Field Ambulance is normally capable of forming two dressing stations where casualties are stabilised and processed before evacuation rearwards.
7. Reserve helicopters.
8. Pre-stocked unit equipment (PUE). By nature of their war role or mobilisation category, for example TA, some units' equipment (such as stores and vehicles) is stocked in central depots either in the United Kingdom or, less frequently now, in Germany.
9. The Defence secure telephone system.
10. MAOTs. A small RAF team providing the ground commander with a link to his supporting RAF aircraft.

Chapter 6: Supply

1. The NAAFI (Navy, Army and Air Force Institute) provide a range of retail shops for the Services in peace time and they are staffed by civilians. They contain a mobilisable element which deploys on exercises and operations (the Expeditionary Forces Institute (EFI)) which provides essential comforts to the servicemen and women.
2. Military vehicles are classified as:
   a. A vehicles – tanks and armoured vehicles
   b. B vehicles – soft skinned vehicles such as landrover and trucks
   c. C vehicles – Engineer plant
3. Fuel consumption unit/oil consumption unit (FCU/OCU). The average

amount of fuel or oil consumed by a given formation in an average battle-field day, in this case 1(UK) Armoured Division.
4. The NATO identification.
5. Composite rations ('Compo') They say an army marches on its stomach and in the case of the British Army this is 'Compo', tinned food designed to meet all the dietary needs without addition. However, it needs to be supplemented with fresh food if possible, to relieve boredom and produce a balance.

Chapter 7: Equipment Support

1. Main Repair Group (MRG). A REME field repair organisation at divisional level capable of extensive automotive and electronic repairs to all types of equipment. It is fairly mobile but operates best if not moved frequently.
2. Forward Repair Group (FRG). A mobile repair organisation providing close support to fighting units. Capable of changing engines and major assemblies on fighting vehicles.
3. The engine and associated components of an armoured vehicle is known as the power pack.
4. In this case a day is a peacetime day for calculating spares holdings.
5. HQ DGEME. Headquarters Director General of Electrical and Mechanical Engineers based at Andover was part of the Army's Logistic Executive and the focus for world-wide equipment management matters. As a result of the reorganisation of the Army following 'Options for Change' it is known as Headquarters Director General Equipment Support and part of Headquarters Quartermaster General. Still located at Andover.

Chapter 8: The Small Cogs

1. Joint Service Publication.
2. Brigade Maintenance Area established north of Jubail and containing a mix of second line logistic units to support 7 Armoured Brigade.
3. US Army Central Command was General Schwarzkopf's Headquarters based in Dhahran and Riyadh.
4. A BFI consists of large fabric fuel tanks to provide a source of bulk fuel in the forward areas.
5. The acquittance role is a legal and auditable document which lists personnel who have drawn money from that account.
6. Unit deployment is normally divided into an advance party who set up facilities for the main body, the balance of the men and equipment and a rear party, left in peacetime barracks to administer the families and provide a 'link' for the unit.
7. Part Two Orders. Any change in personal circumstances of an officer or soldier is published in a Part Two Order as it invariably affects his pay.
8. LOA. An allowance made to adjust a serviceman's pay to local conditions.
9. The American equivalent to NAAFI is the PX (Post Exchange).
10. Lists of unit personnel.
11. An aircraft load of passengers is known as a 'chalk'.

Chapter 10: 1 (UK) Armoured Division Logistic Operations

1. On operations a divisional headquarters is deployed, normally in two elements, so that it is best placed to support the commander in fighting the battle and directing his combat Headquarters service support (CSS). Divisional Main Headquarters which is armoured and commands the battle, may also deploy a small tactical element so that the commander can move forward (Tac HQ). Divisional Rear Headquarter commands the divisional rear area and directs CSS activities; it may also deploy a small divisional rendezvous (RV) (the divisional 'back door') and a Headquarter Divisional Administrative Area (DAA) element. Divisional Rear on Operation GRANBY was armoured.

2. Until the fall of the Berlin Wall and the collapse of the Soviet Union Exercise SUMMER SALES had been one of the main events of the 1 (BR) Corps training year.

3. The British Army consists of arms (armour and infantry artillery, engineers etc) and services (transport, medical, supply maintenance etc).

4. In the early days, tentative plans were drawn up for the roulement (rotation) of the whole brigade group after six months. In the event, this proved unnecessary.

5. The 'bird table' is essentially a large centrally controlled map, round which briefings and planning activities take place. It ensures that staff cells are 'all informed'.

6. An integral part of the Ptarmigan communications system.

7. DP. Distribution Point for combat supplies and other stores formed by the divisional second line transport regiment.

8. IRG. The interface between the unit and its second line logistic support.

9. The main divisional radio net is known as the command net.

10. A unit's vehicles are normally grouped for battle as follows:
    F Echelon – the unit's fighting vehicles (such as tanks).
    A1 Echelon – provide the immediate replenishment of F echelon, normally ammunition and fuel.
    A2 Echelon – backup for A1 and includes some forward repair. In addition the second line interface takes place here.
    B Echelon – The balance of unit stores vehicles.
    B Echelons of a formation are often grouped together under formation control for mutual support and defence.

Chapter 11: The Recovery

1. Linear metres (LIMS). An international measurement of vehicles (tracked and wheeled) for loading on to Roll On/Roll Off (RO/RO) ships.

2. QMG. Quarter Master General, the Army's senior administrative officer and a member of the Army Board. General Sir Edward Jones was QMG during the whole of the Gulf War.

3. CGS – Chief of the General Staff
   AG – Adjutant General
   DMO – Director of Military Operations.

4. AMF(L). ACE Mobile Force (Land). This is the NATO multinational immediate reaction force, a brigade sized force with logistic support including the Ordnance company. It would be employed as part of SACEUR's crisis reaction options.

Index

260 *Gulf Logistics*

List of Units